Study Guide for the
Pre-Professional Skills Tests

► ► ► ► ► ► ► ► ► ► ► ►

A PUBLICATION OF EDUCATIONAL TESTING SERVICE

Table of Contents
Study Guide for the *Pre-Professional Skills Tests*

▶ ▶ ▶ ▶ ▶ ▶ ▶ ▶ ▶ ▶ ▶ ▶

TABLE OF CONTENTS

Chapter 1

Introduction to the *PPST* and Suggestions for Using this Study Guide 7

Chapter 2

Practical Matters: Getting Test Scores, and Tips for Taking the Computer Version 13

Chapter 3

Do Tests Make You Nervous? Try These Strategies 19

Chapter 4

Preparing for the *PPST: Reading* Test 25

Chapter 5

Preparing for the *PPST: Mathematics* Test 57

Chapter 6

Preparing for the *PPST: Writing* Test: The Multiple-Choice Section 105

Chapter 7

Preparing for the *PPST: Writing* Test: The Essay 141

Chapter 8

Practice Test, *PPST: Reading* 159

Chapter 9

Practice Test, *PPST: Mathematics* 183

Chapter 10

Practice Test, *PPST: Writing* 201

Chapter 11

Right Answers and Explanations for the Practice Tests 219

Chapter 12

Are You Ready? Last-Minute Suggestions 255

TABLE OF CONTENTS

Appendix A

Study Plan Sheet 257

Appendix B

For More Information 261

Appendix C

Complete List of Topics Covered 265

Chapter 1

Introduction to the *PPST*® and Suggestions for
Using this Study Guide

► ► ► ► ► ► ► ► ► ► ► ►

Background on the *PPST*®

The *Pre-Professional Skills Tests (PPST®)* in Reading, Writing, and Mathematics are designed to be taken early in a student's college career to measure whether the student has the skills needed to prepare for a career in education. The tests are available in a paper-based or computer-based format.

About the *PPST*

The *PPST* tests reflect the most current research and the professional judgment and experience of educators across the country. This group of tests includes the following:

Test Subject	Test Name and Code	Length of Test	Major Content Areas Covered and Approximate Number and Percentage of Questions in Each Area
Reading	*Computerized Pre-Professional Skills Test: Reading* (5710)	75 minutes	• Literal Comprehension (26 questions, 56%) • Critical and Inferential Comprehension (20 questions, 44%)
	Pre-Professional Skills Test: Reading (0710)	60 minutes	• Literal Comprehension (23 questions, 55%) • Critical and Inferential Comprehension (17 questions, 45%)
Writing	*Computerized Pre-Professional Skills Test: Writing* (5720)	68 minutes (38 minutes multiple-choice, 30 minutes essay)	• Grammatical Relationships (12 questions, 13%) • Structural Relationships (16 questions, 18.5%) • Idiom/Word Choice, Mechanics, and No Error (16 questions, 18.5%) • Essay (1 question, 50%)
	Pre-Professional Skills Test: Writing (0720)	60 minutes (30 minutes multiple-choice, 30 minutes essay)	• Grammatical Relationships (10 questions, 13%) • Structural Relationships (14 questions, 18.5%) • Idiom/Word Choice, Mechanics, and No Error (14 questions, 18.5%) • Essay (1 question, 50%) **Note:** A pencil must be used to write the essay for the paper-based test.

| Mathematics | *Computerized Pre-Professional Skills Test: Mathematics* (5730) | 75 minutes | • Conceptual Knowledge and Procedural Knowledge (21 questions, 45%)

• Representations of Quantitative Information (13 questions, 30%)

• Measurement and Informal Geometry, Formal Mathematical Reasoning (12 questions, 25%)

Note: Calculators are prohibited. |
| | *Pre-Professional Skills Test: Mathematics* (0730) | 60 minutes | • Conceptual Knowledge and Procedural Knowledge (18 questions, 45%)

• Representations of Quantitative Information (12 questions, 30%)

• Measurement and Informal Geometry, Formal Mathematical Reasoning (10 questions, 25%)

Note: Calculators are prohibited. |

How to Use This Book

This book gives you instruction, practice, and test-taking tips to help you prepare for taking the *PPST* tests. In chapters 1, 2, and 3, you will find an overview of the test, information about getting test scores and taking the test on computer, and general test-taking suggestions. Chapters 4, 5, 6, and 7 provide review courses in reading, math, and writing so you can refresh your understanding of the important principles you'll need to know for the test. These chapters also contain sample questions to help you become familiar with the question formats that will actually appear on the test and help you understand the kinds of knowledge and reasoning you will need to apply to choose correct answers. Chapters 8, 9, and 10 contain complete practice tests, and chapter 11 contains the answers to the questions in the practice tests, along with explanations of those answers.

So where should you start? Well, all users of this book will probably want to begin with the following two steps:

Become familiar with the test content. Note what chapters 4, 5, 6, and 7 say about the topics covered in the test. For easy reference, appendix C includes a list of the topics covered in all three subjects—reading, math, and writing—in one place.

Consider how well you know the content in each subject area. Perhaps you already know that you need to build up your skills in a particular area—reading, math, or writing. If you're not sure, skim over chapters 4, 5, 6, and 7 to see what topics they cover. If you encounter material that feels unfamiliar or difficult, fold down page corners or insert sticky notes to remind yourself to spend extra time in these sections.

Also, all users of this book will probably want to end with these two steps:

Familiarize yourself with test taking. Chapter 3 is designed to answer frequently asked questions about the *PPST* tests, such as whether it is a good idea to guess on a test. You can simulate the experience of the test by taking the practice tests in chapter 8, 9, and 10 within the specified time limits. Choose a time and place where you will not be interrupted or distracted. Then, using chapter 11, you can score your responses. The scoring key identifies which topic each question addresses, so you can see which areas are your strongest and weakest. Look over the explanations of the questions you missed and see whether you understand them and could answer similar questions correctly. Then plan any additional studying according to what you've learned about your understanding of the topics.

Register for the test and consider last-minute tips. Consult chapter 2 about how to register for the test, and review the checklist in chapter 12 to make sure you are ready for the test.

What you do between these first steps and these last steps depends on whether you intend to use this book to prepare on your own or as part of a class or study group.

Using this book to prepare on your own:

If you are working by yourself to prepare for a *PPST* test, you may find it helpful to use the following approach:

Fill out the Study Plan Sheet in appendix A. This worksheet will help you to focus on what topics you need to study most, identify materials that will help you study, and set a schedule for doing the studying. The last item is particularly important if you know you tend to put off work.

Use other materials to reinforce chapters 4, 5, 6, and 7. These chapters contain review courses in reading, math, and writing, but you may want to get additional help for the topics that give you the most trouble. For example, if you know you have a problem with spelling, you can find lists of frequently misspelled words in books and on the Internet. Math textbooks can provide instruction and give you additional practice with math problems. Computer-based instruction with a system such as the PLATO® PPST SimTest may also help you improve your skills in reading, math, and writing. See appendix B for more information about the PLATO® PPST SimTest.

Using this book as part of a study group:

People who have a lot of studying to do sometimes find it helpful to form a study group with others who are preparing toward the same goal. Study groups give members opportunities to ask questions and get detailed answers. In a group, some members usually have a better understanding of certain topics, while others in the group may be better at other topics. As members take turns explaining concepts to each other, everyone builds self-confidence. If the group encounters a question that none of the members can answer well, the members can go as a group to a teacher or other expert and get answers efficiently. Because study groups schedule regular meetings, group members study in a more disciplined fashion. They also gain emotional support. The group should be large enough so that various people can contribute various kinds of knowledge, but small enough so that it stays focused. Often, three to six people is a good size.

Here are some ways to use this book as part of a study group:

Plan the group's study program. Parts of the Study Plan Sheet in appendix A can help to structure your group's study program. By filling out the first five columns and sharing the work sheets, everyone will learn more about your group's mix of abilities and about the resources (such as textbooks) that members can share with the group. In the sixth column ("Dates planned for study of content"), you can create an overall schedule for your group's study program.

Plan individual group sessions. At the end of each session, the group should decide what specific topics will be covered at the next meeting and who will be the presenter of each topic. Use the topic headings and subheadings in chapters 4, 5, 6, and 7 to select topics. Some sessions might be based on topics from the review courses contained in these chapters; other sessions might be based on the sample questions from these chapters.

Prepare your presentation for the group. When it's your turn to be presenter, prepare something that's more than a lecture. If you are presenting material from the review course part of a chapter, write five to ten original questions to pose to the group. Practicing writing actual questions can help you better understand the topics covered on the test as well as the types of questions you will encounter on the test. It will also give other members of the group extra practice at answering questions. If you are presenting material from the sample questions, use each sample question as a model for writing at least one original question.

Take the practice test together. The idea of chapters 8, 9, and 10 is to simulate actual administrations of the test, so scheduling a test session with the group will add to the realism and will also help boost everyone's confidence.

Learn from the results of the practice test. Use chapter 11 to score each other's answer sheets. Then plan one or more study sessions based on the questions that group members got wrong. For example, each group member might be responsible for a question that he or she got wrong and could use it as a model to create an original question to pose to the group, together with an explanation of the correct answer modeled after the explanations in chapter 11.

Whether you decide to study alone or with a group, remember that the best way to prepare is to have an organized plan. The plan should set goals based on specific topics and skills that you need to learn, and it should commit you to a realistic set of deadlines for meeting these goals. Then you need to discipline yourself to stick with your plan and accomplish your goals on schedule.

In the next chapter, you will find information about practical matters, including how to register for the test and tips for taking the computer-based version of the test.

Chapter 2

Practical Matters: Getting Test Scores, and Tips for the Computer Version

▶   ▶   ▶   ▶   ▶   ▶   ▶   ▶   ▶   ▶   ▶   ▶

Getting Your Scores

If you take the paper-and-pencil version of the test, your official score report will arrive in the mail approximately four weeks after your test date. Your score report will contain your overall score and six area scores.

If you are taking the computer version of a *PPST* test, you do not have to preregister with Educational Testing Service. To take the computer version, contact the appropriate person in your school or district to find out how you can arrange a day and time for taking the test. Once you are seated at the computer and the school or district administrator has entered the correct codes to start the test, you will be asked to fill in your name, address, and other information on the registration screen. At the end of the testing session, you will receive an unofficial report of your score. Two weeks later, you will receive an official score report in the mail that will contain your overall score and six area scores.

Taking the Test on Computer

You need only a beginner's level of computer skill to take the computer-based version of a *PPST* test. The test runs in an Internet browser. If you have spent an hour surfing the Internet, you know enough about how to work the mouse and how to click on buttons. If you do not have experience with computers, the mouse, and the Internet, visit your public library and ask someone to help you get started. Surf around until you feel comfortable making choices with the mouse.

What the computer-based version looks like

Most of the screens you will see when you take the computer-based version of a *PPST* test will look like this:

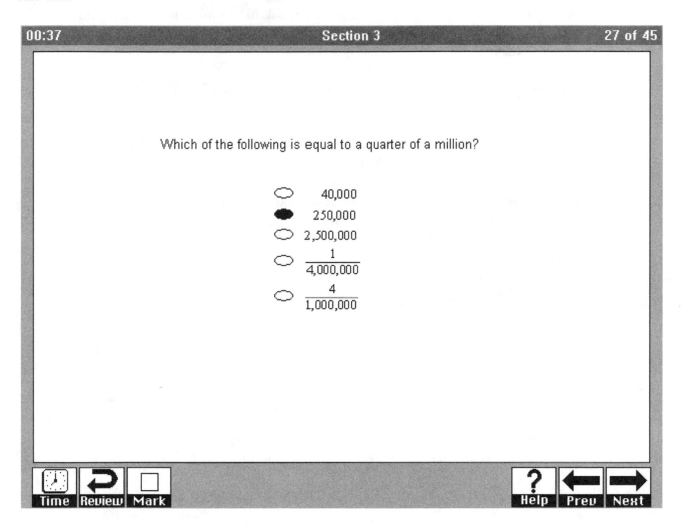

Note how the screen is laid out:

- In the upper right-hand corner, you can see which question you are now working on (question 27 of 45).

- In the upper left-hand corner, you can see how much time you have left (37 minutes). You can hide or display the clock by clicking . (During the last few minutes of the test, the clock remains on continuously.)

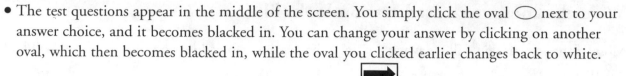

- The test questions appear in the middle of the screen. You simply click the oval ◯ next to your answer choice, and it becomes blacked in. You can change your answer by clicking on another oval, which then becomes blacked in, while the oval you clicked earlier changes back to white.

- When you're ready to move to the next question, click **Next**. To move back to a previous question, click **Prev**.

- To remind yourself of a question you want to check later, click **Mark**. When you return to the question, you'll see that the button has changed to **Mark**.

- Help is always available. Just click **Help** to see instructions about the *PPST* test.

- When you reach the last question, or when time runs out, you will be able to exit the test and receive your score. Once you exit a test, you CANNOT return to it.

- If you want to review questions you have seen (such as those you have marked, or those you have left unanswered), click **Review**. You'll see a screen that looks like this:

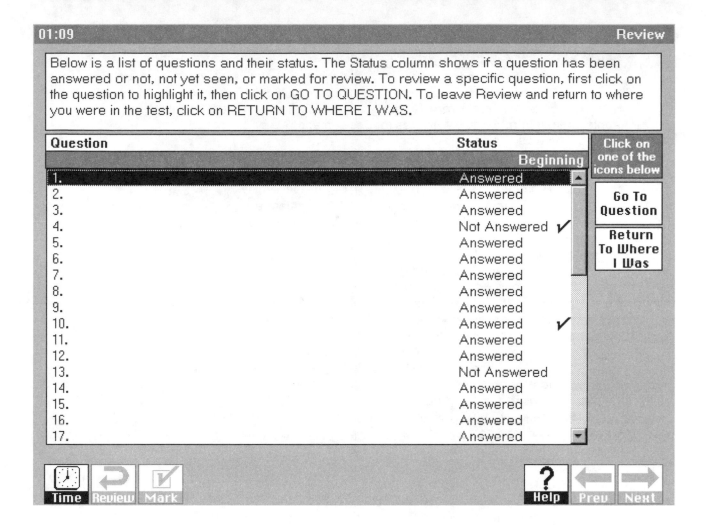

- Click on the question you want to review, then click [Go To Question]. To resume where you left off, click [Return To Where I Was].

In the reading and writing sections, when you are given a long passage of text accompanied by several questions, the screen is divided and looks like this:

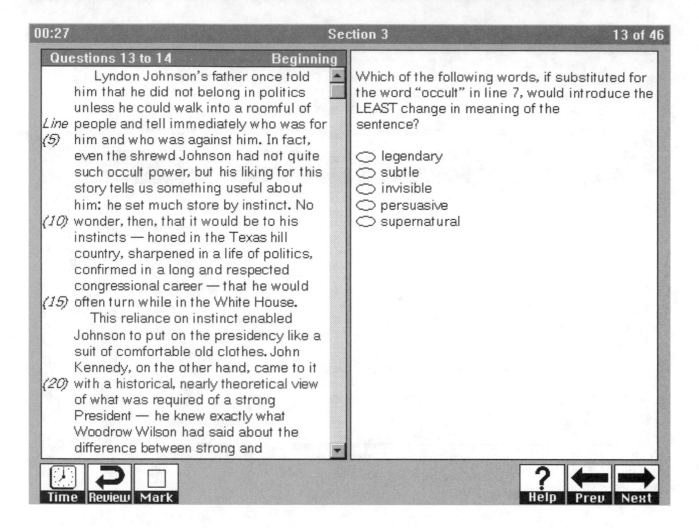

Questions 13 to 14   Beginning

Lyndon Johnson's father once told him that he did not belong in politics unless he could walk into a roomful of people and tell immediately who was for

Line

(5) him and who was against him. In fact, even the shrewd Johnson had not quite such occult power, but his liking for this story tells us something useful about him: he set much store by instinct. No

(10) wonder, then, that it would be to his instincts — honed in the Texas hill country, sharpened in a life of politics, confirmed in a long and respected congressional career — that he would

(15) often turn while in the White House.

This reliance on instinct enabled Johnson to put on the presidency like a suit of comfortable old clothes. John Kennedy, on the other hand, came to it

(20) with a historical, nearly theoretical view of what was required of a strong President — he knew exactly what Woodrow Wilson had said about the difference between strong and

Which of the following words, if substituted for the word "occult" in line 7, would introduce the LEAST change in meaning of the sentence?

○ legendary
○ subtle
○ invisible
○ persuasive
○ supernatural

Time   Review   Mark   Help   Prev   Next

Note that in the heading for the passage (above on the left), it indicates that two questions (13 and 14) are based on the passage. After you answer the first question and click "Next," the right side of the screen changes to show you the next question about the passage.

After you complete the test and exit, you will be able to print your unofficial score report using your Internet browser's Print button.

In the next chapter, you will find some additional suggestions for minimizing anxiety about taking tests.

Chapter 3

Do Tests Make You Nervous? Try These Strategies

▶ ▶ ▶ ▶ ▶ ▶ ▶ ▶ ▶ ▶ ▶ ▶

It's natural to be nervous for a test such as one of the *PPST* tests. You can use your nervous energy to strengthen your performance on the test if you approach it with these facts in mind:

- There are no trick questions on the test. (Some questions may be difficult for you, but they were not written in order to trick you or other test takers.)

- You should have plenty of time to complete the test. The times allotted for the tests are designed so you should not have to feel rushed.

- The test questions are worded very carefully by the test writers and are reviewed many times to make sure that the questions are clear about what they are asking. If a question seems confusing at first, take some time to reread it more slowly.

- You have choices during the test: you can skip a question and come back to it later; you can change your answer to any question at any time during the testing session; you can mark questions you want to return to later.

The sections below give you facts about the test and suggestions for maximizing your performance.

General Test-Taking Suggestions

The *PPST* tests contain a mixture of types of questions. Some of these are simple identification questions, such as "What is the name of the shape shown above?" But other types of questions require you to analyze situations, synthesize material, and apply knowledge to specific examples. In short, they require you to think and solve problems. This type of question is usually longer than a simple identification question and takes more time to answer. You may be presented with something to read (a description of a classroom situation, a sample of student work, a chart or graph) and then asked to answer questions based on your reading. Good reading skills are required, and you must read carefully. Both on this test and as a teacher, you will need to process and use what you read efficiently.

If you know that your reading skills are not strong, you may want to take a reading course. Community colleges and night schools often have reading labs that can help you strengthen your reading skills.

Useful facts about the test

1. **You can answer the questions in any order.** You can go through the questions from beginning to end, as many test takers do, or you can create your own path. Perhaps you will want to answer questions in your strongest subject first and then move from your strengths to your weaker areas. There is no right or wrong way. Use the approach that works for you.

2. **Don't worry about answer patterns.** There is one myth that says that answers on multiple-choice tests follow patterns. There is another myth that there will never be more than two questions with the same lettered answer following each other. There is no truth to either of these myths. Select the answer you think is correct, based on your knowledge of the subject.

3. **There is no penalty for guessing.** Your test score is based on the number of correct answers you have, and incorrect answers are not counted against you. When you don't know the answer to a question, try to eliminate any obviously wrong answers and then guess at the correct one.

4. **It's OK to write in your test booklet.** If you are taking the paper-and-pencil version of the test, you can work problems right on the pages of the booklet, make notes to yourself, or mark questions you want to review later. Your test booklet will be destroyed after you are finished with it, so use it in any way that is helpful to you. If you are taking the test on computer, you can work problems on scratch paper, and you can click the "Mark" button to note questions for later review.

Smart tips for taking the test

1. **Put your answers in the right "bubbles."** It seems obvious, but if you are taking the paper-and-pencil version, you should make sure you are "bubbling in" the answer to the right question on your answer sheet. Check the question number each time you fill in an answer. Use a Number 2 lead pencil and be sure that each mark is heavy and dark and completely fills the answer space. If you change an answer, be sure the previous mark is erased completely. For the computer-based version, be sure that the circle next to your chosen answer is dark after you have clicked on it.

2. **Be prepared for questions that use the words _LEAST, EXCEPT,_ or _NOT._** Some questions may ask you to select the choice that doesn't fit or that contains information that is not true. Questions in this format use the words _LEAST, EXCEPT,_ or _NOT._ The words are capitalized when they appear in test questions to signal a difference in what you are being asked to look for: you are looking for the single answer choice that is different in some specified way from the other answer choices. Here is an example of a question in this format that might be on the math part of the test:

> Some values of x are less than 100.

Which of the following is NOT consistent with the sentence above?

(A) 5 is not a value of x.
(B) 95 is a value of x.
(C) Some values of x are greater than 100.
(D) All values of x are less than 100.
(E) No numbers less than 100 are values of x.

In the question on the previous page, four of the five sentences are consistent with the boxed sentence, and one is NOT. The sentence that is NOT consistent is the correct answer choice—in this case, (E). If no numbers less than 100 are values of x, as stated in (E), there will not be at least one value of x less than 100, as stated in the boxed sentence.

When you encounter a *NOT*, *LEAST*, or *EXCEPT* question, it is a good idea to reread the question after you select your answer to make sure that you have answered the question correctly.

3. **Skip the questions you find to be extremely difficult.** There are bound to be some questions that you think are hard. Rather than trying to answer these on your first pass through the test, leave them blank and mark them in your test booklet so that you can come back to them. (If you are taking the test on computer, you can click the "Mark" button to mark a question and then use the "Review" listing to see which questions you have marked and/or left unanswered.) Pay attention to the time as you answer the rest of the questions on the test and try to finish with 10 or 15 minutes remaining so that you can go back over the questions you left blank. Even if you don't know the answers the second time you read the questions, see whether you can narrow down the possible answers, and then guess.

4. **Keep track of the time.** For the paper-and-pencil version, bring a watch to the test, just in case the clock in the test room is difficult for you to see. (For the computer version, there is a clock on the screen.) Remember that, on average, you have a little more than $1\frac{1}{2}$ minutes to answer each of the questions. One and one-half ($1\frac{1}{2}$) minutes may not seem like much time, but you will be able to answer a number of questions in only a few seconds each. You will probably have plenty of time to answer all of the questions, but if you find yourself becoming bogged down in one section, you might decide to move on and come back to that section later.

5. **Read all of the possible answers before selecting one**—and then reread the question to be sure the answer you have selected really answers the question being asked.

6. **Check your answers.** If you have extra time left over at the end of the test, look over each question and make sure that you have filled in the "bubble" on the answer sheet (or on the computer screen) as you intended. Many test takers make careless mistakes that could have been corrected if they had checked their answers.

7. **Don't worry about your score when you are taking the test.** No one is expected to get all of the questions correct. Your score on this test is not analogous to your score on the SAT or other similar tests. It doesn't matter on this test whether you score very high or barely pass. If you meet the minimum passing scores for your state or district, you will have fulfilled the requirement.

The Day of the Test

You should complete your review process a day or two before the actual test date. And many clichés you may have heard about the day of the test are true. You should

- Be well rested

- Take photo identification with you

- Take a supply of well-sharpened No. 2 pencils (at least three) if you are taking the paper-and-pencil version

- Eat before you take the test

- Be prepared to stand in line to check in or to wait while other test takers are being checked in

You can't control the testing situation, but you can control yourself. Stay calm. The supervisors are well trained and make every effort to provide uniform testing conditions, but don't let it bother you if the test doesn't start exactly on time. You will have the necessary amount of time once it does start.

You can think of preparing for this test as training for an athletic event. Once you've trained, and prepared, and rested, give it everything you've got. Good luck.

Chapter 4
Preparing for the *PPST: Reading* Test

▶ ▶ ▶ ▶ ▶ ▶ ▶ ▶ ▶ ▶ ▶ ▶

Introduction

"Reading comprehension" refers to the ability to *understand, analyze,* and *evaluate* written material. The key to doing well on the *PPST: Reading* test is reading carefully and making correct judgments and conclusions about what you have read. You do not need to be a fast reader in order to succeed on the test, but you do need to understand what you have read and be able to evaluate how each author presents his or her arguments and the evidence used to support them.

Overview of the test

The test consists entirely of reading passages and questions related to the passages. There are no vocabulary questions on the test, such as antonyms (finding the word opposite in meaning) or analogies ("*X* is to *Y* as *Z* is to blank"). You do not have to memorize lists of hard words to prepare for the test. You simply need to be able to read about 20 different reading selections and answer accompanying questions.

There are 40 questions on the test, and you will have 60 minutes to complete them. (If you are taking the computer version, you have 46 questions to answer in 75 minutes.) Your best preparation is to develop the ability to read *carefully*, but with strategies that help you move through the material quickly.

Where the reading passages come from and what they are like

The reading passages are taken from a wide range of reading materials intended for the general reading public. Many passages come from magazines and journals such as *Scientific American, Smithsonian, Archaeology,* and *Psychology Today*.

Other reading passages in the *PPST: Reading* test come from nonfiction books published for general audiences, such as biographies, histories, and books of essays. A relatively small percent of passages are taken from newspapers, usually from lengthy feature articles in major newspapers such as *The New York Times* or the *Washington Post*.

The subject matter of the passages varies. The passages cover a variety of subjects in the areas of social science, humanities, science, and general interest. You should expect to encounter a wide assortment of topics.

You may know a lot about some of the topics and next to nothing about others. That does not matter: *to answer the questions, you do not need to draw on any background or outside knowledge.* Everything you need to know to answer the questions is directly stated or implied in the passages.

In some cases, the information in the passage may conflict with knowledge you have about the subject. If it does, you should not let your knowledge influence your choice of an answer: *always answer each question on the basis of what is stated or implied in the given passage.*

The passages reflect various forms of writing: description, explanation, persuasion, narrative, and personal reflection. Most passages make a single central point and then back it up with supporting examples or observations. There will be a flow of logic or observation, often with transition words such as "but," "however," "therefore," and "in addition."

The length of the reading passages

Each reading passage consists of one or more paragraphs on a single topic, followed by one or more questions.

The passages are of varying lengths:

- Long passages of roughly 200 words (with four to seven questions)

- Short passages of roughly 100 words (with two to three questions)

- Statements of a sentence or two (with one question)

Even the longest passages of 200 words are equivalent in length to a fairly brief newspaper article, so you can be confident that you can read each passage carefully and quickly without running out of time.

Basic Strategies for Taking the *PPST: Reading* Test

Once you've started a set of questions, answer all the questions in the set. When you are taking the reading comprehension test, work through each set of questions completely before moving on to the next set. For tests made up of discrete, unrelated questions, it might make sense to leave some questions unanswered and come back to them; however, once you have read a passage carefully, you should try to finish answering all of the accompanying questions before going on to the next passage.

You should, however, read the passages in whatever order seems best to you. In other words, if a passage seems easy or interesting, you may prefer to begin with that one, and answer all of the questions. Similarly, if a passage seems difficult, you may want to save it for last.

Read through the passage once. For each passage, first read through it carefully but at a fairly quick pace. Then answer each question, referring back to the passage as necessary. Don't analyze the passage in great detail when you first read it. Analyze it only as needed to answer a question.

Cross out choices you think are wrong. When working on a question on the paper test, cross out choices you definitely know to be wrong. If you cross them out in your test booklet, you will not waste time re-reading choices you've already decided are wrong. Once you eliminate the obviously wrong choices you have a better chance of getting the question right if you have to make an educated guess.

If it helps you focus, you may also want to mark parts of the passage that seem important. For instance, you might want to underline transition words, such as "however" or "therefore," to call attention to the structure of the author's argument. Do not, however, spend too much time marking the passage.

Expect variety. Don't panic if you are not familiar with the topic of the passage. Even if the passage is on multicolored eels found near the New Zealand coast, don't be put off! Plunge in and read carefully. You will have all the information you need to answer the questions.

Also, be prepared to shift your mindset between topics. You might encounter a dense passage describing a medical discovery and then a lighter passage about childhood memories of a hometown.

Pace yourself. Do not spend too much time on any one passage or question. If you find that a certain passage or question is taking up too much of your time, make an educated guess and move on to another question.

Answer all the questions. Be sure to answer every question. Because the test is scored according to the number of correct answers, you are not penalized for guessing. At the end of the test period, take a moment to check the answer sheet for any unanswered questions.

The Twelve Types of Questions on the *PPST: Reading* Test

It may look as if each question on the *PPST: Reading* test is different from all the others, but there are really only twelve question types. Below you'll see that the twelve types fall into two main categories. After an explanation of these categories, you'll get an in-depth explanation of each type, plus several practice questions.

The twelve types of questions fall into two major categories:

- Literal comprehension skills (Types 1-4)

- Critical and inferential comprehension skills (Types 5-12)

Literal comprehension is the ability to understand accurately and completely what is explicitly stated in a passage. It also involves the ability to recognize how a passage is organized and how it uses language.

To answer this kind of question, you must concentrate on what is written and how it is written. A little over half of the questions measure this kind of comprehension.

The *PPST: Reading* test assesses the following literal comprehension skills:

Type 1: Recognizing the <u>main idea</u> or primary purpose of a passage

Type 2: Recognizing a <u>supporting idea</u> or detail in a passage

Type 3: Recognizing how particular <u>vocabulary</u> words or phrases are used in a passage

Type 4: Recognizing the <u>organization</u> of a passage

Critical and inferential comprehension questions test the ability to understand aspects of a passage that are not explicitly stated. When you read critically or inferentially, you must understand implications, make predictions, analyze an author's argument, and compare situations and arguments.

To answer this kind of question, you do not need any specialized knowledge; clear and careful thinking is sufficient. A little under half of the questions measure this kind of comprehension.

The *PPST: Reading* test assesses the following critical and inferential comprehension skills:

Type 5: Drawing an <u>inference</u> or implication from a passage

Type 6: Evaluating supporting <u>evidence</u>—its relevance or appropriateness

Type 7: Identifying an <u>assumption</u> made by the author

Type 8: Distinguishing <u>fact from opinion</u>

Type 9: Identifying the <u>attitude</u> of the author toward the topic

Type 10: <u>Extending and predicting</u> based on passage content

Type 11: Drawing a <u>conclusion</u>

Type 12: Making an <u>application</u> to another situation

In-depth Preparation for All Twelve Types of Questions
Type 1: Main Idea questions

There are two kinds of Main Idea questions:

- Main idea

- Primary purpose

Main idea questions ask about the central point of a passage. The main idea may be explicitly stated, or you may have to figure it out. It might help first to identify the topic of the passage (in a few words) and then identify the author's point about that topic (in a complete sentence). That will be the main idea. For example, the topic of a passage might be "the person who invented laptop computers" and the author's point (the main idea) might be "The person who invented laptop computers did not get support from co-workers when trying to sell the idea to the company's marketing department."

Primary purpose questions ask about the author's purpose. The author may explicitly state the purpose, or you may have to figure it out. Sometimes the question will ask you to identify a general phrase describing the purpose (using language such as "explain an event" or "refute an argument"); sometimes the question will ask you to identify a specific statement describing the purpose (using language such as "refute a traditional theory about glaciers").

How to recognize Main Idea questions

Here are the ways in which Main Idea questions are usually asked:

- Which of the following statements best summarizes the main idea of the passage?

- Which of the following statements best expresses the main idea of the passage?

- The main idea of the passage is…

Here are the ways in which Primary Purpose questions are usually asked:

- In the passage, the author is primarily concerned with which of the following?

- The primary purpose of the passage is to…

Keep in mind that the question asks about the *main* idea and the *primary* purpose, not minor ideas and secondary purposes. For example, the way a harpsichord works might be described, but the author might do so *in order to* explain why pianos became more popular than harpsichords in the 1700's. So the primary purpose is not to describe harpsichords, but to explain the rising popularity of pianos.

Look for the choice that is a *complete* description of the main idea or primary purpose of the passage. This will require that you read the *entire* passage.

Expert tips for Main Idea questions

- Don't just choose answers that are true. Some choices may be true, but they may not express the main idea of the given passage.

- Don't choose an answer just because you think the author would agree with the idea expressed; that may not be the main point the author was making in the passage.

- Don't look for the answer choice that has wording that is most similar to that used in the passage. Often, *all* choices will have wording similar to that used in the passage. You will have to read both the passage and the choices carefully to understand exactly what is meant by the words. Merely skimming the passage will not enable you to determine the main idea of the passage.

- With primary-purpose questions, pay attention to the specific meanings of words such as "compare," "examine," "explain," and "refute," which are often used in the answer choices.

- Be sure that the choice you select does not go *beyond* the passage—sometimes a choice may present information that is not, in fact, in the given passage. That will not, therefore, be the main idea or primary purpose.

Try a Main Idea question

Shakespeare wrote four types of plays: histories, comedies, tragedies, and tragicomedies. Some scholars contend that Shakespeare's choice of three of these types of dramatic forms reflects his various psychological states. As a young man making a name for himself in London, he wrote comedies. Then, saddened by the death of his son, he turned to tragedies. Finally, seasoned by life's joys and sorrows, he produced tragicomedies. But a look at the theater scene of his day reveals that Shakespeare was not so much writing out of his heart as into his pocketbook. When comedies were the vogue, he wrote comedies; when tragedies were the rage, he wrote tragedies; and when tragicomedies dominated the stage, he produced tragicomedies.

The primary purpose of the passage is to

(A) examine Shakespeare's life in light of his dramatic works

(B) contest a theory that attempts to explain why Shakespeare wrote the kinds of plays he did

(C) explain the terms "comedy," "tragedy," and "tragicomedy" as they are used in discussions of Shakespeare's plays

(D) compare Shakespeare's plays with the works of other dramatists of his day

(E) discuss what is known about Shakespeare's psychological states

Explanation:

The first two sentences classify Shakespeare's plays into four categories and offer a theory, endorsed by "some scholars," concerning why Shakespeare chose to write three of these four kinds of plays. The next three sentences provide support for this theory by showing correspondence between Shakespeare's likely psychological states and the plays he wrote at various times in his life. The word "But" in the next sentence indicates a change of direction in the passage: the author now suggests that the first theory may be wrong, and goes on to provide an alternate theory—that Shakespeare may well have written the kinds of plays he wrote not because they reflected a particular psychological state but because he thought they would be financially successful. The primary purpose of the passage, then, is best described in B, which states that the author's purpose is to "contest a theory" (and B correctly describes the theory being contested; that is, a theory about why Shakespeare wrote the kinds of plays he did).

Choice C can be eliminated because although the terms listed in C are used in the passage, they are not explained.

Choice D can be eliminated because the passage is not concerned with comparing Shakespeare's plays with those of another dramatist.

While choices A and E do to some extent reflect the content of the passage, neither expresses the complete primary purpose of the passage. (And, in fact, A has the examination backwards: Shakespeare's works are examined in light of his life, not the other way around.)

Type 2: Supporting Idea Questions

Supporting ideas are ideas used to support or elaborate on the main idea. Supporting Idea questions can focus on facts, details, definitions, or other information presented by the author. Whereas questions about the main idea ask you to determine the meaning of a passage or a paragraph as a whole, questions about supporting ideas ask you to determine the meaning of a particular part of the passage.

Think of a lawyer during a court case examining an expert medical witness on the stand. The lawyer asks specific questions about supporting details: "What are the usual symptoms of the disease?" "What medicines are typically used to combat the disease?" "Why would some people take longer to be cured than others?" These specific questions do not comprise the main argument of the lawyer's case, which may be to show a hospital's negligence in the care of a patient, but they are critical supporting facts.

How to recognize Supporting Idea questions

Here are the ways in which Supporting Idea questions are usually asked:

- According to the passage, which of the following is true of *X*?

- The passage mentions all of the following as characteristics of *X* EXCEPT…

- According to the author, the kinds of data mentioned in line *n* are significant because they…

- The author's description of *X* mentions which of the following?

- The passage states that one of the consequences of *X* was…

• According to the passage, *X* is immediately followed by…

Expert tips for Supporting Idea questions

• You may well need to refer back to the passage and find out exactly what is said about the subject of the question—since the question is asking about a detail, you may not recall the detail from your first reading of the passage.

• Eliminate the choices that present information contradictory to what is presented in the passage.

• Eliminate the choices that present information not given in the passage.

• Don't just select a choice that presents information that is given in the passage; your choice must answer the specific question that is asked.

Try two Supporting Idea questions

Predominantly Black land-grant colleges in the United States have a long tradition of supporting cooperative education programs. These programs combine academic courses with work experience that carries academic credit. This tradition has made these colleges the leaders in the recent movement in American education toward career-oriented curriculums.

According to the passage, predominantly Black land-grant colleges in the United States are leaders in career-oriented education because they

(A) have had cooperative education programs as part of their curriculums for many years

(B) were among the first colleges in the United States to shift away from career-oriented curriculums

(C) offer their students academic credit for their work experience prior to entering college

(D) have a long tradition of cooperation with local business and community leaders

(E) provide opportunities for students to work on campus to earn money for tuition

Explanation:

The first sentence tells us that Black land-grant colleges have supported cooperative education programs for a long time. The second sentence describes cooperative education programs. The final sentence tells us that it is this tradition of support for cooperative education programs that has made these colleges leaders in the career-oriented education movement. Of the five choices, A best states the reason that the colleges are leaders in career-related education.

Choice B can be eliminated because it contradicts information in the passage.

Choice C can be eliminated because although it may be an accurate statement about these colleges, it does not account for their leadership in career-oriented education.

The passage says nothing about local business and community leaders; therefore, D can be eliminated.

Although E may be a correct statement about these colleges, this information is not explicitly stated in the passage, and, even if it were, it would not help explain why the colleges are *leaders* in career-oriented education. Providing students with jobs on campus would not necessarily be beneficial to them in developing skills for a future career.

The women's movement emerged in the United States in the 1830's, a period of intense reform and evangelism. Women were encouraged to speak out at religious revival meetings, and many women thus gained public speaking experience. When women sought and were denied leadership and the right to speak out in the abolitionist and temperance societies to which they belonged, they organized their own reform groups, and later worked to improve their own status.

According to the passage, women formed their own reform societies because women

(A) were denied membership in other reform societies

(B) disagreed with the aims of the societies to which they belonged

(C) were not permitted to act as leaders of the organizations of which they were members

(D) were preoccupied with issues that pertained only to the status of women

(E) wished to challenge the existing political order by questioning the political motives of their opponents

---

Explanation:

This question asks you to identify information that is explicitly stated in the passage. The last sentence states that women formed their own reform societies because they were "denied leadership and the right to speak out" in the societies to which they already belonged. Thus, choice C is the best answer.

Choice A can be eliminated because the passage indicates that women were members of temperance and abolitionist societies.

Choices B, D, and E can be eliminated because the passage provides no information about the specific views of the women or about a desire on their part to challenge the existing political order.

Type 3: Vocabulary Questions

Vocabulary questions require you to identify the meanings of words as they are used in the context of a reading passage. These questions not only test your understanding of the meaning of a particular word; they also test your ability to understand how the word is being used in context.

Authors make choices about the language they use, and they sometimes deliberately choose unusual words or figures of speech (words not intended to be understood literally). When you are asked about an unusual word or a figure of speech, you will be given a sufficient context to help you identify the meaning of the word.

How to recognize Vocabulary questions

Here are the ways in which Vocabulary questions are usually asked:

- Which of the following words could be substituted for "*Y*" in line *n* without substantially altering the meaning of the statement?

- The author most probably uses the word "*Y*" in line *n* to mean...

- In line *n*, the word "*Y*" most nearly means...

Expert tips for Vocabulary questions

- Remember that the question is not simply asking about the meaning of a specific word; it is asking about its meaning *in the context of the passage*. Therefore, do not simply choose the answer choice that provides a correct meaning; you must understand which meaning the author is using in the passage.

- Often all the choices will offer acceptable meanings of the word. Your job is to choose which meaning makes the most sense as the word is used in the passage.

- Reread the relevant sentence in the passage, using the word or phrase you have chosen. Confirm that the sentence makes sense in the context of the passage as a whole.

Try two Vocabulary questions

President Lyndon Johnson's father once told him that without the ability to walk into a roomful of people and tell immediately who was a supporter and who was an opponent, one did not belong in politics. In fact, even the shrewd younger Johnson never had such occult power, but his liking for this story tells us something useful about him: he set much store by instinct. No wonder, then, that it would be to his instincts—honed in the Texas hill country, sharpened in a life of politics, confirmed in a long and respected congressional career—that he would often turn while in the White House.

Which of the following words, if substituted for the word "occult" in line 3, would LEAST change the meaning of the sentence?

(A) legendary

(B) subtle

(C) invisible

(D) persuasive

(E) supernatural

Explanation:

The "occult" power described in the first sentence is clearly not a power that people ordinarily have. It could, therefore, best be described as "supernatural." Choice E is, therefore, the best answer.

Choices A and D can be eliminated because they are not synonyms of "occult" in any context.

Choice B can be eliminated because the process of dividing people into two categories, "for" and "against," is not "subtle," but rather a crude and direct means of dealing with others.

Choice C can be eliminated because powers of the mind are always "invisible" and there is no reason why the author would attribute a high degree of invisibility to one power when all are equally invisible.

In *Understanding Media*, Marshall McLuhan sheds a brilliant light, punctuated by occasional shadows of obscurity, on the essential nature of electronic media; the chapter on radio looks harder at that medium than anything since Arnheim's *Radio*.

The phrase "shadows of obscurity" most probably refers to McLuhan's

(A) use of imagery

(B) lack of clarity

(C) depth of understanding

(D) wide-ranging interests

(E) waning reputation

Explanation:

This question asks you to identify the meaning of a figure of speech (the author does not mean to suggest *real* shadows). The passage as a whole presents an evaluation of Marshall McLuhan's *Understanding Media*. The "brilliant light" shed by McLuhan is a figure of speech that can be interpreted as an illuminating discussion of electronic media. The passage states that this brilliant light is "punctuated by" something else, meaning that it is interrupted by something that contrasts with it. The "shadows of obscurity" can thus be interpreted as confusing or unclear parts of McLuhan's discussion. Thus B is the best answer.

Choice A can be eliminated because the passage is discussing McLuhan's work in general and not particular aspects of his style, such as imagery.

Choice C can be eliminated because while "shadows" might refer to "depths," "understanding" is *contrary* to "obscurity."

Choice D can be eliminated because "wide-ranging interests" captures the meaning of neither "shadows" nor "obscurity."

Choice E can be eliminated because the passage is about the merits of McLuhan's book rather than about McLuhan's reputation.

Type 4: Organization Questions

Organization refers to how the content of a reading passage is put together to achieve the author's purpose. The individual sentences and paragraphs that make up the passages have a logical and coherent relationship to one another.

Sometimes you will be asked to identify how a passage as a whole is constructed: for instance, it introduces then describes a theory; it compares and then contrasts two points of view; it offers an idea and then refutes it, and so on.

Sometimes you will be asked to identify how one paragraph is related to another: for instance, the second paragraph gives examples to support a statement offered in the first paragraph; the second paragraph refutes a theory presented in the first paragraph. The answers may be expressed in general terms (e.g., a hypothesis is explained and then challenged) or in terms specific to the passage (e.g., "How children learn one kind of activity is described and then this method is recommended for teaching children another kind of activity").

You may also be asked, as another way of testing your ability to recognize organization, to identify why an author mentions a particular piece of information (to support an assertion would be one reason) or why an author quotes someone (to give an example of a person who holds a certain opinion would be a reason).

To answer Organization questions, pay attention to how sentences and paragraphs are connected. Sometimes certain words make the connections explicit: "for example," "however," "a second reason," "furthermore," and so on. They may tell you whether a sentence or paragraph is giving an example, offering a contrast, offering additional information, extending a point, and so on. You may even want to underline those kinds of words as you read through the passage for the first time. However, you should keep in mind that such key words might not always be present. When you cannot find key words, you must ask yourself how one sentence or paragraph is connected to another.

How to recognize Organization questions

Here are the ways in which Organization questions are usually asked:

- Which of the following statements best describes the organization of the passage?

- Which of the following best describes the way in which the claim is presented?

- The author mentions *X* most likely in order to…

Expert tips for Organization questions

- Pay careful attention to the words used in the answer choices. They are usually the key to finding the right answer.

- Know the precise meanings of these terms: "definition," "comparison," "analogy," "summary," "refutation," "chronological," "controversial," "criticism," and "generalization." These words are often used in the choices of Organization questions.

• Sometimes it may help to recall the main idea or primary purpose of the passage—the organization of the whole as well as of the parts should serve that idea or purpose.

Try two Organization questions

One promising energy source would require sophisticated redesign of the basic windmills that have pumped water for centuries. Coupled with advanced storage batteries, large windmills might satisfy the total energy needs of rural areas and even small cities where strong and prevalent winds can be counted on. Wind power has several advantages. First, no new technology is really required. Second, the energy source is inexhaustible. Third, relatively little capital investment is needed to install or operate windmills.

But wind power has major disadvantages, too. Most obviously, it will work only in areas where wind is strong and prevalent. Furthermore, the amount of electricity that could be generated by wind power would simply be insufficient to meet major nationwide energy needs.

However, a network of sea-based windmills, placed on buoys and driven by the same prevailing winds that once powered sailing vessels, could provide a substantial fraction of the world's electrical energy—especially if the buoy-based windmills could be linked to land by superconducting power transmission cables.

Which of the following best describes the organization of the passage?

(A) A series of interrelated events are arranged chronologically.

(B) A controversial theory is proposed and then persuasively defended.

(C) An unforeseen problem is described and several examples are provided.

(D) A criticism is summarized, evaluated, and then dismissed.

(E) A problematical issue is discussed and a partial solution suggested.

Explanation:

Choice E is the best answer. "A problematical issue is discussed" summarizes the first two paragraphs, in which both the positive and negative aspects of a complicated situation are examined. This discussion is followed, in the third paragraph, by the suggestion of "a partial solution," which may solve some of the problems involved in using windmills to generate electricity.

Choice A can be eliminated because the passage is concerned with examining an issue from different sides rather than with narrating specific events. Nor is there any sense of chronology in the passage.

Choice B attributes a one-sided approach to the author, who actually presents different points of view; furthermore, although the passage implies that there may be disagreement about the usefulness of the windmills, it does not anywhere indicate that the issue is controversial. In addition, the passage focuses more on concrete aspects of a problem than on a theory.

Choice C can be eliminated because there is no evidence in the passage that the problems discussed in the second paragraph were unforeseen.

Choice D can be eliminated because the passage does not summarize, evaluate, or dismiss any criticism that is mentioned, nor does the entire passage deal with criticism.

Whatever their disadvantage with respect to distributing education tax dollars equally among school districts, in one respect at least, local property taxes are superior to state taxes as a means of funding public schools. Because local property taxes provide public schools with a direct source of revenue, these public schools are relatively free from competition with other government services for tax dollars. School administrators do not have to compete for a share of the state tax dollars, which are already being spent on health, criminal justice, public safety, and transportation. They are not placed in the position of having to argue that school programs must have priority over other public services financed by state taxes.

The author mentions the tax dollars spent on health, criminal justice, public safety, and transportation most likely in order to highlight the

(A) government services with which public schools do not have to compete for tax dollars

(B) unequal distribution of local property tax dollars among various public services

(C) high expense of maintaining schools as compared to other public services

(D) government services over which public schools have priority

(E) disadvantage of distributing education tax dollars among various public services

---

Explanation:

The first sentence of this passage states that using local property taxes for schools has advantages over using state taxes. The second sentence explains this advantage: "public schools are relatively free from competition with other government services for tax dollars." The next sentence elaborates, listing some of those "other government services"—"health, criminal justice, public safety, and transportation." Thus, choice A is the best answer.

Choices B and E do not reflect the passage's content: the potentially unequal distribution of local property-tax dollars (a disadvantage) is among school districts, not among various public services.

Choice C can be eliminated because the author is not making a point about the relative cost of education.

Choice D can be eliminated with similar reasoning: the author does not say that public schools have priority over government services (merely that the freedom from competition frees school administrators from having to make that argument).

Type 5: Inference Questions

An inference is a statement that is clearly suggested or implied by the author; an inference is *based on* information given in the passage but is not stated in the passage. To answer inference questions, you may have to carry statements made by the author one step beyond what is presented in the passage. For example, if a passage explicitly states an effect, a question could ask you to infer its cause. Be ready, therefore, to concentrate not only on the explicit meanings of the author's words, but also on the logical implications of those words.

We make inferences in conversation all the time. Consider this conversation between two students:

Sean: "Did you get an A on the quiz?"

Chris: "Didn't you hear the professor say that no one got an A?"

Sean should be able to infer that Chris did not get an A on the quiz, even though Chris did not explicitly say so.

Here's another conversation that illustrates an inference:

Lee: "This is the first year that the university is offering a course in writing poetry."

Sara: "So my sister, who graduated last year, couldn't have taken a course here in writing poetry."

Sara can make an inference about her sister's particular situation from Lee's general statement.

How to recognize Inference questions

Pay special attention when you see words such as "infer," "suggests," and "implies" in a question. These are often signals for inference questions.

Here are the ways in which Inference questions are usually asked:

- Which of the following can be inferred about *X* from the passage?

- The passage strongly suggests that *X* would happen if…

- The author of the passage implies which of the following about *X*?

- It can be inferred from the passage that *X* is effective in all of the following ways EXCEPT…

Expert tips for Inference questions:

- Make sure your answer doesn't contradict the main idea of the passage.

- Make sure your answer doesn't go too far and make assumptions that aren't included in the passage. (For example, in the conversation between Lee and Sara about poetry courses, Sara would have gone too far if she had said, "So all English majors will now be required to take the course in writing poetry." This cannot be inferred from Lee's statement.)

- Don't just choose a statement that sounds important or true. It must be inferable from the passage.

- You should be able to defend your selection by pointing to explicitly stated information in the passage that leads to the inference you have selected.

- Use the "if-then" test to verify your answers. To do this test, complete the following statement: if X (information in the passage), then Y (your selected choice). Does your "if-then" make sense?

Try two Inference questions

Histories of the Middle East abound in stereotypes and clichés, particularly with respect to women. The position of women in the Middle East is frequently treated as though Middle Eastern societies formed a single unit that could be accurately represented in a simple description.

The author of the passage suggests which of the following about histories of the Middle East with regard to their treatment of women?

(A) A general problem with such histories was first noticed in their descriptions of the role of women.

(B) The experience of women in Middle Eastern societies is much more diverse than such histories have often assumed.

(C) The study of women's roles and experience has recently become a central focus in such histories.

(D) Such histories report that the position of women in Middle Eastern societies has undergone a major transformation.

(E) Until recently, such histories typically neglected to discuss the position of women.

Explanation:

In the first sentence, the author asserts that histories of the Middle East are filled with oversimplified generalizations, particularly with regard to women. In the second sentence, the author explains that the error lies in the way historians of the Middle East discuss women as though all Middle Eastern societies were similar. By saying "as though," the author suggests that Middle Eastern societies are different and that the experiences of women in the countries are different, so that it is a mistake to assume that the experiences are similar. Thus, B is the best answer.

Choice A can be eliminated because the author does not suggest that the problem with histories of the Middle East was discovered as a result of the way those studies treat women.

Choices C and E can be eliminated because although the passage suggests that women are discussed in studies of the Middle East, it does not suggest that such studies either typically neglected or focused on women.

Choice D can be eliminated because the passage does not indicate that such histories recently began to focus on women.

In the 1960's and 1970's, electoral support for public education was strong, mainly as a result of certain trends in the United States population. For example, enrollments in primary and secondary schools reached their zenith in these years, when public school students constituted one out of every four members of the United States population. Moreover, parents of children in public school and public school employees comprised approximately 40 percent of eligible voters in the United States.

The author implies that one of the results of large enrollments in public schools in the 1960's and 1970's was

(A) a deterioration in the quality of education offered by nonpublic schools

(B) an increase in the demand for higher education

(C) an increase in the number of eligible voters in the United States

(D) broad electoral support for public education programs

(E) overall improvement in the quality of higher education

Explanation:

The author says that electoral support for public education was strong during the 1960's and 1970's because of certain trends in the United States population. The author then goes on to cite, as an example of those trends, the high levels of enrollment in public schools during this period. The author thus implies a cause-and-effect relationship between large enrollments in public schools and broad electoral support for education—implies, that is, that one of the results of large enrollment in public schools was broad electoral support for education. This answer is given in choice D.

Choices A, B, C, and E can be eliminated because the passage does not suggest anything about the quality of education offered in nonpublic schools, the demand for higher education, the number of eligible voters, or the quality of higher education, respectively.

Type 6: Evidence Questions

In the questions that assess your ability to evaluate supporting evidence, you will sometimes be given hypothetical pieces of evidence and asked which of them is relevant to supporting an argument made in a passage. To answer such a question, you must have a clear understanding of the argument made in the passage and must make a judgment about what kinds of acts, statistics, reasons, examples, or expert testimony would provide strong support for that argument.

For example, if a person argued that dancers experience fewer injuries than other athletes because they are more coordinated, then evidence about the injury rates of various athletes and their relative coordination would be relevant.

Other questions of this type ask you to identify which of several pieces of evidence strengthens or weakens an argument made in a passage. Evidence that provides support for the conclusion would strengthen an argument; evidence that contradicts or casts doubt on the conclusion would weaken an argument.

For example, in the case of argument mentioned above about injury to dancers, evidence that dancers engage in more injury-reducing warm-up exercises than other athletes would weaken the argument, as it casts doubt on the conclusion that coordination (and not warm-up) is the reason for fewer injuries.

How to recognize Evidence questions

Here are the ways in which Evidence questions are usually asked:

- Which of the following, if true, would most weaken the author's argument concerning X?

- The author's argument would be strengthened if it could be proved that…

- Which of the following facts, if true, would most help to explain X?

- Which of the following, if true, supports the conclusion drawn in the passage?

- In order to assess the claim made in the passage, it would be most useful to know which of the following?

Expert tips for Evidence questions

- Remind yourself of the author's claim and the evidence used to support the claim.

- Then test each choice to see whether it provides an example that directly affects the chain of reasoning and supporting evidence.

- Usually a new piece of evidence will either strengthen the author's claim, weaken the author's claim, or be irrelevant to whether the claim is valid or not.

Try an Evidence question

In our increasing awareness of ecological health, many industrial practices have come under close examination, and mining is no exception. Though drilling is required in both cases, base-metal mining involves toxic chemical leachates for separating the metal from the rock, whereas diamond mining does not—diamonds can be separated from surrounding rock using only crushers, screens, and all-natural water. Thus, base-metal mining is environmentally destructive, but diamond mining does not harm the environment.

Which of the following, if true, would most weaken the author's argument concerning the effect of diamond mining on the environment?

(A) The process of drilling and getting the drill rig to and from the site destroys ecological habitats.

(B) Base metals have utilitarian value, but diamonds are functionally almost worthless.

(C) Toxic chemical leachates contaminate not only soil, but groundwater as well.

(D) There have been proposals to use abandoned mine shafts as garbage dumps.

(E) Logging can be as ecologically destructive as mining.

Explanation:

The author argues that whereas base-metal mining is harmful to the environment, diamond mining is not environmentally destructive. Therefore, evidence to the contrary would weaken the argument. Since choice A provides evidence indicating that diamond mining is harmful to the environment, it is the best answer.

Choices B, C, and E may well be true, but they are irrelevant to the argument made in the passage about the impact of diamond mining on the environment.

Choice D may seem at first reading to weaken the argument, but the statement describes environmental destruction caused not by the mining process itself, but by the use of the mines subsequent to mining; furthermore, the destruction described is merely *potential* damage. Choice D is not, therefore, the best answer.

Type 7: Assumption Questions

These questions will ask you to recognize the ideas or perspectives that underlie an author's arguments. These assumptions are unstated ideas or facts that the author accepts as true or takes for granted. Indeed, they must be accepted as true in order for the author's argument to be valid.

If a person argued, "We could increase student performance if all students got eight hours of sleep every night," this person would be assuming that at least some students are not getting eight hours of sleep every night.

How to recognize Assumption questions

Here are the ways in which Assumption questions are usually asked:

- Which of the following assumptions is most likely made by the author of the passage?

- In arguing *X*, the author makes which of the following assumptions?

- The argument in the passage is based on which of the following assumptions?

Expert tips for Assumption questions

- Ask yourself which choice would have to be true for the author's argument to be valid.

- Sometimes the assumption is something you identified as a "missing step" while you were reading the passage.

Try an Assumption question

In 1888, just as its hospital was nearing completion, what was to become The Johns Hopkins School of Medicine ran out of funds; the Baltimore and Ohio Railroad, on which the parent university had been depending for money, was experiencing financial difficulty. The railroad's financial troubles proved a stroke of luck for the cause of women's rights. When the directors did open the school in 1893, it was because five women had raised more than $500,000 through a multi-city campaign. They had insisted, as a condition of this endowment, that Hopkins be the first school of medicine in the nation to admit men and women on equal terms.

Which of the following is an assumption made by the author of the passage?

(A) Even if it had not experienced financial difficulties, the Baltimore and Ohio Railroad would not have furnished The Johns Hopkins University with additional funds.

(B) The Johns Hopkins School of Medicine would have excluded women if the fund-raisers had not insisted that the school admit women.

(C) In 1888 The Johns Hopkins University was suffering from a shortage of funds in all its schools.

(D) The establishment of The Johns Hopkins School of Medicine would spur the development of other schools of medicine.

(E) The women fund-raisers themselves wished to be trained as doctors.

Explanation:

Choice B is the best answer. It is clearly supported by the last sentence of the passage: since the fund-raisers had to *insist* that Johns Hopkins admit women, we can tell that the author assumes that the admission of women was directly caused by the fund-raisers' insistence and would otherwise not have taken place. The author therefore makes the assumption stated in choice B.

Choices C and D are the easiest to eliminate because the passage neither states nor implies anything to support them. Neither is an *assumption* underlying the content of the passage.

Choice A is closer to the content of the passage, but it is clearly incorrect, since the phrase "on which the parent university had been depending" indicates that the railroad would, under normal circumstances, have furnished the funds.

Choice E is a plausible statement; it may possibly have been true—however, it could just as easily have been untrue. Nothing in the passage actually suggests it: all we know is that the fund-raisers insisted on a general policy of equal admissions opportunities. Therefore, choice E is not an assumption underlying the passage content.

Type 8: Fact/Opinion Questions

Often a piece of writing will contain both facts and opinions, and you will be asked to distinguish one from the other.

Facts can be verified (as objectively true or false) and are often presented in a straightforward fashion without emotion.

Opinions are beliefs or judgments that are subjective in nature and sometimes presented with emotion.

Here are two statements, both related to music studies. One is an opinion about the effect of music studies; the other is a presentation of facts about music study.

- Opinion: "Nothing can match the sense of accomplishment a young person feels after mastering the basics of a musical instrument and playing in a first recital."

- Fact: "Studies have shown a positive correlation between learning to play a musical instrument and achieving above-average evaluations in other subjects."

How to recognize Fact/Opinion questions

Here is the way Fact/Opinion questions are usually asked:

- Which of the following statements, taken from the passage, is most clearly an expression of opinion rather than fact?

Expert tips for Fact/Opinion questions

- Remember that you do not need to use any outside knowledge to answer the questions. You aren't expected to be able to verify facts with your own knowledge or with reference materials. However, you should be able to recognize pieces of evidence that are *presented* as facts versus judgments that have inadequate factual support.

- Ask yourself, "Could I reasonably argue with this statement?" If yes, then the statement is probably an opinion. If the statement seems to be presenting factual evidence, then it is probably a fact.

- Words such as "believe" or "probably" and comparisons such as "is more problematical" or "is the best of all" often indicate that authors are stating their opinions.

- Facts often can be stated in terms of quantity or measurable qualities, such as dates or numbers.

Try a Fact/Opinion question

William Bailey, an American Realist painter, studied at Yale in the 1950's. His still lifes depict smooth, rounded containers that sit in a field of uniform color. Bailey denies a close connection to Giorgio Morandi, another American Realist, but admits that they share "a belief in the power of the mute object." While Morandi painted from direct observation, Bailey painted from memory. This difference in method makes Bailey's objects superior to Morandi's for they are thus purified, immutable, and mysterious.

Which of the following statements, taken from the passage, is most clearly an expression of opinion rather than fact?

(A) William Bailey, an American Realist painter, studied at Yale in the 1950's.

(B) His still lifes depict smooth, rounded containers that sit in a field of uniform color.

(C) Bailey denies a close connection to Giorgio Morandi, another American Realist, but admits that they share "a belief in the power of the mute object."

(D) While Morandi painted from direct observation, Bailey painted from memory.

(E) This difference in method makes Bailey's objects superior to Morandi's for they are thus purified, immutable, and mysterious.

Explanation:

Choice E is the best answer because it expresses a subjective judgment about Bailey's objects (as well as about the causal effect of his method); one might disagree with the statement (and claim, for example, that Bailey's objects are not "purified, immutable, and mysterious" or that they are so but not because of his method of painting from memory).

Choices A, B, C, and D are statements of fact: each is either objectively true or false.

Type 9: Attitude Questions

Authors often have feelings about their subjects; that is, they may feel enthusiastic, angry, critical, uncertain, and so forth. The words an author chooses help you recognize his or her attitude. If, for example, an author describes a new invention as "unfortunate" and "misguided," you can say that the author's attitude toward the invention is critical or unfavorable.

How to recognize Attitude questions

Here are the ways in which Attitude questions are usually asked:

- The author's attitude toward X can best be described as...

- The author's attitude toward X is most accurately reflected in which of the following words, as they are used in the passage?

Expert tip for Attitude questions

Look for clue words in the passages. Words such as "successful," "fortunately," and "courageous" probably indicate a positive attitude toward the topic. Words or phrases such as "shortsighted," "inadequate," and "falls short" probably indicate a negative attitude toward the topic.

Try an Attitude question

Parents usually do not insist that their children learn to walk by a certain age. Parents feel confident that the children will learn to walk within a reasonable period of time, when their bodies are ready for such an undertaking. Teachers should adopt the same attitude when teaching children in school how to read. If teachers did this, children might learn to read much more quickly and experience less anxiety while doing so.

The author's attitude toward teachers who try to force children to learn how to read once they reach a certain age can best be described as

(A) sympathetic

(B) accepting

(C) disapproving

(D) neutral

(E) enthusiastic

Explanation:

The word "should" in the third sentence indicates that the author is prescribing that, when teaching children how to read, teachers adopt the same attitude as that usually adopted by parents—not insisting that something be learned by a certain age, but rather letting the child do it when ready. The author would, therefore, disapprove of teachers who try to force children to read at a certain age, making choice C the best answer.

Choices B and E can be eliminated because they express positive attitudes toward teachers who force children to learn to read at a certain age.

Sympathy toward teachers who try to force children to learn to read at a certain age is not suggested by the author, so choice A can be eliminated.

Choice D, neutrality, is contradicted by the author's use of the word "should"—which clearly indicates an attitude of some sort.

Type 10: Extending/Predicting Questions

This type of question tests your ability to recognize ideas or situations that extend (extrapolate) information that has been presented in the passage. For example, such questions can ask you to predict what is most likely to occur in the future if what the author says in the passage is accurate. These questions can also ask you to use information presented in the passage to determine whether the author or an individual mentioned in the passage would agree or disagree with a particular statement that has not been discussed in the passage.

This kind of extending or predicting occurs frequently in casual conversations. Consider this exchange:

Terry: "Did you like the concert last night?"

Rosalyn: "Yes, but it was much too loud for me. My ears hurt the whole time, and for hours afterward."

Terry could safely predict that Rosalyn would prefer *all* concerts she attends to be at comfortable noise levels. Terry could also generalize that Rosalyn's experience at the concert is similar to someone who attends an outdoor theater performance and finds the spotlights too bright, making his or her eyes uncomfortable. At both the concert and the outdoor theater performance, an aspect of the performance made the attendee physically uncomfortable.

To answer extending and predicting questions, you must do more than recall what you have read. You must be able to understand the essential nature or characteristics of ideas or situations appearing in the passage. You then must use that understanding to evaluate the choices in order to determine which choice is most consistent with information you have already been given in the passage.

How to recognize Extending/Predicting questions

Here are the ways in which Extending/Predicting questions are usually asked:

- On the basis of the description of *X* in the passage, the author would be most likely to make which of the following recommendations for future action regarding *X*?

- With which of the following statements about *X* would the author be most likely to agree?

Expert tips for Extending/Predicting questions

- Make sure you find a choice that is highly consistent with the passage.

- For example, the passage might discuss the importance of providing an enriched environment for children, pointing out that interesting challenges stimulate the development of the child's cognitive capacities. One might predict, then, that children who have been raised in an enriched environment are likely to be more developmentally advanced than those children who have not been raised in an enriched environment.

- Don't choose an answer choice just because it sounds related and important. The answer choice may in fact <u>over</u>extend the principles expressed in the passage.

Try an Extending/Predicting question

Carl Filtsch, composer Frederic Chopin's favorite pupil, was once asked by a visitor why he played one of Chopin's compositions so differently from his teacher. His reply delighted Chopin: "I can't play with someone else's feelings."

The statement above suggests that Chopin would have agreed with which of the following ideas about musical performance?

(A) The most important element of a good performance is fidelity to the composer's intentions.

(B) The quality of a musical performance can be best judged by the composer of the piece.

(C) Performances of the same composition by two different musicians should sound different.

(D) A piano teacher must teach a student not only the notes in a composition but also their emotional interpretation.

(E) A composer's interpretation of his or her own compositions is not as profound as another musician's interpretation.

Explanation:

The passage indicates that Chopin was pleased to hear his student say that the student's rendition of a musical composition differed from Chopin's because the student could play only with his own feelings and not with those of his teacher. Chopin's delight in this reply suggests that he would agree that each individual's rendition of a musical composition should sound different because each individual brings his or her own feelings to the piece. Thus, C is the best answer.

Choice A can be eliminated because the passage indicates that Chopin feels that each musician should play a piece with regard to his or her own feelings rather than with regard to the composer's intentions.

Choice B can be eliminated because the passage does not provide information from which to deduce Chopin's views on how a performance should be judged.

Choice D can be eliminated because Chopin's response to his student's remark suggests that Chopin believes that it is up to each individual, not a teacher, to bring his or her own emotional interpretation to a piece.

Choice E can be eliminated because Chopin's response to the student's remark suggests that Chopin would not necessarily agree that a composer's interpretation of a piece is more profound than another musician's interpretation.

Type 11: Conclusion Questions

This type of question asks you to determine which of several conclusions can best be drawn from the information presented in a passage, assuming that information is accurate: if everything the author says is true, what is a necessary consequence that follows from what the author says?

How to recognize Conclusion questions

Here are the ways in which Conclusion questions are usually asked:

- Given the information in the passage, which of the following must be concluded about *X*?

- Which of the following conclusions is best supported by the passage?

Expert tips for Conclusion questions

- Be sure to find a choice that is highly consistent with the passage. Mentally add your choice to the end of the passage—does it fit?

- For example, the passage might present the findings of research that links an audience's comprehension of an advertisement with the advertisement's effectiveness: at the normal rate of 141 words per minute, listeners comprehend 100 percent of the advertisement; at 282 words per minute, listeners comprehend 90 percent of the advertisement; at 423 words per minute, listeners comprehend 50 percent of the advertisement. One might conclude that especially if advertisers incorporate some repetition of key points into their messages, their ads will be highly effective even if read at twice the normal rate—such a sentence would indeed fit well at the end of the passage.

- Don't choose an answer choice just because it sounds related and important. It may in fact <u>over</u>extend the principles expressed in the passage.

Try a Conclusion question

Scientists consider both landslides and surface-creep movement instrumental in the formation of rock glaciers. Evidence of landslides can be distinguished from that of surface-creep movement because landslides leave a more definite and deeper surface of rupture, partly due to their faster rate of movement. Those studying the origins of rock glaciers have noted that some glaciers are well-defined, while others are not, that is, some show evidence of deep ruptures, while others do not.

Given the information in the passage, which of the following must be concluded about rock glaciers?

(A) Not all rock glaciers originate in the same way.

(B) Landslides initiate the formation of rock glaciers, then surface-creep movement follows.

(C) Neither landslides nor surface-creep movement can account for the formation of rock glaciers.

(D) While the definition and depth of rupture can be measured at rock glacier sites, the rate of movement cannot.

(E) Further study is required in order to determine the origins of rock glaciers.

Explanation:

The passage suggests two possible mechanisms for the formation of rock glaciers (first sentence) and describes the effects that distinguish them (second sentence). Since observations reveal both kinds of effects (third and fourth sentences) at rock glacier sites, one can conclude that both formation mechanisms have been occurring. Thus, choice A is the best answer.

Choices C and E can be eliminated because the passage indicates that scientists believe that both landslides and surface-creep movement initiate rock glaciers.

There is no evidence given to support the conclusion that landslides, rock glaciers, and surface-creep movement occur consecutively, hence B can be eliminated.

Choice D can be eliminated because there is nothing in the passage to suggest that the rate of movement cannot be measured.

Type 12: Application Questions

This type of question requires you to recognize a general rule or idea that underlies a specific situation described in the passage and apply that rule or idea to other situations not described in the passage. Specifically, this kind of question measures your ability to discern the relationships between situations or ideas presented by the author and other situations or ideas that might parallel those described in the passage.

How to recognize Application questions

Here are the ways in which Application questions are usually asked:

- The information in the passage suggests that *X* would be most useful to *Y* in which of the following situations?

- It can be inferred from the passage's description of certain *X*s that all *X*s must be…

Expert tips for Application questions

- Look for the most reasonable and consistent choice. The principle from the passage must be directly applicable to the new situation.

- Look for a situation that has characteristics similar to those in the passage. For example, if the passage describes the problems associated with trying to locate the remains of shipwrecks, look for a situation among the choices that has similar features (unknown locations, no eyewitnesses or maps, and some medium like water that makes finding the object difficult).

Try an Application question

Part of the appeal of certain vacation sites is the solitude that can be experienced there. But as more people discover and visit such locations, demand for vacations at those locations will likely decrease. Paradoxically, as soon as the sites become popular, they will necessarily become unpopular.

If the analysis in the passage were applied to gemstones, one would expect the demand for certain gems to decrease when they become

(A) rare

(B) fashionable

(C) beautiful

(D) expensive

(E) useful

Explanation:

Choice B is correct because becoming fashionable implies becoming popular, and once that happens, according to the analysis in the passage, unpopularity follows (demand will decrease).

Choice A reverses the logic of the passage. Choices C, D, and E are not relevant to the level of demand; they merely offer possible characteristics of the gems.

Now that you've prepared

Now that you are done working through the twelve question types, you are ready to put your preparation to work. In the real *PPST: Reading* test, the questions appear in no particular order by type, and they are not labeled by type. You will likely recognize the type of question, though, and you can put your preparation to work.

The practice test in chapter 8 is an actual *PPST: Reading* test from the past. You can simulate actual test conditions, take the test, and then see how you scored. Good luck!

Chapter 5
Preparing for the *PPST: Mathematics* Test

▶ ▶ ▶ ▶ ▶ ▶ ▶ ▶ ▶ ▶ ▶ ▶

Introduction

The emphasis in the *PPST: Mathematics* test is on interpretation rather than computation. Thus, you will not be expected to carry out intricate calculations, but you may be asked to choose appropriate calculations or estimate answers. Many college courses involve some mathematics, but you are seldom required to do long division or add complicated fractions. You are more likely to find very large numbers (e.g., the national debt) or very small numbers (e.g., atomic particles) to compare, a graph to interpret, or a formula to evaluate. The categories tested in the *PPST* represent the kinds of mathematics that might be encountered in any college course, not just in mathematics courses.

The mathematical preparation expected of you is limited to the usual topics of contemporary elementary school mathematics and at least one year of high school mathematics. The questions come from five broad content areas—arithmetic, algebra, geometry and measurement, data interpretation, and reasoning—and require the kind of mathematical competence that you may need in your coursework or in everyday life.

You will have 60 minutes to complete the 40 questions in the paper-and-pencil test. On the computerized test you will have 75 minutes to complete 46 questions. Approximately 45 percent of the questions test conceptual knowledge and procedural knowledge, 30 percent test representations of quantitative reasoning, and 25 percent test measurement and informal geometry and reasoning in a quantitative context. The test is scored on the basis of the number of correct answers; there is no penalty for incorrect answers.

The test questions are chosen from the following five categories, but questions may fit into more than one category.

Category I: Conceptual Knowledge

This category includes knowledge of order, equivalence, numeration and place value, and number and operation properties.

Each number represents a particular value that determines its place when numbers are ordered. When we count "1, 2, 3, 4, 5,…," we follow the order of the counting numbers. You should be familiar with the order not only of the counting numbers, but also of integers and fractions.

Integers

Integers consist of the counting numbers, zero, and the negatives of the counting numbers, as shown below:

$$\ldots, -4, -3, -2, -1, 0, 1, 2, 3, 4, 5, \ldots$$

Fractions and Decimals

Fractions, sometimes called rational numbers, include not only the integers but also the numbers between integers. A number line is a handy way to show how fractions are ordered. Here is an example:

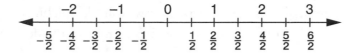

In this example, each unit has been partitioned into two equal parts, and the midpoint of each unit has been given a fraction name with 2 as the denominator. On the number line, you can see that $\frac{5}{2}$ is between 2 and 3 and that $-\frac{1}{2}$ is between 0 and –1. If each unit were partitioned into three equal parts, the number line would look like this:

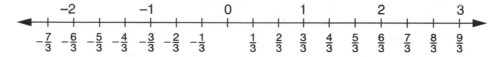

This number line shows, for example, that $\frac{5}{3}$ is between 1 and 2 and that $-\frac{4}{3}$ is less than –1. You should also notice that each integer has a fraction name. For example:

$$-1 = -\frac{2}{2} = -\frac{3}{3}$$

$$\text{and } 3 = \frac{6}{2} = \frac{9}{3}$$

If the units on a number line were partitioned into fourths, we could continue the sequence as follows:

$$-1 = -\frac{2}{2} = -\frac{3}{3} = -\frac{4}{4}$$

$$\text{and } 3 = \frac{6}{2} = \frac{9}{3} = \frac{12}{4}$$

Also, in this case, $\frac{1}{2}$ would have the name $\frac{2}{4}$, $\frac{3}{2}$ would have the name $\frac{6}{4}$, and so on—that is, each number can be given many equivalent names. Here is another example that could come from other subdivisions:

$$\frac{1}{10} = \frac{10}{100} = \frac{100}{1,000}$$

Number lines can be useful for showing both order and equivalence, and you might find it helpful to try some examples of your own, using various kinds of subdivisions.

We use two different systems of notation for numbers: fraction names, such as $\frac{6}{2}$ and $\frac{5}{10}$, and decimal names. In our number system, all numbers can be expressed in decimal form. A decimal point is used, and the place value for each digit depends on its position relative to the decimal point. For example, in the number 25.36, 25 means $(2 \times 10) + (5 \times 1)$ and .36 means $\left(3 \times \frac{1}{10}\right) + \left(6 \times \frac{1}{100}\right)$. (For decimals less than 1, use 0 to the left of the decimal point to make it more noticeable.)

Number Properties

Number properties include knowledge of factors and multiples, primes and divisibility, even and odd numbers, and zero and one.

Operation Properties

Operation properties include knowledge of the commutative, associative, and distributive principles.

Category II: Procedural Knowledge

This category includes the skills needed to match real-life problems with the appropriate mathematical procedures, operations, and quantities. It also includes finding the solution to applied problems, determining information needed, and interpreting and adjusting results of computation. Ratios, proportions, percents, equations and inequalities, computations, patterns, and simple probability are important in this skill area. Algorithmic thinking—for example, following or interpreting procedures and finding or applying patterns in sequences—is also tested in this area. Algorithms often involve repetition of an operation. The ability to estimate and to determine that a problem-solving method or a solution is reasonable is also important.

Estimation skills are useful in many situations. At the supermarket, for example, you might want to estimate the total cost of your groceries as you shop; when taking a test, you might want to estimate the average amount of time you want to spend on each question. In the case of shopping, you might want to *over*estimate the cost to be sure you have enough money. On the other hand, in the case of a test, you may want to estimate how much time you need per question and then try to work under that time to give yourself a little extra time at the end. Whatever your purpose, estimating means selecting some numbers "close to" the given numbers and also numbers that will make the computation easy, because a lot of estimation is done mentally.

Comparisons may have to be more precise, as when you need to determine how much larger, or smaller, one number is than another, or how many times greater one number is than another. This may require some computation, but estimation skills can help you verify your answer.

You should be able not only to solve application problems but also to adjust your answer if the conditions of the problem change, and you should be able to select alternative methods of solution.

Although you will not be expected to know many formulas for the *PPST: Mathematics* test, you should be able to evaluate a given formula or equation, or interpret one. As an example of equivalence of equations, you should recognize that each of the following is equivalent to the equation $2x = 4y + 6$:

$$x = 2y + 3$$
$$2x - 4y = 6$$
$$2x + 1 = 4y + 7$$
$$2x - 2 = 4y + 4$$

Category III: Representations of Quantitative Information

This category includes reading and interpreting visual displays of quantitative information, such as graphs, tables, and diagrams; finding the average, range, mode, or median; making comparisons, predictions, extrapolations, or inferences; applying variation; and recognizing connections between symbols and words, tables, graphs, data, equations, number lines, and the coordinate plane.

Many college textbooks contain graphs to represent given sets of data, illustrate trends, and the like. Here are two examples:

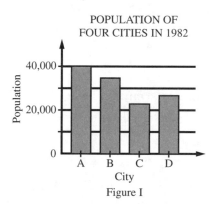

Figure I

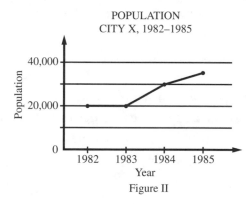

Figure II

Note that an appropriate kind of graph must be used to present data. From the bar graph in Figure I, it can be seen that the population of City B is approximately 35,000, and that the population of City C is less than that of the other three cities. The graph does not show trends, however. The line graph in Figure II does suggest that the population of City X, after showing no change from 1982 to 1983, began to increase. It can also be seen that the increase between 1983 and 1984 was greater than the increase between 1984 and 1985. Note, also, that the data in each graph could be presented in a table, but the visual presentation of a graph is often preferable.

Consider the following problems that illustrate variation:

1. If 1 ice-cream sundae takes 3 scoops of ice cream, how many scoops will 2 sundaes take?

2. If 1 person takes 3 hours to do a piece of work, how long will it take 2 people to do the work?

When events happen in a very regular way so that you can predict the outcome, it is sometimes possible to write an equation that fits. In the example of the ice cream sundaes, if every sundae is made with 3 scoops of ice cream, then the number of scoops (N) will be 3 times the number of sundaes (S), and we can write

$$N = 3 \times S, \text{ or just } N = 3S.$$

Of course, this equation, which illustrates direct variation, would not fit the example of doing a piece of work. For one thing, the more people who work, the *less* time it should take. Also, it is not likely that all the people will work at the same speed, so it is not as easy to predict how long the job will take even if you know how many workers there are. *If* everyone worked at the same speed, you would expect the job to take half as long if 2 people worked, one-third as long if 3 people worked, and so on. Assuming each person worked at the same speed, you would expect that

$$\text{Time } (T) = \frac{3 \text{ hours}}{\text{Number of workers } (N)}, \text{ or } T = \frac{3}{N}.$$

This is an example of inverse variation.

Translating from words to symbols and from symbols to words is an important and useful skill. For example, if Ann is exactly 3 years older than Joe, she will always be 3 years older than Joe, and we can express the relationship by the equation

$$A = J + 3$$

where A represents Ann's age and J represents Joe's age.

It follows that Joe will always be 3 years younger than Ann, and an equivalent equation would be

$$J = A - 3.$$

The formula $D = 5t$ could represent the distance D traveled by someone or something moving at a constant speed of 5 miles per hour for t hours, and $t = \frac{D}{5}$ would be the time it takes to go D miles at 5 miles per hour.

Average, Median, Mode, and Range

Given a list of numbers, it is possible to find the average (arithmetic mean), median, mode, and range. For example, for the list

$$2, 10, 7, 3, 3$$

the average is

$$\frac{2+10+7+3+3}{5} = 5$$

The median is 3, since it is the middle number when the numbers are ordered from least to greatest; the mode is 3, the number that appears most often; and the range is 8, the difference between the greatest number and the least number.

xy-Coordinate System

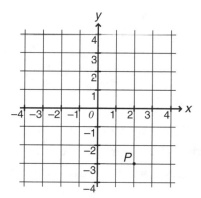

The figure above shows the *xy-coordinate system*, or the *rectangular coordinate plane*. The horizontal number line is the *x*-axis, and the vertical number line is the *y*-axis; the point of intersection of the axes is the *origin*. Each point in the plane has an *x*-coordinate and a *y*-coordinate. A point is identified by an ordered pair (x, y) of numbers in which the *x*-coordinate is the first number. The *x*-coordinate gives the distance to the left (if negative) or to the right (if positive) of the *y*-axis, and the *y*-coordinate gives the distance below (if negative) or above (if positive) the *x*-axis. In the figure above, point P has coordinates $(2, -3)$.

Category IV: Measurement and Informal Geometry

This category includes knowledge of customary and metric systems of measurement; reading calibrated scales; using geometric concepts and properties, such as spatial relationships, symmetry, the Pythagorean theorem, and angles; and solving measurement problems, including linear, area, and volume formulas and rates.

There are two systems of measurement in common use: the U.S. Customary System and the metric, or SI, system. Many measurements today are given in the metric system, and you should know the basic units, together with common measures that are derived from them. In all scientific measurement, all units of measure are related to each other by powers of 10. This makes it easy to convert between units of measure.

Metric Standard Units:

- meter (length)

- gram (mass or weight)

- liter (volume)

- degrees Celsius (temperature)

Common prefixes:

- milli- (one one-thousandth, or 0.001)

- centi- (one one-hundredth, or 0.01)

- kilo- (one thousand, or 1,000)

The standard units of measure in the United States are called the U.S. Customary System. The U.S. Customary System does not use a common factor to convert from one unit to another, so it is important to know the relationships between the units of measure.

Length:

- 12 inches = 1 foot

- 3 feet = 1 yard

- 5,280 feet = 1 mile

- 1,760 yards = 1 mile

Weight:

- 16 ounces = 1 pound (lb)

- 2,000 pounds = 1 ton

Liquid capacity:

- 8 fluid ounces = 1 cup

- 2 cups = 1 pint

- 2 pints = 1 quart

- 4 quarts = 1 gallon

The following chart may be helpful:

Attribute Measured	U.S. Customary Units
Length or Distance	inch foot yard mile
Capacity or Volume	pint quart gallon
Mass (Weight)	ounce pound ton
Temperature	degree Fahrenheit

Attribute Measured	Metric (SI)	
	Basic Units	Some Derived Units
Length or Distance	meter	millimeter centimeter kilometer
Capacity or Volume	liter	milliliter
Mass (Weight)	gram	milligram kilogram
Temperature	degree Celsius	

To solve measurement problems in everyday life, you need to know what characteristic or attribute to consider. If you have a square garden plot and want to know the amount of fence it will take to enclose it, you will be calculating the total *length* of the fence needed to go around the plot. But if you already have a fence and want to paint it, the amount of fence will have to include the *height* of the fence, as well as its total length.

In order to select an *appropriate* unit of measure, you need to recognize the attribute that is important for the problem and know the units used to measure that attribute. Different units of measurement are used for attributes that are different—weight and height, for example. These are familiar examples, and you probably know many of the units used to measure each of these. You probably think of your age as being measured in years, but the ages of young children are sometimes expressed in months.

Sometimes different words are used for the same type of attribute: length, width, and height are examples. These words are used to describe the position of an object in space or to indicate relative lengths. Each of the rectangles in the following figure can be said to have length 4 and width 3; the bottom of the box is also 4 by 3, and the height of the box is 2.

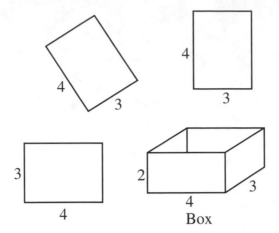

Units of linear measure—inches, feet, miles, meters, kilometers, and so on—are used for length, width, and height. Units of linear measure are also used to measure distance. Distance may be measured along a path, such as a highway or sidewalk, or it may be the "straight line" distance, as from point *A* to point *B* in the figure below.

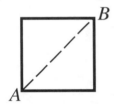

A box that is 2 feet by 3 feet by 4 feet can be thought of as a container with a certain capacity (also called volume). Capacity can be measured in units such as cubic inches, cubic feet, or cubic yards. If you had wooden blocks, each with volume 1 cubic foot (1 foot by 1 foot by 1 foot), you could cover the bottom of the box with 12 of the blocks, as shown below.

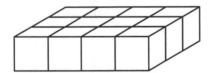

To find the capacity of the box, add another layer of blocks to fill the box, as shown below.

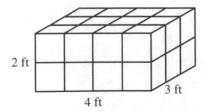

Since two layers contain 24 blocks, the volume of the box is 24 cubic feet.

The 24 blocks form a rectangular solid. If you wanted to paint it, you would need to measure the surface, not its volume. The solid pictured has a top, a bottom, and four sides. The front and back sides of the solid are alike; they are rectangular and measure 4 feet by 2 feet. The two ends are also alike; they are rectangular and measure 3 feet by 2 feet. Finally, the top and bottom are alike; they measure 3 feet by 4 feet.

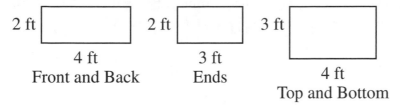

The areas of the front and back are each 8 square feet, the area of each end is 6 square feet, and the areas of the top and the bottom are each 12 square feet. Therefore, the total area of the six surfaces is $8 + 8 + 6 + 6 + 12 + 12 = 52$ square feet.

The lengths could also be in centimeters or meters; in that case, the volume would be in cubic centimeters or cubic meters, and the surface areas in square centimeters or square meters.

Spatial relationships are often important in solving everyday problems. Have you ever had to try several times to get all your belongings into the trunk of your car? If so, and if you succeeded, you probably realize that the shape of the load can be as important as its size. Shape and arrangement may be of practical importance, as in packing the trunk of a car, or it may be important for artistic reasons. As a teacher, for example, you may want to prepare a worksheet for your students that includes charts or graphs. In this case the size of the paper will be a limiting factor, but if you do not want the layout to look too crowded, you will be concerned with arrangement as well as with size. Making patterns for projects is an example of a situation in which you may need to be able to visualize certain spatial relations.

Some of the spatial relations with which you should be familiar are those among lines. Two lines in the same plane may be parallel, or they may intersect. Two intersecting lines may also be perpendicular. These relations are used to identify certain kinds of geometric figures, such as parallelograms and right triangles.

You will not be expected to know a great deal of the vocabulary of spatial relations for the *PPST: Mathematics* test, but you will need to recognize some of these relations.

You may have noticed that beverages are now often sold by the liter, that labels on canned goods often give the mass (weight) in grams and that the specifications for many late-model cars are expressed in metric units. You should know the meanings of the common metric prefixes: milli-, centi-, and kilo-. As illustrated in some of the sample problems, you may need to convert some units. For example, you should be able to convert 250 centimeters to other equivalent metric units.

Category V: Formal Mathematical Reasoning in a Quantitative Context

This category deals with connectives and quantifiers, Venn diagrams, validity, and conclusions, including generalizations and counterexamples.

The term "deductive reasoning" may not be as familiar as some other terms we have discussed, but you have probably had quite a bit of experience with the process, since it is an integral part of mathematics. For example, knowing that

$$\frac{1}{2} = \frac{3}{6}$$

and $\quad \dfrac{1}{3} = \dfrac{2}{6}$

you can conclude that $\dfrac{1}{2} + \dfrac{1}{3} = \dfrac{3}{6} + \dfrac{2}{6}$.

In school, you probably first learned to add fractions with the same denominator and then, using arguments such as that shown above, developed a way to add fractions with different denominators.

As another example, you probably first learned you could find the area of a rectangular region by using the formula $A = lw$, then used this to develop a formula for the area of a region enclosed by any parallelogram. The reasoning is based on this series of diagrams:

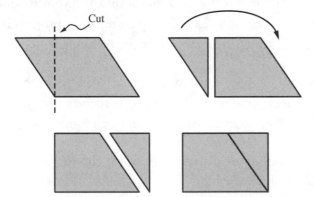

Because the region enclosed by the parallelogram in the first figure can be separated into two pieces that can be rearranged to form a rectangular region, the area can be calculated in the same way. The formula is written as $A = bh$, however, to emphasize that the measurement called the "width" of the rectangle is actually the *height* of the parallelogram and not the measurement of a side. The next step in this particular chain of reasoning would be to deduce the formula for the area of a triangular region. Many people find that following such chains is an aid to memory because the chains show how topics are related.

You should note that certain basic assumptions were made in each of these examples, and the reasoning proceeded from them. These assumptions often take the form of generalizations—in the second example, it was that "the area of any rectangular region can be calculated by the formula $A = lw$." As the examples show, generalizations can be useful, but only if they faithfully represent the mathematical situation. Thus, it is important to be able to tell whether some general statement is, in fact, valid. For example, the statement "all squares are rectangles" is valid because it agrees with the definitions of "square" and "rectangle," but the statement is not valid if turned around—it is *in*valid that "all rectangles are squares." Some, but not all, general statements are valid if reversed, as this example shows. It is sometimes difficult to verify that a general statement is *always* valid, because it would take too long to test every possible case. However, it takes only one case to show that a false generalization is false. The figure below, for example, shows that it is invalid that "all rectangles are squares."

Many generalizations are written with the words "if...then"; for example, the statement "all squares are rectangles" can be expressed this way:

If a figure is a square, then it is a rectangle.

Sometimes it is easier to test a generalization when it is expressed in the "if...then" form, and sometimes it is easier to write a generalization very precisely by using that form.

Here is an example:

$$\text{If } x > 3, \text{ then } x^2 > 9$$

Note that neither of these "if...then" statements is valid if it is turned around. We have already seen that it is false to say that "if a figure is a rectangle, then it is a square." It is also false to say that "if $x^2 > 9$ then $x > 3$" because $(-5)^2 = 25$ and $25 > 9$ but $-5 < 3$. You should notice that each of the following is FALSE:

If a figure is not a square, then it is not a rectangle.

If x is not greater than 3, then x^2 is not greater than 9.

The following examples can be used to show that the statements are false:

[ ] is not a square, but it *is* a rectangle.

-5 is not greater than 3, but $(-5)^2$ *is* greater than 9.

Sometimes people think that when a generalization in "if…then" form is valid, the negative of that generalization is also valid. Sometimes that is so, but, as we have just seen, it is not always so. As you study for the *PPST: Mathematics* test, it can be helpful to follow the chains of reasoning and test yourself on whether the generalizations you find are still true if turned around or changed to negative forms.

Review for the *PPST: Mathematics* Test

The following section provides a review of some of the mathematic concepts of arithmetic, algebra, and geometry, but it is not intended to be a textbook. You should use it to familiarize yourself with the kinds of topics tested in the *PPST: Mathematics* test. If you want more detailed information, however, you should consult a textbook.

Symbols you should know

Some symbols that may be used on the test are as follows:

= is equal to	≤ is less than or equal to
≠ is unequal to	≥ is greater than or equal to
< is less than	⊥ is perpendicular to
> is greater than	∟ is a right angle

Words and phrases you should know

Integers	the numbers $\ldots, -4, -3, -2, -1, 0, 1, 2, 3, 4, \ldots$
Positive Integers	the numbers $1, 2, 3, 4, \ldots$
Negative Integers	the numbers $-1, -2, -3, -4, \ldots$
Whole Numbers	all positive integers, and zero
Zero	an integer that is neither positive nor negative
Odd numbers	the numbers $\ldots, -3, -1, 1, 3, 5, 7 \ldots$—that is, integers that are not divisible by 2
Even Numbers	integers that are divisible by 2—that is, $\ldots, -4, -2, 0, 2, 4, 6, 8, \ldots$
Consecutive Integers	integers in sequence, such as 3, 4, 5, or $-1, 0, 1$; they can be represented in general as $n, n+1, n+2, \ldots$ (where n is any integer)
Prime Number	a positive integer that has exactly two different positive divisors, 1 and itself; for example, 2, 3, 5, 7, 11, 13

Real Numbers	all numbers, including fractions, decimals, etc., that correspond to points on the number line
Factor	a divisor of an integer; for example, 1, 3, 5, and 15 are factors of 15, but 2 is not a factor of 15 (-1, -3, -5, and -15 are, however, factors of 15). Zero is not a factor of any integer.
Multiple	the product of an integer and another integer; some multiples of 4 are -8, -4, 0, 4, 8, 12 and 16, but 2 is not a multiple of 4 (2 is, however, a factor of 4). Zero is a multiple of every integer.
Mean	the average of a group of numbers—that is, the sum of n numbers divided by n
Median	the middle number of a list of numbers, when the numbers are ordered from least to greatest. For example, for the list 1, 3, 3, 4, 6, 9, 11, the median is 4. Note that when there is an even number of numbers, there is no single middle number. In such instances, the median is the average (arithmetic mean) of the *two* middle numbers. Thus, for example, for the list 1, 3, 3, 4, 6, 9, 11, 18, the median is $\dfrac{4+6}{2}$, or 5.
Mode	the number that occurs most often in a group of numbers
Range	the greatest number minus the least number in a group of numbers
Reciprocal	the inverse of a number—that is, one of a pair of numbers whose product is 1; the reciprocal of 5 is $\dfrac{1}{5}$; the reciprocal of $\dfrac{2}{3}$ is $\dfrac{3}{2}$
Exponent	a superscripted number that indicates the number of times a number is multiplied together—in other words, 3^4 indicates $3 \times 3 \times 3 \times 3$
Square	a number multiplied by itself; in other words, 5^2 or $5 \times 5 = 25$
Fraction	a number of the form $\dfrac{a}{b}$, where a and b are integers ($b \neq 0$); a is the *numerator* and b is the *denominator*; if the numerator is larger than the denominator, the fraction is called an improper fraction
Variable	a letter, such as x or n, that is used to represent an unknown quantity
Ratio	a comparison of two or more quantities; for example, if there are 20 women and 15 men in a classroom, the ratio of the number of women to the number of men is 20 to 15, or 20:15, or $\dfrac{20}{15}$

Proportion	a statement of equality between two ratios; for example, if another classroom contained 4 women and 3 men, the ratios of the number of women to the number of men in both classrooms would be equivalent; 20:15 = 4:3 is a proportion. Proportions can be used to solve problems such as the following: If it takes a student 2 days to read 1 book, how many days will it take the student to read 5 books at the same rate? This can be expressed as $\frac{2}{1} = \frac{x}{5}$.

Using cross-multiplication, we can see that if it takes 2 days to read 1 book, then it will take 10 days to read 5 books.

Percent	amount per hundred, or number out of 100; can be expressed as a fraction with a denominator of 100, or as a decimal. For example,

$$35\% = \frac{35}{100} = 0.35; \ 200\% = \frac{200}{100} = 2; \ 0.6\% = \frac{0.6}{100} = 0.006.$$

Percent change	change represented as the amount changed divided by the original amount,

or $\frac{\text{the amount of change}}{\text{the original amount}}$. For example, an increase from 100 to 150 is

$\frac{50}{100}$, or 50%; a decrease from 150 to 100 is $\frac{50}{150}$, or $33\frac{1}{3}\%$.

Operation properties: *associative* (grouping): $(a+b)+c = a+(b+c)$; $(a \times b) \times c = a \times (b \times c)$

commutative (order): $a+b = b+a$; $a \times b = b \times a$

distributive: $a \times (b+c) = (a \times b) + (a \times c)$

Some mathematical topics with which you should be familiar

Arithmetic—how and when to add, subtract, multiply, and divide; percents and ratios; average (arithmetic mean); odd and even numbers; primes, divisibility; simple ideas of probability; ordering and magnitude of whole numbers, fractions and decimals

Algebra—negative numbers; expressing relationships using variables and interpreting such expressions (formulas and equations, for example); use of positive integer exponents; square roots

Geometry—spatial relationships, such as parallel and perpendicular lines, intersections of sets of points (a line and a circle for example), and order along a path; properties of common geometric figures (rectangles and cubes, for example); special triangles (isosceles, equilateral, and right); locating points on a coordinate grid

Measurement—U.S. Customary and common metric units; perimeters, areas, or volumes of common figures (triangles, circles, cubes, etc.); angle measure, comparisons among units of measurement; reading measuring instruments

Data Organization and Interpretation—interpretation of graphs, tables, stem-and-leaf plots, scatter plots, and other visual displays of data; mean, median, mode, and range

Other—reasoning; recognizing insufficient or extraneous data for problem solving; estimation

Algebra review

Algebra is a generalization of arithmetic in which letters (variables) often represent numbers, and rules of arithmetic are followed. This allows words to be translated into algebraic expressions or equations. For example, "The sum of 8 and another number is 10" can be expressed as $8 + x = 10$. Similarly, the expression $1.04S$ can be used to represent a salary S after it is increased by 4%.

Rules to remember in solving equations:

- Combine like terms.

- Isolate the unknown term on one side of the equation (for example, x).

- When two fractions make up both sides of the equation, cross-multiply to solve the equation.

- When you multiply or divide two numbers, both of which have a positive sign or a negative sign, the result is positive.

- When you multiply or divide two numbers, one of which has a positive sign and the other of which has a negative sign, the result is negative.

Strategies for solving word problems:

Decide what information is included in the problem and what information is unknown. Substitute a variable for the unknown quantity. Then write an equation to express the relationship given in the problem and solve the equation.

Probability review

Probability problems ask you to predict the outcome of events. The probability of a particular result is determined by dividing the total number of ways the outcome can occur by the total number of possible outcomes. For example, if there are 3 yellow balls and 2 red balls in a jar, the probability of drawing a red one at random is 2 out of 5.

Geometry and measurement review

Definitions of common terms:

Line
A straight line extends infinitely in both directions.

Line segment
A segment has two endpoints. The part of line *l* from *P* to *Q* is a line segment.

Parallel lines
These are two lines in the same plane that do not intersect.

Perpendicular lines
These are two lines that intersect to form four angles of equal measure, and each angle has a measure of 90°.

Ray
A ray has a single endpoint and extends infinitely from that point.

Angles
An angle is created by the intersection of two lines, rays, or segments. The point where they intersect is called the *vertex*. When two lines, rays, or segments intersect, the opposite angles have equal measure.

A *straight angle* measures 180° and is a straight line. A 90° angle is called a *right angle*, an angle of less than 90° is an *acute angle*, and an angle of more than 90° is an *obtuse angle*. Angles whose measures total 90° are called *complementary angles*, while angles whose measures total 180° are called *supplementary angles*.

Triangles
The sum of the measures of the three angles of a triangle is 180°. *Equilateral triangles* have 3 equal sides, so that each angle is 60°. *Isosceles triangles* have 2 equal sides, giving them two angles of equal measure. *Right triangles* have a 90° angle, and the side opposite the right angle is called the *hypotenuse*.

Perimeter
Perimeter is a measurement of the distance around an object. To find an object's perimeter, add the measurements of all the sides.

Circumference
Circumference is the distance around a circle (its perimeter). Circumference can be found without measuring the distance around the circle if the length of the diameter or of the radius is known.

Linear units of measure
Linear units of measure are used to measure length—for example, an inch, a foot, or a centimeter.

Square units of measure Square units of measure are used to measure the area of a two-dimensional surface (such as a triangle, square, or circle), or the surface area of a three-dimensional figure (such as a prism, cone, or sphere).

Surface area Surface area is the total area of all outside surfaces of three-dimensional objects. For example, a box has six outside surfaces—the sides, or faces, of the box. To find the surface area, you must find the area of each face, then add these values.

Formulas you should know:

$a^2 + b^2 = c^2$ The Pythagorean theorem: in a right triangle, the sum of the squares of the legs equals the square of the hypotenuse.

$A = \dfrac{1}{2} bh$ The area of a triangle is equal to one half the base times the height.

$A = lw$ The area of a rectangle or square is equal to the length multiplied by the width.

$V = lwh$ The volume of a rectangular solid is equal to the length multiplied by the width, multiplied by the height.

$C = \pi d$ The circumference of a circle is found by multiplying the circle's diameter by pi.

$A = \pi r^2$ The area of a circle is found by multiplying the square of the radius by pi.

$\text{Distance} = \text{Rate} \times \text{Time},$ Use these formulas to solve word problems involving time, rate, and distance.

$\text{Time} = \dfrac{\text{Distance}}{\text{Rate}},$

$\text{Rate} = \dfrac{\text{Distance}}{\text{Time}}$

Helpful Advice for Taking the Mathematics Test:

Review the mathematics topics, words and phrases, and symbols that you are expected to know, as listed above; work on any weaknesses you believe you have in those areas.

If you work through the practice questions carefully, you will probably find some mathematics that you already know, but you may also find some things that you need to review more closely. This should help you organize your review more efficiently.

You may need to consult some mathematics texts or other sources for assistance.

You will not be required to identify which type of question is being asked, but being aware of the different types of questions as you prepare for the test will likely help you succeed in answering the questions correctly.

As you take the test you should do the following carefully:

- identify the specific task in each test question

- organize the given information in order to solve the problem

- execute each calculation carefully

- monitor your pace in order to remain on schedule

- use estimation as a means of checking your work

The following suggestions may help you choose the best answer—and remember, try to answer every question.

In a question that involves both decimals and fractions, convert the decimals to fractions or the fractions to decimals. For example, converting $\frac{1}{2}$ to 0.5 may help you determine whether it is greater than or less than 0.7.

You may also wish to convert given fractions to those with common denominators in order to compare them. For example, converting $\frac{1}{2}$ to $\frac{3}{6}$ may help you determine whether it is greater than or less than $\frac{5}{6}$. Likewise, to determine whether $\frac{1}{3}$ is greater than or less than $\frac{2}{5}$, convert both numbers to fractions with 15 as the denominator—that is, $\frac{5}{15}$ and $\frac{6}{15}$.

Remember that negative numbers are less than positive numbers.

Drawing a number line often helps in determining "greater than," "less than," and "equivalent" questions.

You may not need to perform time-consuming calculations to answer the question. If, for example, you are simply asked which of the given fractions is least, you may see at a glance that all are greater than 1 except one—that one would be the correct answer. Or, if a question asks which of the given numbers is greatest, you need not calculate by how much it is greater than each of the others.

Don't be intimidated by the visual presentation of data; take some time to figure out what the chart, graph, etcetera, is saying before you read the accompanying question.

To solve irregular area measurement problems, it may help to visualize the piece that's not there—the piece that would make the area regular. Calculate the area of the missing piece and subtract it from the area as if it were regular; the difference will be the area of the irregular piece. For example, if you have to figure out the area of a rectangle that has a corner missing, figure out the area of the missing corner (use the formula for calculating the area of triangles, $A = \frac{1}{2}bh$), then subtract it from the area of the rectangle; you will then know the area of the rectangle with the missing corner.

For word problems asking you to calculate area measurements, draw a sketch. It does not have to be drawn to scale; the important thing is that you have a place in which to put the given numbers.

Remember that some, but not all, general statements are valid if reversed. For example, it is true that "All squares are rectangles," but it is not true that "All rectangles are squares."

It is often difficult to verify that a general statement is always valid, because it would take too long to test every possible case; however, it takes only one case to show that a generalization is false.

Sometimes it is easier to test a generalization when it is expressed in the "if… then" form. For example, "If a figure is a square, then it is a rectangle" or "If $x > 3$, then $x^2 > 9$."

To succeed on the *PPST: Mathematics* test and many other mathematics tests, you will need to be able to apply mathematics to real-world situations. There are several things you can do to prepare for the test. You can review the mathematical skills that will be required for the test. You can work on any weaknesses you believe you have in those skills. You can study test-taking skills and practice working problems under a variety of self-imposed time limits. If you believe your performance will be hurt by a fear of tests, or some other weakness, you can seek advice from your university testing center. Finally, you will need to assure that you arrive at the test center relaxed and rested so that you do your best on the test.

You should note that no single test can cover all of the topics listed here; rather, only a sample of the topics will be included.

Directions for the Paper-and-Pencil Version of the *PPST: Mathematics* Test

You should familiarize yourself with the following directions before taking the test.

Directions: Each of the questions or incomplete statements below is followed by five suggested answers or completions. Select the one that is best in each case and then fill in the corresponding lettered space on the answer sheet with a heavy, dark mark so that you cannot see the letter.

Special Note: Figures that accompany problems in the test are intended to provide information useful in solving the problem. They are drawn as accurately as possible, except when it is stated in a specific problem that its figure is not drawn to scale. Figures can be assumed to lie in a plane unless otherwise indicated. Position of points can be assumed to be in the order shown, and lines shown as straight can be assumed to be straight. The symbol ∟ denotes a right angle.

Remember, try to answer every question.

The following questions are representative of the questions in the test. They are arranged by category here, but they appear in random order in the test. Some of the questions that appear in this section are not multiple-choice questions; however, all the questions on the actual test are multiple-choice questions.

Category I: Conceptual Knowledge

---

1. Which of the following is equal to a quarter of a million?

   (A) 40,000

   (B) 250,000

   (C) 2,500,000

   (D) $\dfrac{1}{4,000,000}$

   (E) $\dfrac{4}{1,000,000}$

Since one million is 1,000,000, a quarter of a million is $\dfrac{1}{4} \times 1,000,000$, or 250,000. The answer is B.

2. Which of the following fractions is least?

 (A) $\dfrac{11}{10}$

 (B) $\dfrac{99}{100}$

 (C) $\dfrac{25}{24}$

 (D) $\dfrac{3}{2}$

 (E) $\dfrac{501}{500}$

It is not necessary to perform time-consuming calculations to answer the question. Of the five fractions given, four are greater than 1. Only one of the fractions, $\dfrac{99}{100}$, is less than 1, so it must be least. The answer is B.

3. Of the five numbers listed below, which is greatest?

 (A) 0.02

 (B) 0.009

 (C) 0.036900

 (D) 0.01078

 (E) 0.0601

E is the correct answer. If we write the expanded form of three of these, we begin to see why this is so:

$$(A)\ 0.02 = \left(0 \times \frac{1}{10}\right) + \left(2 \times \frac{1}{100}\right)$$

$$(B)\ 0.009 = \left(0 \times \frac{1}{10}\right) + \left(0 \times \frac{1}{100}\right) + \left(9 \times \frac{1}{1,000}\right)$$

$$(E)\ 0.0601 = \left(0 \times \frac{1}{10}\right) + \left(6 \times \frac{1}{100}\right) + \left(0 \times \frac{1}{1,000}\right) + \left(1 \times \frac{1}{10,000}\right)$$

Which of the five numbers in the question is least? B is correct, because there are no $\dfrac{1}{100}$'s, whereas there are in each of the other numbers shown.

4. Which of the following numbers is between $\frac{1}{3}$ and $\frac{2}{5}$?

(A) $\frac{1}{2}$

(B) $\frac{1}{4}$

(C) $\frac{6}{15}$

(D) $\frac{11}{30}$

(E) $\frac{20}{60}$

The answer is D. If you think about the location of $\frac{1}{3}$ and $\frac{2}{5}$ on a number line, you might

notice that both $\frac{1}{3}$ and $\frac{2}{5}$ are less than $\frac{1}{2}$, so answer choice A can be ruled out. Also, $\frac{1}{4}$ is less

than $\frac{1}{3}$, and $\frac{20}{60} = \frac{1}{3}$, so B and E can be eliminated. To check the remaining two choices, rewrite

$\frac{1}{3}$ and $\frac{2}{5}$ as fractions with the denominators 15 and 30 (or note that $\frac{6}{15} = \frac{2}{5}$, leaving only $\frac{11}{30}$).

5. In which of the following are the two numbers equivalent?

I. 0.7 and 0.70

II. $\frac{1}{3}$ and 1.3

III. 4.5 and $4\frac{1}{2}$

Examination of each of the pairs shows that I and III have two numbers that are equivalent:

I. $0.7 = 7 \times \frac{1}{10} = \left(7 \times \frac{1}{10}\right) + \left(0 \times \frac{1}{100}\right) = 0.70$ or just $0.7 = \frac{7}{10} = \frac{70}{100} = 0.70$

II. $\frac{1}{3}$ is less than 1, but $1.3 = 1 + \frac{3}{10}$, which is greater than 1, so $\frac{1}{3} < 1.3$. These are not equivalent.

III. $4.5 = 4 + \frac{5}{10} = 4 + \frac{1}{2} = 4\frac{1}{2}$

6. 1,200 is how many times 1.2?

 (A)   10

 (B)   100

 (C)   1,000

 (D)   10,000

 (E)   100,000

The answer is C. You can divide 1,200 by 1.2 or multiply 1.2 by each of the answer choices. You can verify your answer by noting that since 1.2 is a little more than 1, and 1,200 is a little more than 1,000, the answer must be 1,000.

Category II: Procedural Knowledge

7. Which of the sales commissions shown below is greatest?

 (A) 1% of $1,000

 (B) 10% of $200

 (C) 12.5% of $100

 (D) 15% of $100

 (E) 25% of $40

This problem can be solved by computing each of the commissions, but looking them all over first may save some time. Since 15% of $100 is greater than 12.5% of $100 (choices C and D), there is no need to consider C; and 10% of $200 (choice B) is $20, which is greater than 15% of $100, or $15. That leaves 1% of $1,000 (choice A) and $\frac{1}{4}$ of $40 (choice E) to consider, both of which equal $10. The answer is B.

8. For a certain board game, two number cubes are thrown to determine the number of spaces a player should move. One player throws the two number cubes and the same number comes up on each of the cubes. What is the probability that the sum of the two numbers is 9?

   (A) 0

   (B) $\dfrac{1}{6}$

   (C) $\dfrac{2}{9}$

   (D) $\dfrac{1}{2}$

   (E) 1

If two number cubes are thrown and the same number appears on both, the sum will always be 2 times the number thrown on either of the cubes and thus must be an even number. Since 9 is an odd number, the sum cannot be 9; therefore, the probability is zero. The answer is A.

9. If $P \div 5 = Q$, then $P \div 10 =$

   (A) $10Q$

   (B) $2Q$

   (C) $Q \div 2$

   (D) $Q \div 10$

   (E) $Q \div 20$

$P \div 5 = Q$ can be expressed as $P = 5Q$. Since we are trying to determine what $P \div 10$ equals, we can divide both sides of the equation $P = 5Q$ by 10 as follows:

$$P \div 10 = \frac{P}{10} = \frac{5Q}{10}$$

Simplifying $\dfrac{5Q}{10}$ results in $\dfrac{Q}{2}$, and therefore $P \div 10 = \dfrac{Q}{2} = Q \div 2$. The answer is C.

10. Which of the following is closest to 34×987?

   (A) 25,000

   (B) 27,000

   (C) 30,000

   (D) 34,000

   (E) 40,000

The answer is D. 34×987 is a little less than $34 \times 1,000$, or approximately 34,000.

11. Which of the following is closest to 0.053×21?

   (A)　　0.1

   (B)　　1

   (C)　　10

   (D)　　100

   (E)　1,000

The answer is B. Since 0.053 is about $\dfrac{50}{1,000}$, which equals $\dfrac{5}{100}$, or $\dfrac{1}{20}$, and 21 is close to 20, we can estimate by finding $\dfrac{1}{20} \times 20 = 1$.

12. Mr. Jones discovered that his heating bill for the month of December was $9.15 higher than his bill for the previous December. Since neither month was unusually warm or cold, he decided that the price of fuel had risen. If the bill for the previous December was $50.00, what was the percent increase in the cost of fuel?

According to the problem, the cost for the cheaper month was $50.00. That cost went up by $9.15. Thus, the problem is to compare $9.15 to $50.00 and express that ratio as a percent:

$\dfrac{9.15}{50.00} = \dfrac{18.3}{100.0}$, which is 18.3%.

13. Two executives, Ms. Smith and Ms. Grambling, arrived at a restaurant, ordered, and were served their meal. A little later, Mr. Lucia, an important client of Ms. Smith's, walked into the dining room. The women invited Mr. Lucia to join them. As they prepared to leave, the waiter brought two checks: one for the earlier order, in the amount of $13.57, and one for Mr. Lucia's order, in the amount of $7.62. Ms. Smith planned to pay for all three meals and wanted to include a tip of about 15%. Approximately how much should she leave?

The problem involves both percent and estimation. The approximate cost of the three meals is $21—about $13.50 for the first two and $7.50 for the third. If Ms. Smith wants to leave about a 15% tip, the tip can be computed mentally as

10% of $21 is $2.10
so 5% of $21 is $1.05
and 15% of $21 is $3.15

The price of the meals, plus tip, therefore, is approximately $25.

14. Carlos left Dallas with a full tank of gasoline and drove to Little Rock before stopping for fuel. He purchased 11.2 gallons of gas, refilling his tank. Since he had forgotten to write down the mileage on his odometer when he left Dallas, he consulted his map and found that the distance was reported as 330 miles. Using this information, he estimated his fuel consumption in miles per gallon. What would be a good estimate?

Without carrying out the actual computation, you can probably see that Carlos' car averaged a little less than 30 miles per gallon. If he had used exactly 11 gallons of gasoline and gone 330 miles, that would have represented a rate of 30 miles per gallon. Because he used a little more than 11 gallons, his car must have averaged a little less than 30 miles per gallon.

15. What if Carlos plans to drive 660 miles farther than he has traveled so far? What is the easiest way to calculate the amount of gas he will use?

There is no need for lengthy calculation; simply doubling what he used for 330 miles (11.2 gallons) will result in the approximate amount he will need to go 660 miles (22.4 gallons).

16. As Carlos was completing his purchase in Little Rock, another motorist asked how far it was to Dallas. Carlos told her the distance was 330 miles, and the motorist wondered how much gas she would use getting there. Since the motorist said her pickup truck used a gallon of fuel every 15 miles, Carlos estimated her consumption as 22 gallons. What method might he have used?

Because the pickup truck gets 15 miles per gallon, it must use twice as much gas as Carlos' car, which gets about 30 miles per gallon. So, if Carlos' car required 11.2 gallons on the Dallas-Little Rock trip, the pickup should use about twice as much.

17. On a scale drawing of a room, the scale is to be 1 inch: 4 feet. If the room is 20 feet long, how long should the drawing be?

    (A)   5 in

    (B)   16 in

    (C)   20 in

    (D)   24 in

    (E)   80 in

The answer is A. If 1 inch represents 4 feet, then the proportion $\frac{1}{4} = \frac{x}{20}$ can be solved for x. By cross multiplication, $4x = 20$ and $x = 5$.

18. If the scale used on a scale drawing is 1 inch: 4 feet and the drawing of the room is $3\frac{1}{2}$ inches wide, how wide is the room?

    (A) $7\frac{1}{2}$ ft

    (B) $12\frac{1}{2}$ ft

    (C)   14 ft

    (D)   15 ft

    (E) $15\frac{1}{2}$ ft

The answer is C. Each inch represents 4 feet, so 3 inches would represent 12 feet, and the $\frac{1}{2}$ inch would represent another 2 feet; $12 + 2 = 14$.

19. In a class of 25 students, 15 are girls. What percent of the students in this class are girls?

    (A) 10%

    (B) 15%

    (C) 25%

    (D) 30%

    (E) 60%

The answer is E. Percent means per hundred, and $\dfrac{15}{25} = \dfrac{60}{100}$, or 60%.

20. In a certain class, there are 15 girls and 10 boys. What percent of the students in the class are girls?

    (A) 10%

    (B) 15%

    (C) 60%

    (D) $66\dfrac{2}{3}\%$

    (E) 150%

The answer is C. This problem is the same as the one above, except that here you must first determine the number of students in the class. But the ratio of the number of girls to the number of students is still 15:25, which is 60:100, or 60%.

21. Correct methods for multiplying 399 by 19 include which of the following?

I.

$$399$$
$$\underline{\times 19}$$
$$3591$$
$$\underline{+ 399}$$

II.

$$19$$
$$\underline{\times 400}$$
$$7600$$
$$\underline{- 19}$$

III.

Step 1.
$$400 \times 10 = 4{,}000$$
$$400 \times 9 = 3{,}600$$

Step 2.
$$4{,}000 + 3{,}600 = 7{,}600$$

Step 3.
$$7{,}600 - 19 =$$

(A) I only

(B) III only

(C) I and II only

(D) II and III only

(E) I, II, and III

The answer is E. All of the procedures are correct, and it is not necessary to complete each computation to determine this. Procedure I is the familiar procedure for multiplication.

For II, the procedure is $19 \times 399 = 19 \times (400 - 1) = (19 \times 400) - (19 \times 1)$.

The procedure for III looks a bit more complicated because it includes extra steps for calculating 19×400.

22. Susan says that the probability that a certain traffic light will be green when she gets to it is 0.20. What is her best prediction of the number of times the light will be green for the next 30 times she gets to it?

    (A) 5

    (B) 6

    (C) 7

    (D) 10

    (E) 15

The answer is B. A probability of 0.20 means that she would expect a green light 20 out of every 100 times, or $\frac{1}{5}$ of the time. Since $\frac{1}{5}$ of 30 is 6, the light would probably be green 6 times out of the next 30 times she gets to it.

23. There are 3 red marbles, 4 yellow marbles, and 3 blue marbles in a bag. If one of these marbles is to be selected at random, what is the probability that the marble chosen will be yellow?

    (A) $\frac{1}{10}$

    (B) $\frac{1}{4}$

    (C) $\frac{1}{3}$

    (D) $\frac{2}{5}$

    (E) $\frac{2}{3}$

The answer is D. There are 10 marbles in the bag, and 4 of them are yellow. Therefore, there are 4 out of 10 chances of selecting a yellow one, and $\frac{4}{10} = \frac{2}{5}$.

24. 1. How many 10-foot lengths of rope can be cut from a coil of rope that is 42 feet long?

    2. How many boxes are needed to transport 42 plants if no more than 10 plants can be placed in a box?

    3. If 10 people share equally in the cost of a gift, what is each person's share for a gift costing $42?

    4. If a 42-foot length of rope is cut into 10 pieces of equal length, how long is each of the pieces?

Notice that the *computation* $42 \div 10$ is appropriate for each of these examples. However, a different interpretation of the *answer* is needed for each of the situations:

1. At most 4 pieces of rope 10 feet long can be cut from a 42-foot length.

2. At least 5 boxes are needed to transport the 42 plants if no more than 10 can be placed in a box.

3. Each of 10 people should pay $4.20 to cover the cost of a $42 gift.

4. Each of the 10 pieces of rope cut from a 42-foot length would be $4\frac{1}{5}$ feet long.

These examples illustrate the fact that in a real-life setting, the "answer" to "$42 \div 10$" may be 4 or 5 or 4.20 or $4\frac{1}{5}$, depending on the context.

25. If $A = 6s^2$ and $s = 3$, then $A =$

    (A)   12

    (B)   15

    (C)   36

    (D)   54

    (E)   324

The answer is D, because if $s = 3$, then $s^2 = 9$, so $6s^2$ is 6×9, or 54.

26. If $D = 5t$ and $D = 20$, then $t =$

   (A) $\dfrac{1}{4}$

   (B) 4

   (C) 15

   (D) 25

   (E) 100

The answer is B, because if $D=20$, then 5 must be multiplied by 4 to get this.

Category III: Representations of Quantitative Information

Car Model	Frequency
K	7
X	9
W	7
J	8

27. The chart above gives data about the distribution of four compact-car models in a company parking lot. Which of the following figures best represents the data given?

(A)
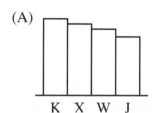
K X W J

(B)
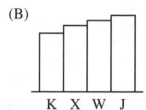
K X W J

(C)
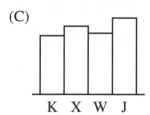
K X W J

(D)
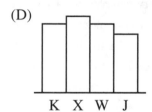
K X W J

(E)
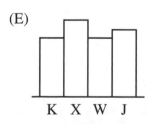
K X W J

The chart shows that one frequency is greater than the others and two frequencies are equal. A quick look at the choices shows that only C, D, and E have both one bar that is taller than the others and two bars of equal height. According to the chart, the frequency of model X is greatest, which eliminates choice C. J is second greatest, so only choice E shows bars whose relative heights all agree with the information in the chart. The best answer is E.

x	y
0	5
2	11
6	23
7	26
10	35

28. Which of the following equations expresses the relationship between x and y in the table above?

(A) $y = x + 5$

(B) $y = x + 6$

(C) $y = 3x + 5$

(D) $y = 4x - 1$

(E) $y = 4x - 5$

Although it is possible to see the relationship between x and y by carefully examining the values in the table, a more systematic approach may be helpful. The correct equation must hold when each of the pairs of values from the table is substituted for x and y in the equations given. Choice A holds for $x = 0$, $y = 5$, but not for $x = 2$, $y = 11$. Choices B, D, and E do not hold for $x = 0$. Choice C holds for all of the values given:

if $x = 0$, then $y = 3(0) + 5 = 5$

if $x = 2$, then $y = 3(2) + 5 = 11$

if $x = 6$, then $y = 3(6) + 5 = 23$, and so forth.

The answer is C.

WIND-CHILL CHART

Temp. (F)	Wind Speed (m.p.h)							
	5	10	15	20	25	30	35	40
50°	48	40	36	32	30	28	27	26
40°	37	28	22	18	16	13	11	10
30°	27	16	9	4	0	–2	–4	–6
20°	–16	4	–5	–10	–15	–18	–20	–21
10°	–6	–9	–18	–25	–29	–33	–35	–37
0°	–5	–21	–36	–39	–44	–48	–49	–53
–10°	–15	–33	–45	–53	–59	–63	–67	–69
–20°	–26	–46	–58	–67	–74	–79	–82	–85
–30°	–36	–58	–72	–82	–88	–94	–98	–100
–40°	–47	–70	–85	–96	–104	–109	–113	–116
–50°	–57	–83	–99	–110	–118	–125	–129	–132

29. The temperature today is 10°F, but it feels as cold as it did last week when the temperature was –10° and the wind speed was 10 miles per hour. According to the chart above, what is the wind speed today?

    (A) 10 m.p.h.

    (B) 15 m.p.h.

    (C) 20 m.p.h.

    (D) 25 m.p.h.

    (E) 30 m.p.h.

According to the chart, if the temperature is –10°F and the wind speed is 10 miles per hour, then the wind-chill factor is –33. The problem states that it feels this cold today although the temperature is 10°F. To solve this problem, look at the row of the chart for 10°F and find the wind-chill factor –33. This factor corresponds to a wind speed of 30 miles per hour. The answer is E.

CHILDREN'S FAVORITE
CARTOONS

Billy Beagle	😊	😊	😊	
Sergeant Starch	😊	😊	🌙	
Kitty Kitty	😊	😊	😊	😊

Each 😊 Represent 10 children.

30. According to the graph above, how many children chose "Sergeant Starch" as their favorite cartoon?

(A) $2\frac{1}{2}$

(B) 3

(C) $20\frac{1}{2}$

(D) 25

(E) 30

The answer is D. If each face in the pictograph represents 10 children, then half a face represents 5 children. There are $2\frac{1}{2}$ faces for Sergeant Starch, and $2\frac{1}{2}\times 10 = 25$.

MARKET SHARE

31. Based on the graph above, if Acme's share is $2,519,000, approximately what was Beta's share?

(A) $3,000,000

(B) $4,000,000

(C) $5,000,000

(D) $6,000,000

(E) $7,000,000

The answer is C. This is a circle graph or pie chart. Because the sector for Beta is about double that for Acme, you can double $2,500,000 for an estimate of Beta's share.

Category IV: Measurement and Informal Geometry

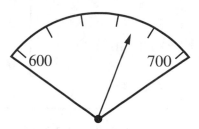

32. On the scale above, the arrow most likely indicates

    (A) $630\frac{1}{2}$

    (B) 635

    (C) $660\frac{1}{2}$

    (D) 670

    (E) 685

The scale given in the problem shows the numbers 600 and 700, which means that the interval between them represents 100 units. The interval is marked off in fifths, so each subdivision represents 20 units, and the reading at each mark can be written on the scale.

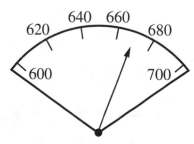

The arrow marks a point approximately halfway between 660 and 680, or 670. The best answer is D.

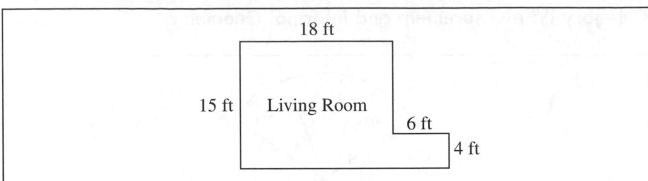

33. The de Falco family wanted to replace the carpet in their living room. The room was shaped as shown in the diagram above. The carpet they liked was available in 12-inch-square carpet tiles that were sold in cartons of 12 per carton. How many cartons of carpet did they need to buy?

The first thing to note, because the room dimensions are in feet, is that the carpet tiles are 1 foot square. You also need to recognize that the floor space can be separated into two rectangular parts. The main part of the living room is a rectangle 15 feet by 18 feet that would require 15×18 or 270 carpet tiles to completely cover the floor. The area in the lower right of the diagram is 4 feet by 6 feet and requires another 24 tiles; so the de Falcos need a total of 294 tiles. Because the tiles come in units of 12 tiles per carton, you must divide 294 by 12 to determine the number of cartons needed. Since the answer is 24.5, the de Falcos must buy 25 cartons.

34. On a trip from Chicago to Seattle, the Bergen family drove westward on Interstate Route I-90. At a rest area just before Spearfish, Ms. Bergen examined the route from Spearfish to Billings on the map. This is what she saw:

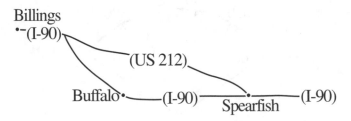

What could Ms. Bergen conclude from the map about the relative distances along US 212 and I-90 from Spearfish to Billings?

An important relation in a triangle is that any one of its sides is always shorter than the sum of the other two. Since the routes shown here form a rough triangle, the route along US 212 is shorter than the route along I-90.

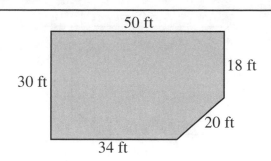

35. Suppose you want to buy sod to make a lawn on the plot of ground pictured above. How much sod would you need?

This is an example of a measurement problem you might encounter in everyday life. To solve it, you must first recognize that it is the *area* of the plot that is to be found. The plot is an odd shape, one for which you did not learn a formula in school, so a bit of work needs to be done. The plot is almost rectangular, but it has a corner missing. This is where spatial visualization comes in, because the missing corner is in the shape of a right triangle:

That is, the area of the plot can be found by calculating the area of a rectangular plot and then subtracting the area of the triangular piece. The area of a rectangular plot 50 feet by 30 feet is 1,500 square feet, but what is the area of the corner? You need to recall that the formula for the area of a triangular region is $A = \frac{1}{2}bh$, so all that is needed now is to determine the base and height of the piece. It is a right triangle, so its base and height can be considered to be as shown here:

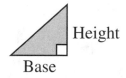

The completed rectangle is 50 by 30, and we know some other measurements:

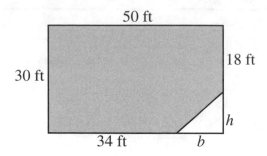

Thus, $h = 30 - 18 = 12$ feet

and, $b = 50 - 34 = 16$ feet

Therefore, the area of the plot to be sodded is $1,500 - 96$, which is 1,404 square feet. You should notice that to solve the problem you need spatial skills to visualize the missing piece, and also knowledge of formulas and how to evaluate them. You should also note that the 20 feet given in the problem was not needed for the solution.

---

36. Ramon wants to buy fabric for drapes in his den. He has one window 60 inches wide. The top of the window is 6 feet 8 inches above the floor. He wants the drapes to hang from 2 inches above the window to 1 inch from the floor. He also wants the drapes to extend 4 inches on either side of the window. He needs to allow 6 inches at the top and the bottom for hems, and he plans to add 50% to the width to allow for pleats and side hems. What are the dimensions of the piece of fabric needed before it is hemmed and pleated?

Without a picture to guide you, this may seem just a jumble of numbers, and making a sketch might be the most helpful thing to do first. The sketch does not need to be drawn to scale; the important thing is that you have a place to put in the numbers given. Beginning with the figure on the left, we can see what some of these numbers represent:

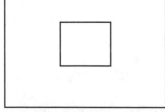

Room and Window

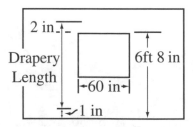

With the help of the sketch, you see that the height of the piece of fabric would be 6 feet 8 inches plus 2 inches (extra at the top) less 1 inch (height from the floor), but plus 12 inches (hem allowance). So the vertical dimension is 7 feet 9 inches. The horizontal dimension is 60 inches + 8 inches (in order to allow for the extra coverage) or 68 inches. However, we must increase this by 50% to allow for pleats and side hems. That is, the width must be 68 inches + $\frac{1}{2}$ (68 inches), which is 102 inches, or 8 feet 6 inches. Thus, the dimensions of the piece of fabric to be bought are 7 feet 9 inches by 8 feet 6 inches.

> 37. About how many cubic yards of coal can be stored in a silo 20 feet in diameter and 40 feet high? (A silo is a storage tower having the shape of a cylinder.)

In this problem you need to use the formula for the *volume* of a cylinder, $V = Ah$, where A represents the area of the base and h represents the height of the cylinder. The base is circular, and the formula for the area of a circular region is $A = \pi r^2$, where r represents the radius. You are given that the diameter is 20 feet, so you need to recall that a diameter is twice the length of a radius. You also need to recall that π is approximately 3.14. You should also notice that the problem asks, "how many cubic yards?" while the dimensions of the silo are given in feet. Before you substitute into the formula, convert the dimensions from feet to yards as shown below, recalling that 3 feet = 1 yard.

$$\text{Diameter} = 20 \text{ feet} = \frac{20}{3} \text{ yards}$$

$$\text{Radius} = \frac{1}{2}(\text{diameter}) = \frac{1}{2}\left(\frac{20}{3}\text{ yards}\right) = \frac{10}{3} \text{ yards}$$

$$\text{Height} = 40 \text{ feet} = \frac{40}{3} \text{ yards}$$

The area of the base of the silo is $3.14 \times$ the square of the radius, or $3.14 \times \frac{100}{9}$ or $\frac{314}{9}$ square yards.

The silo is $\frac{40}{3}$ yards tall, so the volume is $\frac{314}{9}$ square yards $\times \frac{40}{3}$ yards $= \frac{314}{9} \times \frac{40}{3}$,

or approximately $35 \times \frac{40}{3} = \frac{1,400}{3}$, or approximately 467 cubic yards.

38. To convert centimeters to millimeters, you should

   (A) divide by 10

   (B) multiply by 10

   (C) divide by 100

   (D) multiply by 100

   (E) multiply by 1,000

The answer is B. 100 centimeters = 1 meter and 1,000 millimeters = 1 meter; 100 centimeters = 1,000 millimeters; so 1 centimeter = 10 millimeters.

39. If pesos are exchanged at 600 to the dollar, how do you convert pesos to dollars?

   (A) Divide by 6

   (B) Multiply by 6

   (C) Divide by 600

   (D) Multiply by 600

   (E) Multiply by 100

The answer is C. 600 pesos = 1 dollar. 1 peso = $\frac{1}{600}$ dollar.

40. On the scale above, the arrow most likely points to

(A) $60\frac{1}{2}$

(B) $62\frac{1}{2}$

(C) $63\frac{1}{2}$

(D) 65

(E) 70

The answer is E. The arrow points to a number that is about halfway between 60 and 80. Alternatively, each subinterval on the scale represents 4 units; so the arrow is pointing halfway between 68 and 72, or 70.

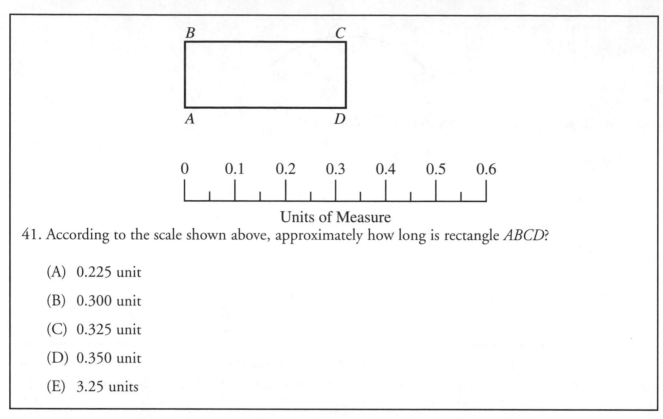

Units of Measure

41. According to the scale shown above, approximately how long is rectangle *ABCD*?

    (A) 0.225 unit

    (B) 0.300 unit

    (C) 0.325 unit

    (D) 0.350 unit

    (E) 3.25 units

The answer is C. Each subinterval on the scale represents 0.5 unit. *AD* extends from 0 to about halfway between 0.30 and 0.35, or 0.325.

Category V: Formal Mathematical Reasoning in a Quantitative Context

> Some values of *x* are less than 100.

42. Which of the following is NOT consistent with the sentence above?

    (A) 5 is not a value of *x*.

    (B) 95 is a value of *x*.

    (C) Some values of *x* are greater than 100.

    (D) All values of *x* are less than 100.

    (E) No numbers less than 100 are values of *x*.

The sentence says that *some* values of *x* are less than 100, which means that there is *at least one* value of *x* that is less than 100. This value can be 5, but it does not have to be, or it can be 95, so choices A and

B both are consistent. While at least one value of x must be less than 100, some values can be greater than 100, or all values can be less than 100, without contradicting the sentence. Thus choices C and D are consistent. If no numbers less than 100 are values of x, however, there will not be at least one value of x less than 100, so choice E is not consistent with the sentence. The best answer is E.

Now that you've prepared

Now that you are done working through the five categories of questions, you are ready to put your preparation to work. In the real *PPST: Mathematics* test, the questions appear in no particular order by category, and they are not labeled by category. You will likely recognize the category of question, though, and you can put your preparation to work.

The practice test in chapter 9 is an actual *PPST: Mathematics* test from the past. You can simulate actual test conditions, take the test, and then see how you scored. Good luck!

Chapter 6

Preparing for the *PPST: Writing* Test:
The Multiple-Choice Section

▶   ▶   ▶   ▶   ▶   ▶   ▶   ▶   ▶   ▶   ▶   ▶

Introduction

The multiple-choice section of the *PPST: Writing* test is designed to measure your ability to recognize correct standard written English, which is the language of most college textbooks and the language you will be expected to use as a professional. No question asks you to define grammatical terminology or to label particular elements of grammar; you simply need to recognize what is correct and what is incorrect.

This chapter contains a review course on basic grammar and sentence construction, a close-up examination of the two types of questions (**Usage** and **Sentence Correction**), and practice questions with explanations of right answers.

Overview of the multiple-choice section

The multiple-choice section of the test consists entirely of individual sentences. There are no essays or long paragraphs.

There are 38 sentences, and each is the basis of a single multiple-choice question. You have 30 minutes to complete these 38 questions. (If you are taking the computer version, you have 38 minutes in which to answer 44 questions.) You will need to develop the ability to work carefully and confidently, without frequently second-guessing yourself, at a fairly quick pace.

Where the sentences come from and what they are like

The sentences used in the *PPST: Writing* test are rarely written from scratch by the question writers. The vast majority are taken from college-level books, magazines, and newspapers.

The sentences cover a wide variety of topics, ranging from science, history, social sciences, and literature to the arts. You should not be worried about or intimidated by their content. Each sentence makes a statement or presents an idea that you can understand without having any specialized knowledge. Do not be put off by subjects that seem foreign to you or by names that are unfamiliar. Your task is to understand how the different parts of the sentence work together.

The two types of questions

The multiple-choice section of the test consist of two subsections.

- The first subsection (**Usage**) consists of sentences that contain four underlined parts. Appearing after each sentence is a fifth underlined choice, "No error." For each sentence, you have to determine which underlined part, if any, contains an error. Some of the sentences will not contain any errors; that is, all of the underlined parts will be correct. If this is the case, you should select the fifth choice, "No error," as your answer.

- The second subsection (**Sentence Correction**) gives you sentences in which some or all of the words have been underlined. Each sentence is followed by five choices: the first is the same as the underlined part, and the others are rewrites. Your job is to decide whether the original is the best way to express the meaning of the sentence or whether one of the other four choices would be better.

An in-depth look at each question type, with specific expert tips for each, can be found after the review course.

What's being tested?

The two question types, **Usage** and **Sentence Correction**, are the basis for assessing a whole range of skills and knowledge in standard written English.

The following list indicates the major areas covered by the questions. Each element in the list is covered in the review course that follows.

Parts of Speech

- Noun
- Verb
- Adjective
- Adverb
- Pronoun
- Preposition
- Conjunction
- Interjection

Parts of Sentences:

- Subject
- Predicate
- Phrases and Clauses

Grammar

- Forms of adjectives and adverbs
- Comparisons
- Subject-verb agreement
- Verb tense
- Parallelism

- Noun-pronoun agreement
- Negation
- Modification

Sentence fragments and run-on sentences

Punctuation

- Comma usage
- Colon usage
- Semicolon usage
- Apostrophe usage

Capitalization

Word usage (diction)

Idiomatic expressions

Clarity of expression

- Redundancy
- Wordiness

It is also important to know what is **not** tested on the multiple-choice section of the test.

- Spelling is not tested. Everything on the test is spelled correctly. Don't be tempted to choose an answer based on what you think is a spelling error.

- Extremely subtle and often-ignored distinctions, such as the difference between "shall" and "will" or the difference between "due to" and "because," are not tested.

Review Course on Grammar and Sentence Construction

This review course covers many of the common elements of grammar and sentence construction that you need to know to do well on this test. The review course may use some grammar terms that are new to you. You do **not** need to know these terms to do well on the *PPST: Writing* test. These terms are mentioned in case you want to consult a grammar handbook for more help. It is often easier to find out information about a particular grammar concept if you know what it is usually called in a grammar book.

Parts of Speech

Every word in a sentence can be classified as a part of speech. There are eight parts of speech:

- Noun
- Verb
- Adjective
- Adverb
- Pronoun
- Preposition
- Conjunction
- Interjection

In the *PPST: Writing* test, you will need to know how to identify the first six parts of speech on this list (you will not need to know how to identify conjunctions or interjections). However, it is helpful to recognize conjunctions and interjections because they often serve as signals for particular kinds of punctuation.

Let's review the parts of speech and how to recognize them.

Noun

A **common noun** is a word that names a person, place, thing, or concept. Examples of nouns include *nurse* (person), *office* (place), *book* (thing), *happiness* (concept).

A **proper noun** is a noun that gives the name of a specific person, place, thing, or concept; it is always capitalized. Examples of proper nouns include *Ellen* (person), the *Grand Canyon* (place), the *Washington Monument* (thing), *Buddhism* (concept).

You will need to know when a noun should be a proper noun, and when it should not. For example, *judge*, when used by itself, is a common noun and should not be capitalized. However, if *judge* is used as a part of someone's title, as in *Judge Harry Jones*, it then becomes a proper noun and should be capitalized.

Verb

A **verb** is a word that tells what a subject does or is. Examples of verbs include *walk, feel, led, is running, had eaten*. The base form of a verb is the phrase "*to + verb*": *to show, to fall, to seek, to read*. From this base form, the verb can change its form for one of several purposes. These include the following:

A verb can show time through its tense.

Example:	to learn	Present tense:	Tammy <u>learns</u>.
		Past tense:	Tammy <u>learned</u>.
		Past perfect tense:	Tammy <u>has learned</u>.
		Future tense:	Tammy <u>will learn</u>.

An **irregular verb** does not follow this pattern; the base form changes in different ways. Here are some common irregular verbs you should know for the *PPST: Writing* test:

Present	Past	Past Participle
be	was/were	(have/had) been
do	did	(have/had) done
go	went	(have/had) gone
lay	laid	(have/had) laid
lie	lay	(have/had) lain
rise	rose	(have/had) risen
swim	swam	(have/had) swum

The following verb pairs are often confused. The difference between those in each pair is that the first one takes a direct object and the second one does not.

Present	*Past*	*Past Participle*	
set (put)	set	set	*Set the glass down.*
sit (be seated)	sat	sat	*Please sit down.*
lay (put)	laid	laid	*She laid the papers down.*
lie (recline)	lay	lain	*An hour ago I lay down for a nap.*
raise (lift)	raised	raised	*The glasses have been raised.*
rise (get up)	rose	risen	*The Sun has risen.*

A verb can indicate the number of the noun engaging in the action (singular—one; or plural—more than one).

Singular: The runner <u>sprints to</u> the finish line.

Example: to <u>sprint</u>

Plural: The runners <u>sprint to</u> the finish line.

Adjective

An **adjective** is a word that describes a noun or pronoun. Adjectives are said to *modify* nouns and pronouns because they help change a reader's understanding of a noun. Notice how your image of the dog changes in the following sentences:

Examples: A <u>tired</u> dog sat on the porch next to the door.

An <u>angry</u> dog sat on the porch next to the door.

A <u>happy</u> dog sat on the porch next to the door.

Adverb

An **adverb** is a word that modifies a verb, an adjective, another adverb, or a clause. Adverbs are used to add detail and specificity to the action of a sentence.

Examples: The adverb modifies a verb: Dan finished his dessert <u>quickly</u>.

The adverb modifies an adjective: The puzzle left him <u>completely</u> confused.

The adverb modifies another adverb: The cat climbed the tree <u>very</u> quickly.

The adverb modifies a clause: <u>Suddenly</u>, the lights went out.

Most adverbs end in *-ly*. They are often formed by adding *-ly* to an adjective.

Pronoun

A **pronoun** is a word that stands in for or refers to a noun. A pronoun can be personal (stands in for a noun) or possessive (refers to a noun).

Examples: He baked a cake. (The pronoun *he* stands in for a noun, so it is a personal pronoun.)

Leticia fixed her car. (The pronoun *her* shows Leticia's possession of her car, so it is a possessive pronoun.)

Personal pronouns usually change their form depending on whether they are used as the subject (the person or thing performing the action) or object (the person or thing receiving the action) of a sentence.

Personal pronouns to use as subjects: *I, we, you, he, she, it, they*

Personal pronouns to use as objects: *me, us, you, him, her, it, them*

Examples: He fell out of the boat. (*He* is the subject of the sentence.)

Alice gave the extra ticket to me. (*Me* is an object of the sentence.)

Possessive pronouns usually change form depending on whether they are used as adjectives or stand alone.

Possessive pronouns to use as adjectives: *my, our, your, his, her, its, their*

Possessive pronouns to use standing alone: *mine, ours, yours, his, hers, its* (rarely used), *theirs*

Examples: Her book won the Pulitzer Prize. (*Her* modifies *book* and thus acts as an adjective.)

Alice took my sandwich and gave me hers. (*Hers* stands alone; it is an object of the sentence and is being used in place of the phrase *her sandwich*.)

Pronouns must agree in number with the noun for which they are standing in or to which they are referring. If a pronoun is used to stand in for *the students*, it should be a plural pronoun because it is referring to more than one student. The pronoun *they* is a plural pronoun and should be used in this case.

Example: General Motors is one of our biggest companies. It has about 365,000 employees. (*It* refers to *General Motors*, which is a single company even though the name ends with *s*. Therefore the singular pronoun *it* is used, rather than the plural pronoun *they*.)

Pronouns must also agree in gender with the noun for which they are standing in or to which they refer. If a pronoun is used to stand in for the male name *Mark*, it should be a masculine pronoun, *he*.

Following is an explanation of the most often confused pronouns.

Who and *whoever* are used as subjects.
Who is it?

Whom and *whomever* are used as objects.
Whom did you invite?

Its is a possessive pronoun.
The dog ate its dinner.

It's is not a pronoun, but a contraction.
It's not my dog.

Anytime you encounter the word *it's*, substitute *it is* and check whether it makes sense.

Restrictive and nonrestrictive pronouns

Pronouns are often used to introduce information about the nouns to which they refer.

Examples: Bring me the pear <u>that</u> looks ripest.

I do not like *Romeo and Juliet*, <u>which</u> is too sad for me to enjoy.

In the first example, the sentence does not make much sense without the information that follows the pronoun. *Bring me the pear* does not explain <u>which</u> pear is desired. The information *that looks ripest* limits or restricts the reader's understanding of the *pear* being referred to; therefore, the pronoun is **restrictive**.

By contrast, note that in the second example, *Romeo and Juliet* is very clearly a particular play, and the information that follows (*which is too sad for me to enjoy*) is nice to know, but not necessary. (The fact that *which is too sad for me to enjoy* is set off by a comma is another clue that it is extra information.) *Romeo and Juliet* does not need any additional restrictive information, so the pronoun that follows is **nonrestrictive**.

Most pronouns can be either restrictive or nonrestrictive without any change in form.

Examples: My cousin <u>who</u> lives in Dallas called me last week. (*Who* is restrictive, because we assume that the writer has more than one cousin and is giving the information to indicate which cousin is being discussed.)

Charles Dickens, <u>who</u> wrote *David Copperfield*, was born in 1814. (*Who* is nonrestrictive, because the famous name indicates exactly which person is being discussed.)

On the other hand, with *that* (restrictive) and *which* (nonrestrictive), you do need to be careful to use the correct pronoun.

Preposition

A **preposition** is a word used most often in front of a noun or pronoun to identify a relationship such as time or space. Prepositions help provide more detail about an action.

Examples: Portia drove <u>to</u> the bank. (The preposition *to* helps to show *where* Portia was driving).

Josh hasn't seen Ken <u>since</u> Friday. (The preposition *since* helps to indicate *when* Josh last saw Ken).

Common prepositions include *about, at, before, for, in, like, of, on, to, with.* Consult a grammar handbook for a more detailed list of prepositions.

Conjunction

There are two types of conjunctions: coordinate and subordinate.

Coordinate conjunctions join two coordinate elements—for example, two independent nouns, verbs, phrases, or clauses. Coordinate conjunctions include *and, but, or, nor, for,* and *also.*

Example: I brought a notebook <u>and</u> a pen.

Subordinate conjunctions join subordinate elements to the principle elements of sentences.

Example: I will go <u>because</u> you asked.

Correlative conjunctions are conjunctions that are used in pairs. Correlative conjunctions include *either...or, neither...nor,* etc.

Example: <u>Either</u> he <u>or</u> I must go.

Interjection

An **interjection** is a word that expresses emotion. It is inserted into a sentence or stands alone. Interjections usually are punctuated by exclamation points.

Examples: <u>Wow!</u> Dante received an A on his research paper.

Trina lost control of her sled—<u>look out!</u>

Examples of interjections include: *wow!, oh my!, ha!,* and *neat!*

Parts of Sentences

Subject and predicate

Every complete sentence has to have two essential parts in order to be a complete sentence: a **subject** (a person, place, or thing that is performing an action) and a **predicate** (the action that the subject performs or an assertion about that subject).

For example, in the sentence

Raoul has been working in his garden.

Raoul is the **subject** of the sentence. Raoul is performing an action (he *has been working* in his garden).

...has been working in his garden is the **complete predicate**. It characterizes Raoul. As a complete predicate, it includes both the main verb (*has been working*) and any modifiers of the action, or anyone or anything receiving the action of the verb (in this case *in his garden* modifies the action by saying where it happened).

...has been working... is the **simple predicate**. It consists only of the main verb in the sentence.

The subject of a sentence can be a common noun (*book, table, lamp*) a proper noun (*Reggie, Janet, the Secretary of Education*), or a pronoun (*I, you, they*); it may consist of a word, phrase, clause, or combination of nouns (*Tyrone and Laura, the first person who comes into the room, the woman wearing the baseball cap*). The simple predicate is always the main verb. The **complete predicate** includes the simple predicate but may also include adverbs, adjectives, prepositions, and prepositional phrases.

Phrases and clauses

Phrases and clauses are both parts of sentences. A **phrase** is a group of words that does not contain a subject and a predicate. *According to Susan* is a phrase.

A **clause** is a group of words that contains both a subject and predicate and that is used as part of a sentence.

Example: If she is late, we will miss the movie.

The example is made up of two clauses. The first clause (*If she is late*) is grammatically and logically incomplete on its own. This is called a **dependent** or **subordinate** clause. While the second clause (*we will miss the movie*) is an **independent** or **principal** clause and therefore could stand alone as a sentence, it does not express the complete meaning. In other words, we will miss the movie only if she is late. Both clauses of the sentence are necessary to express the complete thought.

The dependent or subordinate clause is introduced by a subordinating word that relates it to another clause. *She is late* would be an independent clause or a simple sentence. Adding the word *if* makes the clause subordinate to the second part of the sentence.

Grammar

Grammar is a system of rules that governs how words are used to form sentences. Grammar can be intimidating because it is often discussed using a highly specialized vocabulary; however, you do not need to know all of the grammar rules and vocabulary to identify and correct grammar mistakes effectively. Here are some of the aspects of grammar that are most important for students who are learning how to write and speak effectively.

Forms of adjectives and adverbs

Adjectives and adverbs usually have three forms: the **positive**, the **comparative**, and the **superlative**. The comparative form is used to compare two things, and the superlative is used to compare something to three or more.

Positive	Comparative	Superlative
big	bigger	biggest
interesting	more interesting	most interesting
good	better	best
badly	worse	worst

She was good at tennis.
Of the two, she was the better player.
She is the best tennis player on the team.

The classrooms were painted badly.
The hallways were even worse.
The lounge was the worst of all.

Subject-verb agreement

Subjects and verbs have to indicate the same number; if a noun consists of a single thing, then the verb that goes with the noun must also be in a singular form. A sentence has a **subject-verb agreement error** when one word in a subject-verb pair is singular and the other word is plural.

Incorrect:	Birds flies.	This sentence is incorrect because the subject, *Birds*, is in a plural form while the verb, *flies*, is in a singular form.

You can correct sentences by changing the form of one of the words to make both words singular or both words plural.

Correct:	Birds fly.	(Both the subject and the verb are plural.)
	A bird flies.	(Both the subject and the verb are singular.)

For the most part, English speakers have internalized this grammar point, and subject-verb agreement just sounds right. For example: I go, you go, she goes, we go, they go. Speakers tend to make subject-verb agreement errors when the subject and verb are separated by a clause.

Example: Many employees at the law firm take long lunches.

Even though *law firm* is the noun next to the verb, *employees* is the subject, and *take* agrees with the plural subject.

Compound subjects are sometimes tricky. When two subjects are joined by *and*, the subject is generally plural.

Example: Coffee and tea are available.

On the other hand, some words and phrases, such as *plus*, *as well as*, or *in addition to*, do not make true compound subjects.

Example: Coffee, as well as tea, is available.

(The commas around the phrase *as well as tea* are another hint that only *coffee* is the subject of the verb.)

When compound subjects are joined by *or* or *nor*, the verb agrees with the closest subject.

Example: Neither cookies nor tea is available.

Verb tense

Each verb in a sentence must be in the proper tense. If two or more actions in a sentence occur at the same time, the verbs that indicate those actions must be in the same tense (for example, past tense or present tense). A sentence has a **verb tense error** if a verb in the sentence is in the wrong tense. Keeping all of the verbs in the same tense clarifies when the action in a sentence is taking place.

Incorrect: During the committee meeting last week, Jessie <u>suggested</u> going to the beach, while Tracy <u>votes</u> for going to a museum.

(Both underlined verbs should be in the past tense because the phrase *During the committee meeting last week* indicates that both actions occurred in the past.)

You can correct the sentence by changing *votes* to the past tense.

> Correct: During the committee meeting last week, Jessie <u>suggested</u> going to the beach, while Tracy <u>voted</u> for going to a museum.
>
> (Both verbs are now in the past tense. Verbs in the past tense often end in *-ed*.)

Parallelism

When a sentence contains a series of items, all the items should be in parallel form. Keeping all phrases and clauses in the same form creates **parallelism** by clarifying the relationship among the parts of the sentence.

> Incorrect: Nadia enjoys <u>traveling</u> and <u>to visit</u> friends.
>
> (This sentence is not parallel because *traveling* and *to visit* are not in the same form.)

You can correct sentences by putting both words in the same form.

> Correct: Nadia enjoys <u>traveling</u> and <u>visiting</u> friends.
>
> (Both words are now in an *-ing* form.)

Parallel grammatical structure is crucial for clear and concise sentences.

> Incorrect: He was good at English, history, and playing soccer.
>
> Correct: He was good at English, history, and soccer.

Noun-pronoun agreement

All pronouns and the nouns to which they refer must have the same number; both words must be singular or both words must be plural. If both words do not have the same number, the sentence has a **noun-pronoun agreement** error.

> Example: I tried to go to <u>the supermarket</u> near my house, but <u>they</u> were closed.
>
> (The sentence is incorrect because the noun, *supermarket*, is singular, and the pronoun, *they*, is plural.)

You can correct the sentence by making the pronoun singular.

> Example: I tried to go to the <u>supermarket</u> near my house, but <u>it</u> was closed.
>
> (Both noun and pronoun are singular. Note that the verb, *were*, also had to become singular to agree with the pronoun.)

Negation

The negative particles are *not* and *no*. The negative particle is placed after the auxiliary verb in a sentence.

> Example: The dog **will** *not* **come** when called.

Come is the verb, *will* is the **auxiliary verb** (it "helps" the verb *come* by putting it into the future tense), and *not* is the negative particle.

A form of the verb *to do* often performs an auxiliary function in forming the negative.

> Example: I **do** *not* **want** dessert.

Never can be used with the main verb.

> Example: I *never* **want** dessert.

Contractions are common in negation: *don't, haven't, isn't, can't.*

In English, only one negative is allowed per sentence.

> Example: I *don't* **go** to school.

If a double negative is used, the expression becomes affirmative.

> Example: I *never don't* **go** to school.

I never don't go to school means *I always go to school.*

Modification

Adjectives modify nouns, and *adverbs* modify verbs.

> Examples: Her smile looked happy. (Adjective)
>
> She smiled happily. (Adverb)

Speakers often confuse the pairs of modifiers *good* (adjective) and *well* (adverb), and *bad* (adjective) and *badly* (adverb).

> Examples: Peach cobbler tastes so good. (Adjective)
>
> She throws the ball well. (Adverb)
>
> He played tennis badly. (Adverb)
>
> I feel bad for his partner. (Adjective)

A modifier should be placed as close as possible to the word it modifies. It should be clear which word in the sentence the modifier is modifying.

Examples: The copyeditor only found two errors.

The copyeditor found only two errors.

The first sentence suggests that the copyeditor did nothing with the errors except to find them *(only found; did not correct)*. The second sentence suggests that there were *only two errors* to be found.

Adjectives usually precede the nouns they modify.

Example: I heard a loud noise.

If a modifier does not have a clear subject it is called a **dangling modifier**.

Incorrect: As an adult, childhood was a happy memory.

It is not clear what or who the phrase *as an adult* modifies. The sentence seems to imply a subject.

Correct: As an adult, Marty remembered his childhood fondly.

Sentence fragments and run-on sentences

Run-on sentences and **sentence fragments** are punctuated as sentences, but they have either too much or too little information to be one sentence. Run-on sentences should be split into two or more sentences. Sentence fragments need to have their missing elements added in order to form complete sentences.

A new blender. Absolutely free!

These two sentence fragments can be made into a sentence with the addition of a verb:

A new blender is available absolutely free of cost to each customer.

Run-on sentences occur when two independent clauses are joined with no connecting word or punctuation between them.

Incorrect: She called he didn't answer.

Correct: She called but he didn't answer.

Comma splices occur when two independent clauses are joined by a comma. The two clauses must be separated by a semicolon.

Incorrect: He wasn't at home, therefore he didn't answer the phone.

Correct: He wasn't at home; therefore, he didn't answer the phone.

Punctuation

Punctuation separates the different parts of a sentence and distinguishes between sentences. While there are many rules for punctuation, we will concentrate on three of the most common punctuation errors: comma usage, semicolon usage, and using apostrophes to show possession.

Comma usage

Commas are used to separate elements of a sentence. For example, they may be used to separate a series of words in a list or two separate clauses. A **clause** is a group of words that contains both a subject and a verb. Below are the four most common ways to use commas.

1. Use commas between two independent clauses that are connected by a **conjunction** such as *and, but, yet, or, nor, so,* or *for.* An **independent clause** is a clause with a subject and verb that does not depend upon another part of the sentence to clarify its meaning; it can stand alone as a complete sentence.

> Incorrect: Gemma won the election for student body president but Dana has more experience in leadership roles.
>
> Correct: Gemma won the election for student body president, but Dana has more experience in leadership roles.

The sentence above should have a comma because it contains two independent clauses connected by the word *but* (a coordinating conjunction). You can tell that it has two independent clauses because each clause has a subject paired with its own verb: the independent clause *Gemma won the election for student body president* has a subject (*Gemma*) paired with a verb (*won*), and the independent clause *Dana has more experience in leadership roles* also has a subject (*Dana*) paired with a verb (*has*).

A good test to determine whether a sentence requires a comma is to break it into two sentences where you think the comma might need to go (before the coordinating conjunction). If you end up with two complete sentences (*Gemma won the election for student body president. Dana has more experience in leadership roles.*) then you need a comma. Make sure you don't forget about the coordinating conjunction; a sentence of this type with a comma but no coordinating conjunction is incorrect.

Note: In very short sentences, the comma may be omitted, but it is not incorrect to put a comma as long as there are two independent clauses connected by a coordinating conjunction.

2. Use commas after an introductory element for a sentence when that element appears before the subject of the sentence.

>Incorrect: Before the race started Cliff stretched his muscles.
>
>Correct: Before the race started, Cliff stretched his muscles.

Some writers do not use a comma after very short introductory elements. However, you should use a comma if the introductory element is long or if the comma would help clarify the meaning of the sentence.

3. Use commas before and after a clause or phrase that provides additional information that is not essential to the meaning of the sentence.

>Incorrect: My cousin an experienced pilot landed the plane safely.
>
>Correct: My cousin, an experienced pilot, landed the plane safely.

Since the phrase *an experienced pilot* is not essential to understanding that the speaker's cousin landed the plane safely, it should be surrounded by commas.

4. Use commas to separate items in a series. When three or more items are used in a series, commas should separate the items.

>Incorrect: Seth has traveled to France Italy and the Czech Republic.
>
>Correct: Seth has traveled to France, Italy, and the Czech Republic.

Some writers omit the comma before the last item in a series (before *and the Czech Republic*), but it is not incorrect to use a comma there.

Colon usage

The **colon** (:) means *as follows*. The colon is used to introduce a list or to anticipate a statement. It is also used after the salutation of a business letter: *Dear Madam or Sir:*

>Example: There is one main challenge for the new dog owner: housebreaking.

Semicolon usage

The **semicolon** (;) is used to separate two independent clauses that are closely related in subject matter. (Remember, an **independent clause** is a clause with a subject and verb that does not depend on another part of the sentence to clarify its meaning; it can stand alone as a complete sentence.)

Incorrect: Darrell wanted to wear his lucky tie for his job interview, unfortunately, the tie was at the cleaners.

Correct: Darrell wanted to wear his lucky tie for his job interview; unfortunately, the tie was at the cleaners.

The sentence contains two complete independent clauses: *Darrell wanted to wear his lucky tie for his job interview*, and *unfortunately, the tie was at the cleaners*. You can tell that they are independent clauses because either clause could stand alone as a sentence. Therefore, they should be separated by a semicolon, not a comma.

Apostrophe usage

The **apostrophe** (') can be used to show that a noun belongs to someone or something. Here are some common rules for using apostrophes.

Use apostrophes in the following situations:

1. To show possession for singular nouns: attach *-'s*

    Examples: the bird's wing, the host's party

2. To show possession for plural nouns that do not end in *-s*: attach *-'s*

    Examples: men's shoes, the mice's cheese

3. To show possession for plural nouns that end in *-s*: attach *-'*

    Examples: the dogs' howling, the players' rivalry

Do not use apostrophes in the following situations:

1. *Do not* use apostrophes for possessive pronouns:

    Examples: Use *yours*, not *your's*, to show possession: *This coat must be yours.*

2. *Do not* use apostrophes to make nouns plural:

    Examples: Use *ten fingers*, not *ten finger's*

Capitalization

Capitalization is used to mark the beginning of a sentence. The first letter of the first word of a sentence is capitalized. A quoted sentence within a sentence also begins with a capital letter.

Capitalization is also used to distinguish proper nouns and titles. A proper noun is the individual title of a person, place, or thing.

Examples: United States
Rutgers University
Nathaniel Hawthorne
The Scarlet Letter
Lake Erie
the Victorian Age
The New York Times

Word Usage (diction)

Word usage refers to using words with meanings and forms that are appropriate for the context and structure of a sentence. A common error in word usage occurs when a word's meaning does not fit the context of the sentence. This often occurs with homonyms (words that sound alike but have different meanings).

Incorrect: Mark likes candy better <u>then</u> gum.

Correct: Mark likes candy better <u>than</u> gum.

Incorrect: The dog chased <u>it's</u> tail.

Correct: The dog chased <u>its</u> tail.

In addition to *than/then* and *it's/its*, some other commonly misused words include *they/their/they're*, *your/you're*, *except/accept*, and *affect/effect*.

For contractions (*it's, they're, you're*), you can spell out the contraction to make sure you are using the correct word (*it's ▶ it is; they're ▶ they are; you're ▶ you are*). For other words, however, you will need to learn the correct usage by looking up the word in the dictionary to find out its meaning.

Idiomatic Expressions

Some words take particular prepositions in idiomatic usage. To English speakers, the correct form should sound right.

Incorrect: similar as

Correct: similar to

Incorrect: different than

Correct: different from

You should be able to identify when a certain preposition should be used. For example, dinner is *in* the oven, but *on* the table. A person is *in* love, but *at* home.

Clarity of Expression

Wordiness, redundancy, and awkwardness impede clarity of expression.

Wordiness

Always express your meaning in the clearest way possible. Omit unnecessary words. Wordy phrases should be simplified or eliminated.

Incorrect: We missed our appointment due to the fact that the train was late.

Correct: We missed our appointment because the train was late.

Incorrect:	at that point in time	for the purpose of	at all times
Correct:	then	for	always

Vague nouns and modifiers such as *factor*, *situation*, *really*, and *very* can simply be deleted from most sentences in which they are used.

Redundancy

Incorrect: I was really exhausted.

Correct: I was exhausted.

Really exhausted is redundant because *exhausted* is already an extreme state.

Incorrect: Combine the butter and sugar together in a bowl.

Correct: Combine the butter and sugar in a bowl.

Combine already means to mix together.

In-depth Preparation for the Two Major Question Types

Type 1: Usage Questions

In each **Usage** question, four elements of the sentence are underlined. Here is an example:

The larger fireflies of eastern <u>North</u> America belong, <u>for the most part</u>, to the genus *Photurus*, a
         A   B

group <u>in which</u> the males show much more variation in flash pattern <u>as</u> in body structure and color.
       C   D

<u>No error</u>
  E

To answer the question, you have to determine whether there is an error and, if so, where it is. You are not required to specify what the error is, nor do you have to suggest a way to fix it. You just have to identify where the error, if any, is.

Note that choice E is "No error"; you should choose E if you think the sentence is correct as shown. In every **Usage** question, E is the "No error" choice.

In the question about fireflies above, choice A is testing capitalization: Is the continent correctly referred to as "North America" or "north America"? Choice B is testing diction—is the phrase used correctly? Choice C is testing subordination—does the wording "in which" correctly link the idea "group" to the following information about males in that group? Choice D is testing a comparative construction: Should the phrase beginning with "more" be completed by a phrase beginning with "as" or "than"? The error is in choice D. Substituting "than" for "as" at D would make the sentence grammatically correct ("...the males show much more variation in flash pattern *than* in body structure and color" is correct). Choice D is the answer.

Usage questions typically present specific, discrete errors rather than expressions that may be ineffective. Stylistic problems, such as wordiness and vagueness, are generally tested in **Sentence Correction** questions.

Expert Tips for Usage Questions

- Before you choose an answer, be sure to look at all parts of the sentence to see how they fit together.

- If you see a line under a blank space, it means that you are to decide whether some punctuation mark is needed there.

- If you see a line under a single punctuation mark, you must consider three possibilities: (a) no punctuation mark is needed in that spot, so the mark shown is an error; (b) some punctuation mark is needed, but not the one shown; and (c) the punctuation mark is correct.

- Sometimes the underlined part consists of a single word, sometimes more than one word. Remember, where an underlined part is several words long, not all the elements underlined have to be wrong for that part to be incorrect. The error may depend on only one word or element.

- The "No error" answer choice is always E in a usage question. Do not be afraid to choose E if, after careful consideration, you think the sentence looks and sounds correct. Not every sentence has an error; there are some E answers in every Usage section.

- If you think that an answer choice contains an error, you should be able to correct the error mentally in one of the following ways.

  a. You can delete an element, such as one of the words in an underlined phrase.

  b. You can change the form of an element that is already there, such as changing it's to its.

  c. You can replace an element, such as changing than to then.

  d. You can add an element, such as a comma.

Try Usage questions

1. The club members <u>agreed</u> that <u>each would contribute</u> ten days of volunteer work
                  A   B

   <u>annually each year</u> at the <u>local hospital.</u> <u>No error</u>
      C   D   E

The error in this sentence occurs at C. The phrase "annually each year" is redundant, because "annually" and "each year" convey the same information. The sentence would be correct with either "annually" or "each year" at C. The error is one of redundancy.

2. Tennis players <u>have complained</u> for years <u>about</u> the surly crowds and the raucous noise at
               A   B

   matches <u>,</u> distractions that seriously affect their ability to concentrate and <u>for playing</u> well. <u>No error</u>
      C   D   E

The error occurs at D. The phrases "to concentrate" and "for playing" are connected by "and"; therefore, they should be parallel verbal forms. The correct phrase at D is "to play."

3. Anesthesiologists are in <u>so short supply</u> that operating rooms <u>are used</u> <u>only three or four days</u> a
                        A   B   C

   week in <u>some</u> hospitals. <u>No error</u>
        D   E

The error in this sentence occurs at A. The correct modifier for the noun phrase "short supply" is "such." "Such" is used to modify nouns or noun phrases, which may include nouns that are modified by adjectives (for example, "such tall trees"), whereas "so" is used to modify adjectives alone (for example, "so tall").

---

4. The school magazine will print <u>those who win</u> prizes for poetry, short stories, and drama <u> ;</u>
                                    A   B
    nonfiction, however, <u>will not</u> be <u>accepted for</u> publication. <u>No error</u>
                          C   D   E

The error occurs at A. In the phrase "those who win," the pronoun "those" indicates the people who win prizes. But the magazine will not print the *people* who win; it will print what the winners have written, or the submissions of those who win prizes. The error in this question is the illogical use of a pronoun.

---

5. Fireworks <u>,</u> which were probably <u>first created</u> in ancient China in order to frighten off devils,
              A   B
    were not used <u>as</u> entertainment purposes <u>until around</u> A.D. 1500. <u>No error</u>
                   C   D   E

The error occurs at C. The phrase "used as… purposes" is unidiomatic. The correct word at C is "for."

---

6. If <u>smaller amounts</u> of pesticide <u>would have</u> been used by the farmers, the streams <u>around</u>
        A   B   C
    Merchantville would not now be <u>so polluted</u>. <u>No error</u>
                                    D   E

The error in this sentence occurs at B. The conditional "would," when used as it is here with "if," suggests that a specific action can still be performed ("if only the farmers would use smaller amounts of pesticide"). But the actions of the farmers were completed in the past and cannot be changed. Consequently, "would" is incorrect here. The correct verb form here is "had been used."

---

7. <u>Plagued by</u> robbers, Paris in 1524 passed an <u>o</u>rdinance <u>requiring citizens</u> to burn candles<u> </u>
        A   B   C   D
    in windows fronting on the streets. <u>No error</u>
                                          E

Because this sentence contains no grammatical, idiomatic, logical, or structural errors, the best answer is E. Note that at B a single letter is underlined in order to test whether that letter should be a capital. In this case a capital letter is incorrect. Also note that at D the underline of a blank space is designed to test the need for a mark of punctuation at that point. In this particular case no punctuation is needed.

8. Diabetes mellitus is a <u>disorder of</u> carbohydrate metabolism that <u>inflicts</u> <u>approximately</u> 3 percent
$\qquad$ A $\qquad\qquad\qquad\qquad\qquad$ B $\qquad$ C

<u>of the population.</u> <u>No error</u>
$\quad$ D $\qquad\qquad$ E

The error in this sentence occurs at B. The verb "inflict" means "to cause to be suffered" and is used to describe a step that is *actively* taken by a person or similar agent. (Example: "He inflicted punishment on the prisoners.") Diabetes mellitus, however, does not cause something to be suffered in this way; rather, it is a disease that *is* suffered. The correct word here is "afflicts," which means "distresses" or "affects." The error in this question is one of diction.

9. For a writer, the <u>rarest</u> privilege <u>is not merely</u> <u>to describe</u> her country and time but to help
$\qquad\qquad\qquad$ A $\qquad\qquad$ B $\qquad\qquad$ C

shape <u>it.</u> <u>No error</u>
$\quad$ D $\quad$ E

The error in this sentence occurs at D. The pronoun "it" is wrongly used to refer to two nouns, "country" and "time." The pronoun required here is the plural "them."

10. Researchers in the United States say<u>_</u> that a diet rich in fish oils <u>reduces</u> the <u>amount</u> of fat
$\qquad\qquad\qquad\qquad\qquad\qquad$ A $\qquad\qquad\qquad\qquad\qquad$ B $\qquad$ C

in the blood as <u>effective</u> as a diet rich in vegetable oils. <u>No error</u>
$\qquad\qquad$ D $\qquad\qquad\qquad\qquad\qquad\qquad\qquad$ E

The error in this sentence occurs at D. The word at D describes (or modifies) the verb "reduces," and because verbs are modified by adverbs, the word at D should be in the form of an adverb. In this sentence, the correct word would be "effectively."

11. The company is under pressure to sell <u>its</u> assets <u>to avoid</u> difficulties <u>in making</u> future interest
$\qquad\qquad\qquad\qquad\qquad\qquad\qquad$ A $\qquad$ B $\qquad\qquad\qquad$ C

payments <u>on</u> outstanding loans. <u>No error</u>
$\qquad$ D $\qquad\qquad\qquad$ E

This sentence contains no grammatical, idiomatic, logical, or structural errors, so the best answer is E, "No error."

12. The famous portraitist <u>,</u> John Singer Sargent <u>learned</u> the art <u>of sketching</u> from his mother <u>,</u>
$\qquad\qquad\qquad\qquad$ A $\qquad\qquad\qquad\qquad$ B $\qquad\qquad$ C $\qquad\qquad\qquad$ D

an enthusiastic amateur. <u>No error</u>
$\qquad\qquad\qquad$ E

The comma at A is incorrect. The name "John Singer Sargent" is necessary to identify *which* "famous portraitist" is referred to in the preceding phrase. Elements that are necessary to the sentence in this way are **restrictive** and are not set off by commas. At D, the comma is correct because the phrase that follows "mother" is not needed to identify who his mother is.

---

13. The oldest remains <u>of cultivated</u> rice, <u>dating from</u> about 5000 B.C.E., <u>has been found</u> in eastern
     A B C

China <u> </u> and northern India. <u>No error</u>
D E

This sentence presents a problem in subject-verb agreement. The plural subject "remains" requires a plural form of the conjugated verb at C. The phrase "have been found" would be correct.

---

14. <u>No one</u> is quite sure where the Moon came from <u> </u>, but it is clear that the Apollo lunar samples
     A B

are very similar <u>with the rocks</u> of the Earth's outer mantle. <u>No error</u>
C D E

Choice D presents an error of idiom. The correct expression for the sentence would be "to the rocks."

---

15. The town council is applying <u>for funds</u> from the agency that <u>has been established</u> two years ago
     A B

to coordinate environmental projects <u>in the state</u>. <u>No error</u>
C D E

The error in this sentence occurs at B. The tense of the verb should indicate that the action of establishing the agency was completed at a definite time in the past (two years ago). You could correct the sentence by changing B to "was established."

---

16. Movies, <u>like</u> fairy tales, <u>embody</u> powerful myths <u>that help</u> children <u>struggle against</u> unexpected
     A B C D

difficulties. <u>No error</u>
E

This sentence contains no grammatical, idiomatic, logical, or structural errors, so the best answer is E, "No error."

Type 2: Sentence Correction Questions

In **Sentence Correction** questions, you will not be evaluating the underlined choices for a discrete grammatical error; instead you will be looking at an entire portion of a sentence to determine how it should best be worded. **Sentence Correction** questions look different from **Usage** questions. One or more words of the sentence are underlined, as shown in this example:

By analyzing the wood used in its construction, <u>the settlement was dated by scientists to the seventh century</u>.

(A) the settlement was dated by scientists to the seventh century

(B) the dating of the settlement by scientists has been to the seventh century

(C) scientists dated the settlement to the seventh century

(D) the seventh century was the date of the settlement by scientists

(E) the settlement has been dated to the seventh century by scientists

---

The five choices provide five different ways that the underlined portion could be expressed. Your job is to decide whether the sentence is correct as is or whether one of the other four choices is the correct way to express the meaning of the underlined portion.

Note that choice A is the same as the original underlined portion. This is true for all **Sentence Correction** questions. If the sentence is correct as is, you should choose A.

In the example about old wood above, the original sentence is not correct. The introductory phrase of the sentence, "By analyzing the wood used in its construction," should modify "scientists" because they do the analyzing; therefore, "scientists" should immediately follow the clause. C, the best answer, is the only choice in which "scientists" appears in this position.

The underlined portion of a **Sentence Correction** question may be as short as one or two words or as long as the entire sentence. It is important to read each of the choices carefully. More than one element may change from choice to choice, and if you do not read all of them carefully, you may miss some of these changes.

Expert Tips for Sentence Correction Questions

- Choice A always repeats the underlined portion of the original sentence. Do not be reluctant to choose A if you think that the original is better than any of the variations, but do not choose any answer until you have read every choice.

- If you detect one or more errors in the original sentence, you should be able to correct the sentence mentally, and, in most cases, you should find your corrections among the answer choices. But do not spend more than a few seconds trying to make the corrections before you start reading the choices; you may very well recognize the corrections when you see them, even if you cannot come up with them yourself.

- Don't be alarmed if you mentally correct the sentence but then fail to find an answer choice that would correct it in exactly the same way. Sometimes there are several possibilities for correcting a faulty sentence; however, only one will appear among the answer choices. As long as you can recognize what is correct, you should still be able to answer the question.

- Read all the way through each answer choice; don't stop at the first corrected element. Individual choices may correct some errors while also introducing new errors that do not appear in the original sentence.

- Remember that the answer you choose should not only be error free in and of itself but should also fit correctly and comfortably with the part of the original sentence that is not underlined.

- Don't be tempted into thinking that you can answer a question by looking at the relative lengths of the choices. A long choice does not necessarily signal a sophisticated statement but may in fact be *less* effective than other possibilities because of wordiness or awkwardness. Conversely, don't assume that the shortest answer is both concise and correct.

- Once again, be sure to read all the choices before you choose an answer. It frequently happens that a version strikes you as being correct until something in another version makes you realize that you have overlooked an error.

Try Sentence Correction questions

---

1. <u>To try and appeal</u> to consumers who prefer no additives, some food companies are making unneeded changes in products.

   (A) To try and appeal

   (B) With the intention to appeal

   (C) In an effort to appeal

   (D) Because they made an effort to try appealing

   (E) In that they made an effort to be appealing

The original sentence is incorrect because it includes the phrase "try and appeal" instead of "try to appeal." Choice B is incorrect, because "intention to appeal" should be "intention of appealing." Choices D and E are wordy and present an action, "made an effort," that took place in the past, which is incorrect in this sentence, because both parts of the sentence need to be in the same tense. Only C, the best answer, creates a logical and idiomatic statement.

---

2. Shunning astrologers and fortune-tellers, she insisted that life would be less interesting <u>were we in the possession of knowledge of the future.</u>

   (A) were we in the possession of knowledge of the future

   (B) were we to possess knowledge of the future

   (C) if we were to possess the future's knowledge

   (D) if we possess future knowledge

   (E) if we can possess knowledge of the future

The original sentence is incorrect because the phrase "in the possession of knowledge of the future" is an awkward string of prepositional phrases and because it permits an ambiguous reading—that the people ("we") would be *possessed by* the knowledge. Choices C and D inaccurately replace "knowledge of the future" (knowledge *about* the future) with "the future's knowledge" (knowledge that the future possesses) and "future knowledge" (knowledge that exists in the future). Choices D and E are wrong because "we possess" and "we can possess" fail to indicate that the discussion is hypothetical: "would be" in the first part of the sentence must be matched by a phrase such as "were we to possess" to show that the situation described—that is, possessing knowledge of the future—is not actual. Choice B, the best answer, is both clear and grammatically correct.

3. Conservationists want to preserve stretches of "wild" rivers, those whose banks are still unobstructed by buildings and <u>uncontaminated by wastes in their waters</u>.

(A) uncontaminated by wastes in their waters

(B) whose waters are uncontaminated by wastes

(C) whose waters are without wastes contaminating them

(D) by wastes contaminated their waters

(E) wastes contaminating their waters

The problem in this sentence is faulty parallelism. Two attributes of "wild" rivers are named in the clause beginning with "those whose." Both parts of the clause should have the same grammatical structure. Choices B and C are therefore the only possibilities. Choice C is awkward, and "them" does not have a clear referent (it could refer to "water" or "banks"). Choice B, "whose waters are uncontaminated by wastes," has the same grammatical structure as the first part of the clause, "whose banks are still unobstructed by buildings," and is clear and correct.

4. The fact that some mushrooms are perfectly safe for one person <u>but not for another</u> probably accounts for differences of opinion as to which species are edible and which are not.

(A) but not for another

(B) but not for the other

(C) and not for the other

(D) and unsafe for some other

(E) and some are unsafe for others

The original sentence is clear and grammatically correct. Therefore choice A is the correct answer. Choices B, C, and D change "another" to "the other" or "some other," suggesting incorrectly that one particular person is being discussed. In C, D, and E the appropriate conjunction "but" is changed to "and."

5. In the celery fields of Florida, <u>chameleons are welcome by the growers; they</u> feed upon caterpillars and moths.

(A) chameleons are welcome by the growers; they

(B) the chameleon is welcome to the growers, since they

(C) the chameleons are welcomed by the growers, since they

(D) the growers are welcoming of chameleons, which

(E) the growers welcome chameleons, which

The original sentence is incorrect and confusing. The "are welcome by" is wrong (it should be "are welcomed by"). In addition, it is not clear whether the pronoun "they" refers to the chameleons or the growers. Choices B and C are wrong because the noun referent of the pronoun "they" is still "growers" instead of "chameleons." Choices D and E are correct with regard to the referent, but D uses an unidiomatic form of "welcome." Choice E, the best answer, is clear, idiomatic, and grammatically correct.

6. Martin Luther King Jr. <u>spoke out passionately</u> for the poor of all races.

(A) spoke out passionately

(B) spoke out passionate

(C) did speak out passionate

(D) has spoke out passionately

(E) had spoken out passionate

This sentence presents no problem of structure or logic. The verb tense is correct, and the use of the adverb "passionately" is also correct in this context. In choices B, C, and E, the adjective "passionate" is incorrectly used instead of the adverb. Choice D, while it uses the correct adverb, introduces an incorrect verb form, "has spoke out." Thus, the best answer is A.

---

7. The king preferred accepting the republican flag <u>than giving</u> up the throne altogether.

(A) than giving

(B) than to giving

(C) than to give

(D) rather than give

(E) to giving

The correct form for this kind of comparative statement is "preferred *X* to *Y*." Choices B, C, and E have the correct "to," but B and C can be eliminated because they add "than" before the "to." Only E, the best answer, presents the correct construction.

---

8. <u>The agent, passing through the crowd without being noticed by hardly anyone.</u>

(A) The agent, passing through the crowd without being noticed by hardly anyone.

(B) The agent passed through the crowd without hardly being noticed by anyone.

(C) The agent's passing through the crowd was not hardly noticed by anyone.

(D) No one hardly noticed how the agent passed through the crowd.

(E) The agent was hardly noticed as she passed through the crowd.

This sentence presents two major problems: it is not a complete sentence and the phrase "without…hardly" is not idiomatic. Although B, C, and D are complete sentences, each retains the problem of using "hardly" in an unidiomatic construction. The best answer to this question is E.

---

9. <u>As a consumer, one can accept</u> the goods offered to us or we can reject them, but we cannot determine their quality or change the system's priorities.

(A) As a consumer, one can accept

(B) We the consumer either can accept

(C) The consumer can accept

(D) Either the consumer accepts

(E) As consumers, we can accept

The main problem in this sentence concerns agreement in pronoun number. In the portion of the sentence that is not underlined, the first person plural, "we," is used as the subject in the second part of the compound sentence. The underlined portion of the sentence is therefore wrong in the original, since it uses the singular "consumer" and the singular pronoun "one." To create a sentence free of agreement faults, you must look for a choice that contains "we" and the plural of "consumer." Choice E is the only one that corrects the agreement problem and has a phrase parallel to "we can reject them."

---

10. Since 1977, Mexico has <u>had a building code comparable to California</u>.

(A) had a building code comparable to California

(B) had a building code comparable to that of California

(C) had a building code that is similar to California

(D) a building code comparable to California's

(E) a building code comparable to that of California's

This sentence is correct in its verb tense (present perfect tense, "has had") but it illogically compares Mexico's building code to the whole state of California rather than to California's building code. Choices D and E are wrong because they use the simple present tense, "has," alone. Choice C preserves the illogical comparison. Choice B correctly uses "has had" and creates a logical comparison.

---

11. <u>That its collection of ancient manuscripts can be preserved</u>, the museum keeps them in a room where temperature and humidity are carefully controlled.

(A) That its collection of ancient manuscripts can be preserved

(B) So they can preserve the collection of ancient manuscripts

(C) For preserving its collection of ancient manuscripts

(D) In order that they can preserve the collection of ancient manuscripts

(E) To preserve its collection of ancient manuscripts

This sentence presents an awkward and unidiomatic expression but is correct in that the pronoun "its" agrees with the singular noun "museum." Choices B and D have pronoun reference agreement problems: the plural pronoun "they" doesn't match the singular noun "museum." Between choices C and E, E presents the clearer and more idiomatic expression.

12. <u>The flow of the Hudson River was so reduced by the drought of 1985 that</u> salt water borne on ocean tides moved upstream to within six miles of Poughkeepsie, New York.

(A) The flow of the Hudson River was so reduced by the drought of 1985 that

(B) So reduced was the flow of the Hudson River by the drought of 1985 as to make

(C) The drought of 1985 made such a reduction of the flow of the Hudson River that

(D) Of such a reduction was the flow of the Hudson River by the drought of 1985 that

(E) There was such a reduction of the flow of the Hudson River by the drought of 1985 as to make

The original sentence is correct, therefore choice A is the answer. Choices B, C, D, and E are unidiomatic, wordy, and awkward.

13. Neon glows red-orange <u>upon placing it</u> in a glass tube and charged with electricity.

(A) upon placing it

(B) when placed

(C) as placed

(D) on its placement

(E) after placement

This sentence suffers from lack of parallelism. Both verbs in the sentence ("place" and "charge") should be in the same form. Choices B and C use correct forms of "place," but the "as" in choice C is unidiomatic. Choice B is best.

14. The conflict between somatic and psychological interpretations of mental disorder <u>rage as noisily as ever, and each side make</u> tragic errors of diagnosis and treatment.

(A) rage as noisily as ever, and each side make

(B) rage as noisily as ever, and each side makes

(C) rages as noisily as ever, and each side make

(D) rages as noisily as ever, with each side making

(E) have raged as noisily as ever, with each side making

First, there is a subject-verb agreement error in the original sentence. The subject of the first part of the sentence is "conflict," a singular noun. The correct form of the conjugated verb is "rages." Therefore, "rage" in choices A and B and "have raged" in choice E (which also inappropriately changes the tense of the verb) are both wrong. The second part of choice C contains a subject-verb agreement error (it should be "each side *makes*"). Only choice D avoids errors in subject-verb agreement in both parts of the sentence. Therefore, D is the best choice.

15. Jazz is a rigorous and <u>technical demanding music, deeply affecting such composers like Stravinsky and Gershwin</u>.

(A) technical demanding music, deeply affecting such composers like Stravinsky and Gershwin

(B) technical demanding music, one that deeply affected such composers like Stravinsky and Gershwin

(C) technically demanding music, which deeply affected such composers like Stravinsky and Gershwin

(D) technically demanding music, and such composers as Stravinsky and Gershwin were being deeply affected by it

(E) technically demanding music, one that deeply affected such composers as Stravinsky and Gershwin

In the original sentence there are two errors. The first is the word "technical": since it modifies an adjective ("demanding"), it should be in adverbial form ("technically," as in C, D, and E). The second error is "like" (preceded by "such"): the correct modifier is "as." Choices D and E use "as," but D is awkward and also uses the past progressive tense unidiomatically because in the context of this sentence it implies that some other, unspecified action is occurring at the same time that Stravinsky and Gershwin were affected by jazz. Choice E, which is clear as well as grammatically and idiomatically correct, is the best answer.

Now that you've prepared

Now that you are done working through the mini-review and the two question types, you are ready to put your preparation to work. The practice test in chapter 10 is an actual *PPST: Writing* test from the past. You can simulate actual test conditions, take the test, and then see how you scored. Good luck!

Chapter 7
Preparing for the *PPST: Writing* Test: The Essay

▶   ▶   ▶   ▶   ▶   ▶   ▶   ▶   ▶   ▶   ▶   ▶

Introduction

The essay counts toward one-half of your score on the *PPST: Writing* test, so it is crucial that you maximize your success on this part. Of all parts of the three *PPST* tests, you have probably had the most experience with the essay format. The purpose of the examination is to test your ability to write effectively within a limited period of time. The term "writing sample" is often used to describe the kind of writing you will be asked to produce, and it is useful to think of your response in this way. If you were trying out for a part in a play or for a sports team, you might be asked to read a small section of dialogue or to demonstrate some aspect of your athletic skills. Your overall ability would be evaluated on the basis of samples of what you can do. The writing sample works in the same way. You are not expected to turn out a well-researched, comprehensive essay about a highly specific, specialized topic.

This chapter discusses the scoring criteria and offers some strategies for using your time effectively during the test. The chapter also includes a list of 71 sample essay topics that show the kind of topic you will encounter when you take the test.

Overview of the essay section

In the essay section of the *PPST: Writing* test, you are given 30 minutes to write on an assigned topic. Thirty minutes should allow you sufficient time to read the topic carefully, organize your thoughts prior to writing, write a draft with reasonable care and precision, and briefly check over your response. Note that the result is considered a *draft*, not the kind of highly polished document you would be expected to produce if you were given the assignment to do as homework.

After your draft essay is returned to ETS, it will be evaluated by experienced teachers of writing. Every essay is graded by at least two scorers, neither of whom knows what score the other has given. Each scorer gives a score ranging from 1 (low) to 6 (high). (Essays that do not respond to the specified topic are given a score of 0, regardless of the quality of the writing.) If the two scorers differ by more than one point in the score they assign, the essay is scored *independently* by a third scorer, who is not given any information about what other scores the essay has received. Your essay score is then combined with your multiple-choice Writing score to give you a total *PPST: Writing* score.

What's being tested

The easiest way to find out what skills are being tested in the essay portion of the test is to look at the *PPST: Writing* scoring guide included below, which scorers use in assigning a score of 1 to 6 to each paper. You should also look at the sample question and sample responses included at the end of this chapter.

Here is the official ETS scoring guide used by the *PPST: Writing* essay scorers:

6   A 6 essay demonstrates a *high degree of competence* in response to the assignment but may have a few minor errors.

An essay in this category

- states or clearly implies the writer's position or thesis
- organizes and develops ideas logically, making insightful connections between them
- clearly explains key ideas, supporting them with well-chosen reasons, examples, or details
- displays effective sentence variety
- clearly displays facility in the use of language
- is generally free from errors in grammar, usage, and mechanics

5   A 5 essay demonstrates *clear competence* in response to the assignment but may have minor errors.

An essay in this category

- states or clearly implies the writer's position or thesis
- organizes and develops ideas clearly, making connections between them
- explains key ideas, supporting them with relevant reasons, examples, or details
- displays some sentence variety
- displays facility in the use of language
- is generally free from errors in grammar, usage, and mechanics

4   A 4 essay demonstrates *competence* in response to the assignment.

An essay in this category

- states or implies the writer's position or thesis
- shows control in the organization and development of ideas
- explains some key ideas, supporting them with adequate reasons, examples, or details
- displays adequate use of language
- shows control of grammar, usage, and mechanics, but may display errors

3   A 3 essay demonstrates *some competence* in response to the assignment but is obviously flawed.

An essay in this category reveals *one or more* of the following weaknesses:

- limited in stating or implying a position or thesis

- limited control in the organization and development of ideas

- inadequate reasons, examples, or details to explain key ideas

- an accumulation of errors in the use of language

- an accumulation of errors in grammar, usage, and mechanics

2   A 2 essay is *seriously flawed*.

An essay in this category reveals *one or more* of the following weaknesses:

- no clear position or thesis

- weak organization or very little development

- few or no relevant reasons, examples, or details

- frequent serious errors in the use of language

- frequent serious errors in grammar, usage, and mechanics

1   A 1 essay demonstrates *fundamental deficiencies* in writing skills.

An essay in this category

- contains serious and persistent writing errors, or

- is incoherent, or

- is undeveloped

0   A 0 essay is off topic; that is, it is not a response to the topic specified.

Strategies for Success

While preparing for the test, you should maximize your chances for success by focusing on the same characteristics that the scorers look for when scoring the essays. To help you do this, let's closely dissect the scoring guide—that's where the strategies for success lie.

Strategy 1: Respond to the specific topic

In the scoring guide, the characteristics of a "6-point" versus a "1-point" essay are described in terms of the degree of competence the writer shows in *responding to the assignment*. Notice the description of a score of zero: "not a response to the specified topic." This is the goal of Strategy 1: staying focused on the exact question being asked. It sounds simple, but this focus is critical for success.

Strategy 2: State your position clearly

The first bullet under the description of each score-point, from 6 to 1, makes it clear that responses with higher scores *state their position or thesis clearly*. As you will see in the next section of this chapter, the essay assignment in *PPST: Writing* always involves stating to what extent you agree or disagree with a given statement. The scoring guide specifies that it is critical to make sure you communicate clearly whether or to what extent you agree or disagree—don't leave the reader guessing.

Strategy 3: Plan your essay before you write, so that it is organized, and
Strategy 4: Create a logical flow from idea to idea

The second bullet under the description of each score-point addresses *organization* and *development*. You should strive for logical organization and flow, not just a loose collection of ideas. You might consider taking a few minutes to make an outline or notes before you write. In addition, when you are writing your draft, think about the logical flow from idea to idea. You should consider using transition phrases to link ideas both within and between paragraphs.

Strategy 5: Develop each key idea with one or more examples or clarifying statements

The third bullet under the description of each score-point mentions the use of reasons, examples, or details. Depending on the topic you're given and the arguments you're making, this could take the form of particular examples (such as, "For example, there are literally thousands of species of spiders") or clarifying explanations (such as, "The enforcement of such a policy would put an undue burden on teachers, who already have a great many responsibilities to attend to during the school day"). Be alert for opportunities to expand your key ideas or provide specific details or examples.

Strategy 6: Use variety in sentence construction

The fourth bullet under the two highest score points refers to "sentence variety." This means that in high-scoring papers, the sentences are not all structured in the same way as one another. You should try to vary the length and type of sentences. For example, don't start every sentence with "There is…." Use transitions and, perhaps, begin some sentences with modifying phrases (such as, "Remaining true to their profession, teachers often…"). Consider occasionally combining simple sentences in order to vary the length and rhythm of your sentences.

Strategy 7: Follow the rules of standard written English

The remaining bullets encompass the large territory known as "correct written English." This means correct subject-verb agreement, correct use of modifiers, correct parallelism, correct idiomatic expressions, and so on—all the elements discussed in chapter 6 for the multiple-choice section of the test. Try as much as you can to get these elements correct, especially as you look through your draft before turning in your test. However, do not sacrifice organization, development, details, and sentence variety by spending all of your time thinking about the mechanics.

Now that you have considered the strategies, let's examine the types of topics you'll apply the strategies to.

The Essay Topics

ETS has published the list of topics that is printed below. One of these exact topics, or a similar topic, will be presented to you when you take the test. This is the official ETS list of essay topics, so it makes sense to examine it carefully.

The format for every essay question is the same: you will be asked to discuss the extent to which you *agree* or *disagree* with the opinion presented in the topic and to *support your position* with specific reasons and examples from your own experience, observations, or reading.

It does not matter whether you agree or disagree with the topic: the scorers are trained to accept all varieties of opinions. What matters are the skills we've discussed in the section above: taking a clear stand that responds directly to the question and writing a draft essay that is characterized by good organization, complete development, sentence variety, and correct written English.

None of the topics requires specialized academic knowledge. Most topics are general and are based on common educational experiences or issues of public concern. Don't be intimidated by the topic. Just decide quickly whether or to what extent you agree or disagree with the statement, and then begin working on your essay.

What should you do with this list of 71 topics? To prepare for the essay portion of the test, you should practice writing essays in response to these topics. Try to make your practice conditions as much like the actual testing conditions as possible. Make sure to time yourself, giving yourself 30 minutes to read a question and write a response. After completing an essay, read it over and compare it with the scoring guide. Or better yet, have a friend, professor, or teacher evaluate the essay against the scoring criteria and give you feedback. Identify the skills with which you have trouble, and try to practice them in future writing. Composition professors and staff at college writing labs can also recommend useful textbooks on how to improve one's writing.

Here are the official directions that precede each topic in the test:

Read the opinion stated below. Discuss the extent to which you agree or disagree with this point of view. Support your position with specific reasons and examples from your own experience, observations, or reading.

Each of the following 71 topics is an opinion statement. You will be asked to agree or disagree with one of them (or a statement like one of them) when you take the *PPST: Writing* test.

1. "Celebrities have a tremendous influence on the young, and for that reason, they have a responsibility to act as role models."

2. "Our society is overly materialistic. We center our lives on acquiring material things at the expense of such traditional values as family and education."

3. "Censorship of song lyrics, television shows, and offensive speech is necessary in order to protect the rights of all members of society."

4. "Young people who attend college immediately after high school often lack a clear sense of direction and seriousness about learning. Before hurrying into college, it's better to get a taste of the real world by working or serving in the military for a few years."

5. "Although routines may seem to put us in a rut and stifle creativity, in fact routines make us more efficient and allow creativity to blossom."

6. "An effective leader of any organization—from the military to businesses to social organizations—is someone who is decisive, acts quickly, and remains committed to certain key principles."

7. "Advances in computer technology have made the classroom unnecessary, since students and teachers are able to communicate with each other from computer terminals at home or at work."

8. "Schools should be open for classes all year long."

9. "Schools should focus more on preparing students for specific careers and vocations, and less on teaching subjects such as literature, art, and history."

10. "Although the marvels of technology surround us every day, there are moments when we all would give anything to be freed from that technology."

11. "Colleges should require all students, regardless of their individual majors, to take a common set of required courses."

12. "Schools should require all students to participate in field trips since these outings are an essential part of the curriculum for all grade levels."

13. "In order to prepare students to live in a culturally diverse society, schools should formally require all students to study other cultures and societies in depth."

14. "One clear sign that our society has improved over the past 100 years is the development of disposable products whose convenience has made our lives easier."

15. "The best way to understand the true nature of a society is to study its dominant trends in art, music, and fashion."

16. "Because the traditional grading scale of A through F fosters needless competition and pressure, colleges and universities should use a simple pass/fail system."

17. "To address the problem of chronic truancy, schools should fine the parents of students who are frequently absent from school."

18. "Studying a foreign language should be a college requirement for anyone planning to be a teacher."

19. "We are constantly bombarded by advertisements—on television and radio, in newspapers and magazines, on highway signs and the sides of buses. They have become too pervasive. It's time to put limits on advertising."

20. "In order to understand other societies, all college students should be required to spend at least one of their undergraduate years studying or working in a foreign country."

21. "Every member of society should be required before the age of twenty-one to perform at least one year of community or government service, such as in the Peace Corps, AmeriCorps, USA Freedom Corps, the military, a hospital, a rural or inner-city school, or some equivalent organization."

22. "Citizens of the United States should be allowed to designate how a portion of their tax dollars should be spent."

23. "The only important criterion by which to judge a prospective teacher is his or her ability to get along with the widest possible variety of students."

24. "Rather than relying on taxes, communities should be directly responsible for raising any required funds to pay for all extracurricular public school activities, including after-school sports."

25. "School activities not directly related to course work, such as assemblies and pep rallies, should not be part of the regular school day."

26. "School children should be required to participate in a variety of extracurricular activities so that they can become well-rounded individuals."

27. "All schools should have student dress codes."

28. "It is well within the capability of society to guarantee that all public schools are entirely drug-free."

29. "Opinion polls should not play an important role in the political decision-making process because they indicate only what is popular, not what is the right or wrong position for our leaders to take."

30. "Childhood is a time for studying and playing, not working. Parents should not force their children to do chores."

31. "We are all influenced in lasting ways—whether positive or negative—by the particular kind of community in which we grow up."

32. "Television has had an overwhelmingly negative impact on society."

33. "Grading systems should be replaced with some other method of measuring students' performance because giving grades to students puts too much emphasis on competition and not enough emphasis on learning for its own sake."

34. "Political candidates should not be allowed to use popular actors in their advertising campaigns. Candidates too often win elections because they have actors for friends rather than because they are honestly qualified to represent the public interest."

35. "Television programming should be limited and strictly monitored for offensive content by a governmental supervising agency."

36. "Although we say we value freedom of expression, most of us are not really very tolerant of people who express unpopular ideas or act in nonconforming ways."

37. "Job satisfaction is more important in a career than a high salary and fringe benefits."

38. "College students should not have to decide on a major until after they have taken several classes and examined the various career fields the school has to offer."

39. "Schools should make a greater effort to teach ethics and moral values to students."

40. "Colleges and universities should ban alcoholic beverages on campus, even for students who are of legal drinking age."

41. "Teachers and parents should be more concerned than they are about the gradual trend among high school students toward part-time employment and away from participation in school-sponsored extracurricular activities."

42. "It is the responsibility of the government rather than the individual citizen to find a solution to the growing problem of homelessness in the United States."

43. "Federal regulations should entirely ban all advertising of alcoholic beverages in all media, including television, radio, and magazines."

44. "Schools should put as much emphasis on such subjects as music, physical education, and visual arts as they do on traditional academic courses such as English or math."

45. "Materialism and consumerism have gone too far in American society. We often buy things that we do not need, and we even buy things that we do not especially enjoy."

46. "The failure of public schools is not ruining society. The failure of society has ruined the public schools."

47. "Honesty is universally valued, at least in principle. In practice, however, there are many cases in which governments, businesses, and individuals should not be completely honest."

48. "All employers should institute mandatory drug testing for employees."

49. "All high school students should be required to take some classes in vocational education."

50. "School administrators should regulate student speech in school-sponsored publications."

51. "Computer training should be mandatory for anyone planning to become a teacher, no matter what subject the person will teach."

52. "The world offers us abundant places to learn. We should not expect all of our most important lessons to be learned in the buildings we call schools."

53. "Many public buildings and transportation systems in the United States prohibit or restrict smoking. These restrictions are unfair because they deny smokers their individual rights."

54. "Public schools should be required to offer socially oriented courses, such as sex education and personal finance, because such courses help students cope with problems in society."

55. "Our lives today are too complicated. We try to do too much and, as a result, do few things well."

56. "The United States government has become so corrupt that people who vote in national elections are wasting their time."

57. "The increasing involvement of businesses in the schools, ranging from the establishment of apprenticeships and grants to the donation of equipment and facilities, is a cause for concern because this involvement gives the businesses too much influence over school policy and curriculum."

58. "One of the biggest troubles with colleges is that there are too many distractions."

59. "The best way to improve the quality of public schools in the United States is to institute a national curriculum with national standards so that students, parents, and teachers all across the country know exactly what is expected at each grade level."

60. "Instead of making our lives simpler, computers cause more problems than they solve."

61. "Children learn responsibility and the value of work by being required to do household chores such as making beds, washing dishes, and taking care of pets."

62. "We should ban any speech—whether on the radio, in the movies, on television, or in public places such as college campuses—that encourages violent behavior."

63. "In today's society, the only real function of a college education is to prepare students for a career."

64. "Students suffer from participating in highly competitive extracurricular activities such as debate and sports."

65. "We live in a passive society in which few people take a stand or become involved in social issues."

66. "Students should be required to meet certain academic standards, such as passing all courses or maintaining a C average, in order to participate in extracurricular activities."

67. "Increasing reliance on the use of new technologies in the classroom has distracted from, rather than contributed to, the learning process."

68. "We find comfort among those who agree with us—growth among those who don't."

69. "Film and television studios in the United States nearly always want to dish up a sunny view of life because American audiences would rather not be reminded of problems in society."

70. "Competition is a destructive force in society."

71. "All 18–21 year olds should be required to perform government or community service."

Using Your 30 Minutes—Planning and Writing

Planning your essay—take five minutes

After you have carefully read the topic, you may find it helpful to jot down notes about the points you plan to cover or even to make a brief outline. Space for notes is provided in the test booklet; these notes will not be considered when your essay is evaluated. The space is for your own use, and the kind of outline you write or the kind of notes you make is up to you. You do not have time to make an elaborate outline, but it is important to take time to plan what you are going to write. Skilled writers typically plan first; even when time is an issue, as it is in timed writing tests, spending five minutes on some kind of outline or notes is often a good investment. A simple list of the major points (and supporting examples or reasons) you want to cover can be very helpful as you write your essay. Suppose that you are writing on Topic 71 from the list above ("All 18–21 year olds should be required to perform government or community service."); your notes might look like this:

— Agree

— Chief reason #1: gets them into the community-service habit for life

— Chief reason #2: might help career choice; might help meet people in area of interest

— Chief reason #3: the high numbers of volunteers would really help relieve poverty and other problems

— Examples: Habitat for Humanity; friend who became literacy volunteer in college

— Other reasons:

  • could get school or college credit for their work

  • could choose type of service based on college major

This kind of outline might be all you need to jog your memory as you write.

Writing your essay

On the paper version of the test, some people try to write out their essays in the section for notes and then copy them over into the designated answer area. In these cases, the writers usually run out of time before they can complete the copying, and they are forced to turn in incomplete essays. It is usually best to use the answer area to write out your essay once, writing as legibly as you can. You might plan to give yourself five minutes near the end of the allotted time period for editing and proofreading your essay. Such editing might include checking that the essay is organized—that is, that it proceeds from one point to another in a way that your readers can follow, that your sentences are clearly stated, and that your spelling and punctuation are correct.

The people who evaluate your essay need to be able to read your handwriting, but neatness, as such, does not count. It is expected that you might cross out words and make insertions. Also, it is not necessary for papers to be mechanically perfect: a misspelled word or a forgotten comma in an otherwise well-written paper will not lower your score. Still, careless mistakes can be corrected if you use your time well; you do not want to give your readers the impression that you do not understand the rules that govern written English when, in fact, you just have not taken the time to make corrections.

Sample scored essays

Let's return to Topic 71 in the list of ETS topics, "All 18–21 year olds should be required to perform government or community service," and look at actual test-taker responses at each score level, from a high score of 6 to a low score of 1.

Response that Received a Score of 6

Essay	Explanation of Score
"We wanted her car." This simple reason of wanting a certain car was several teenagers' reason for killing a young nursing student. Several years ago, a woman named Pam was getting out of her car which she had parked at her apartment. She was attacked, stabbed, and left for dead while a group of teenagers took her car. This is one example of young people's way of thinking here in the U.S. This "Generation X" seems to have a lack of morals, low esteem, apathy, and no vision or goals for the future. Perhaps this generation needs a taste of the real world, a chance to see people who are needy and have nothing tangible in life. Perhaps if these young people could see others who are in a poorer state than they are, they themselves would see how much they have, and in turn, treat others with more respect. Is this a job the government can do, or does the decision to see and help others who are in need have to come from the individual "X-ers?" The government's role in the community is to protect the liberty of the people, not to form morals or create better people. Although forcing young people, specifically between the ages of eighteen and twenty-one, to do community service, volunteer at a hospital or inner-city school, or participate in other outreach projects could help society as a whole, several consequences could occur. First of all, the act of forcing individuals to participate in acts is unconstitutional and the government would be stepping over the bounds created for it. The government also declares the age of eighteen as an adult. This is seen through the right to vote, the right to marry without parental consent, and the right to smoke as well. By these two examples alone, the government could not possibly force any and every adult to do community work. Besides the fact of unconstitutionality, another reason why government could not require all people between eighteen and twenty-one years of age to do community projects is simply because of human nature. What benefit in life comes from force? In many times throughout history, when force is used, rebellion follows. An example of this is seen nearly two thousand years ago.	The writer lures the reader into this debate with an intriguing introduction. Think about how more engaging an introduction this is than the normal "I'm against community service." In this essay, the writer uses this first anecdote to show that kids today do need to change their ways, although he goes on to say that he is against mandatory community service. The reasons the writer is against it are clearly stated (it is unconstitutional and against human nature), and each reason is fully explained in a paragraph of its own. Having stated a position and explained the supporting reasons, the essay concludes with a reasonable explanation why mandated community service will not work. The essay is clear and organized, with transitions linking together both ideas and sentences, and there are varied sentences (long and short) and precise word choices ("apathy, compassion, commendable"). Errors are rare and do not interfere with understanding.

After the death of Jesus, his followers proclaimed his name as the Messiah, and they proclaimed him as God. Some of the followers were commanded by authorities to not even mention the name of Jesus. However, since the followers believed in Him with all they had, they could not obey the authorities. As a result, Christianity, the religion of following Jesus, is one of the most well-known religions in the world. Examples such as this one permeate history, and if government were to force people to do outreach projects, it could face the opposite effect of what was intended. One cannot change the heart of a person, even if this person is shown the most helpless being in the world. Helping others will not create compassion. Compassion comes from within, and it is compassion which motivates one to help others.

Young people today need to see beyond themselves. How can this be done? Can any person, government, or thing cause anyone to see that more lies beyond the selfish intentions that most humans have, or does that "seeing beyond themselves" come from within? Seeing and helping the lives of others who are less fortunate is a commendable thing and must come from a loving heart. What success is there when it comes out of duty, out of government law? If the government were to ever create a law that makes young adults participate in some type of outreach project, the government would be replacing compassion with law. There is no doubt that the young adults of today need morals. They need role models. They need to see beyond their selfish selves. Government's responsibility, however, is limited to only protect man's God-given rights of liberty, so perhaps hopefully one day these young people will be able to taste true love that gives and serves from the heart.

Response that Received a Score of 5

Essay	Explanation of Score
Our Founding Fathers obviously thought that each American citizen should be responsible and accountable. Along with the rights that we have as Americans, there are also responsibilities that go along with those rights. However, I do not believe these rights can be mandated or legislated by the government. The definition of a good citizen might be one who is patriotic, a contributor to society, one who obeys the law, and who seeks to live peaceably among other men, as our constitution implies when it reads, "...the pursuit of happiness." This pursuit of happiness cannot be forced upon an individual. It must come from within. If one does not want to be a good citizen of America, that is his or her choice. Rather than the goverment mandating community or government service upon individuals, the most logical and reasonable thing to do would be to begin teaching citizenship early in a child's life; teaching children what good citizens are and what good citizens do. The home should be the first place citizenship should be taught.	This essay is very well written, with precise word choices ("facilitate, revival, zealousness") and sentences that are fluid and rhythmic (for example, varying lengths of sentences from long to short and asking questions to add punch: "Can this be blamed upon them? Absolutely not. The fault lies upon the older adults, the parents, teachers, ministers and business people"). The essay clearly states that there should NOT be mandatory community service, and works hard to give reasons to support that position. However, the essay could be better

Parents ought to serve as examples to their children. They ought to be good citizens themselves and give to their communities and to their country. Teachers should also teach citizenship as soon as students come into the public schools. They should teach responsibility, respect for others, patriotism, and contribution to society.

Facts prove that young people are not being taught good citizenship. The greatest number of people who fail to vote but are eligible falls in the category of those between the ages of 18 and 24. Generally speaking, have these young people been taught that along with their rights as Americans, they also have many responsibilities? If these young people will not even vote, how can we expect them to serve the community or their country? And why are they not voting? Because they are against freedom and responsibility? No. In most cases, it is because they have not been taught the core democratic values of what a good citizen is. Can this be blamed upon them? Absolutely not. The fault lies upon the older adults, the parents, teachers, ministers, and business-people. Values in this democracy are being destroyed from within, by the same people who are advocating them.

It is certain that young people from 18-21 need to be good citizens and serve their communities and their country. It is just as certain that government legislation is not needed to facilitate this change. All that is needed is caring parents, teachers, and other community leaders who will stand upon their foundations in America, upon the basic core values of democracy, and who will teach America's youth the same good things. I believe this change would bring a refreshing national revival to America's youth and compel them to desire to serve their communities and their country with feverency of mind and zealousness of heart.

organized, as the position is never originally stated until a third of the way down the first page, and then much of the explanation to support the position against mandatory community service rambles into a discussion of whose fault it is that kids today are lacking morals. While the essay has a clear position with support, better organization, and more focus could help the essay score even higher.

Response that Received a Score of 4

Essay	Explanation of Score
I teach in a vocational high school setting. After instructing the students how the business world works, the students are ready to experience what they have been trained to do. The students want the ability to purchase products without the help of their parents or guardians. They also want to find a good job, and the ability to make decisions on their own. I have many students who are also contemplating marraige. I feel that these students should be involved in community service, but not a full year of their lives. Requiring these young adults to perform community service work a certain amount of hours each week would be adequate. Many of these people have their lives planned and they are certain what they want to do. In the classroom, I also have students that have no goals or direction. When questioned what they will do upon graduation,	This essay has few errors and is easy to follow. Although there are some interesting ideas (service work could reduce crime, or could broaden the horizons of many underprivileged kids), these ideas are not presented in support of a position. The writer says limited community service should be required, but then says some students wouldn't need it at all and others could use lots of it. This lack of a clear position takes away from the piece as a

many of them reply, "Get a job at McDonalds" or "Hang around awhile". These students would possibly benefit from community or Peace Corps service work. It would allow the students to see what is happening in the community around them. Some of these students have not had the opportunity to travel or experience anything outside their little world. Many students, when given the opportunity to see other regions of the country or world, would now find a direction to aim their lives.

Once these students are involved with an organization, they will be given the chance to see how other parts of the world function. Most young people do not realize until they experience what life is like in under-developed countries. This might help them realize they need to work for what they receive. Also, their training in a high school vocational program can be put to use, such as carpentry skills, computer skills, etc. This will allow the students to gain experience and confidence when they return to the work sector in our country.

If young adults are used for service work, a study should be done to see if the crime rate among young adults drops. Once a person has a goal or job, I feel they will be less likely to have the free time to commit robbery or get involved with illegal drugs. When a person is bored, I feel they are more likely to get into trouble with the law.

When a young adult does get involved in something constructive, instead of destructive, the person, the community and the world will be better off.

whole, even though the writer can write very well and has offered some intriguing ideas. By the final sentence one can infer the writer is for mandatory service, but this is an assumption the reader has to make. This essay would benefit from a more clear main idea (a stance, clearly stated, for or against mandatory community service) and an explanation organized in support of that.

Response that Received a Score of 3

Essay	Explanation of Score
Requiring 18-21 year olds to participate in government or community service for one year is an excellent idea. However, this type of a program may not be suitable for all young adults, it may only be beneficial to those that plan to continue on to college or some sort of specialty school. This would provide these young adults with a broad experience of different cultures in the world, help to prepare them for making future career choices, and also help them to develop into better young adults by learning to relate to others. Today many students who have graduated from high school and are continuing on to college are not prepared to decide on a particular field of study. In many cases we as seventeen year olds do not have the experience or foresight to make a decision on our future. I did not make a final decision on my field of study untill late into my sophomore year. As I look back on my college experience I feel I could have learned more by having that extra year and a half of time dedicated to my major field of study. The more an individual can experience in life, the better off he or she will be in the long run. Our life experiences can help us to see	This essay states that mandatory community service is an "excellent idea" and defends that position with a discussion of the benefits of that year of work for college-bound students. It explains that a year of work may help students to decide on their field of study, an argument that supports the writer's reasoning. But this is the only support given, and while it is clear and helps the writer's main point, additional similar support would make the essay stronger. The essay has few errors and is clear, but it would be better if it supported its idea with more explanation.

things from many perspectives instead of strictly one perspective and this makes life a little easier. With this type of experience in community or government service, the young adults will be more well rounded in thier view of the world in which we live.

I think this idea will help the world to be a better place as well as save much money on wasted college tuition.

Response that Received a Score of 2

Essay	Explanation of Score
Developing a community outreach or government service for young adults for one year I think is a great idea. If organized well it could only make the United States a better country. Young people could learn responsibilty, accountability, and character. Since we live in a democracy something like this could not be enforced, but it could be highly encouraged. For example if from the time they start school until they finish they are taught the opportunities and benefits of doing an outreach project. The government could provide financial assistance for the young adults. They could provide an opportunity for the student to do one year of community service and in return one full year of school. This kind of community service would not have to mean leaving the country or state; although this could be an option. It could be done right in their own community. I also think that there could be options of the length of time the student would put in.	This essay states a clear position in favor of mandatory community service ("I think is a great idea") and gives reasons that support it (the U.S. will be "a better country," students "could learn responsibility, accountability, and character"). But instead of explaining those ideas, the essay goes on to explain how the program would work, not why it should be adopted. This means the reasons to support the position are not explained at all, even though they could do a great deal to help the writer's argument. This leaves the essay feeling incomplete and causes it to earn a much lower score than it would have if the writer had explained the ideas. Vague language also occasionally makes the essay hard to follow.

Response that Received a Score of 1

Essay	Explanation of Score
The government already tells us too much what we should and shouldn't do. They shouldn't also be able to tell us how much we have to help the community, thats something we should just be able to decide on our own. What good does it do if the government decides we should be good people if we dont feel like it. They can't make laws which tell people to be nice, that's crazy. Weather or not people are nice is gonna be there choice, not the Presidents or anyone else's. If people want to do a good thing they ought to but I can't see someone making them do it. Community service is not something that should be legilized or illegal becuase its against human nature.	This essay is against mandatory community service, but its reasons why the government "shouldn't also be able to tell us how much we have to help the community" is just that mandatory service is "against human nature." How it is against human nature is never explained, so no clear reasons are ever given why this writer is against the idea. No reasons equals no explanation, and no explanation means the essay can earn little credit. It is possible to understand the sentences in this essay, but they are disorganized, lack explanation, and add up to little.

Now that you've prepared

Now that you are done working through the strategy for writing your essay and have seen examples of essays at different score points, you are ready to put your preparation to work.

The practice test in chapter 10 is an actual *PPST: Writing* test from the past. You can simulate actual test conditions, take the test, and then look at the sample scored essays in chapter 11. Good luck!

Chapter 8
Practice Test, *PPST: Reading*

▶ ▶ ▶ ▶ ▶ ▶ ▶ ▶ ▶ ▶ ▶ ▶

Now that you have studied the content topics and have worked through strategies relating to the *PPST: Reading* test, you should take the following practice test. You will probably find it helpful to simulate actual testing conditions, giving yourself 60 minutes to work on the questions. You can cut out and use the answer sheet provided if you wish.

Keep in mind that the test you take at an actual administration will have different questions. You should not expect the percentage of questions you answer correctly in the practice test to be exactly the same as when you take the test at an actual administration, since numerous factors affect a person's performance in any given testing situation.

When you have finished the practice questions, you can score your answers and read the explanations of the best answer choices in chapter 11.

Professional Assessments for Beginning Teachers ®

TEST NAME:
Pre-Professional Skills Test **Reading**

Time—60 Minutes

40 Questions

THE PRAXIS SERIES
Professional Assessments for Beginning Teachers®

Answer Sheet B

PAGE 1

DO NOT USE INK

Use only a pencil with soft black lead (No. 2 or HB) to complete this answer sheet.
Be sure to fill in completely the oval that corresponds to your answer choice.
Completely erase any errors or stray marks.

1. NAME
Enter your last name and first initial.
Omit spaces, hyphens, apostrophes, etc.

Last Name (first 6 letters)

F I

(A) (B) (C) (D) (E) (F) (G) (H) (I) (J) (K) (L) (M) (N) (O) (P) (Q) (R) (S) (T) (U) (V) (W) (X) (Y) (Z)

2.

YOUR NAME:
(Print)
Last Name (Family or Surname)   First Name (Given)   M. I.

MAILING ADDRESS:
(Print)
P.O. Box or Street Address   Apt. # (If any)

City   State or Province

Country   Zip or Postal Code

TELEPHONE NUMBER: (   ) Home   (   ) Business

SIGNATURE: _____   **TEST DATE:** _____

3. DATE OF BIRTH

Month	Day	
Jan.		
Feb.		
Mar.		
April		
May		
June		
July		
Aug.		
Sept.		
Oct.		
Nov.		
Dec.		

4. SOCIAL SECURITY NUMBER

(0)(1)(2)(3)(4)(5)(6)(7)(8)(9)

5. CANDIDATE ID NUMBER

(0)(1)(2)(3)(4)(5)(6)(7)(8)(9)

6. TEST CENTER / REPORTING LOCATION

Center Number   Room Number

Center Name

City   State or Province

Country

7. TEST CODE / FORM CODE

0
1

(0)(1)(2)(3)(4)(5)(6)(7)(8)(9)

8. TEST BOOK SERIAL NUMBER

9. TEST FORM

10. TEST NAME

Educational Testing Service, ETS, the ETS logo, and THE PRAXIS SERIES:PROFESSIONAL ASSESSMENTS FOR BEGINNING TEACHERS and its design logo are registered trademarks of Educational Testing Service. The modernized ETS logo is a trademark of Educational Testing Service.

 Copyright © 1993 by Educational Testing Service. Princeton, NJ 08541. Printed in U.S.A.

MH99232   Q2572-06   51055 • 08916 • CV99M500
I.N. 202973

1   2   3   4

CERTIFICATION STATEMENT: (Please write the following statement below. DO NOT PRINT.)

"I hereby agree to the conditions set forth in the *Registration Bulletin* and certify that I am the person whose name and address appear on this answer sheet."

_____

_____

_____

SIGNATURE: _____ DATE: _____/_____/_____

                                                                          Month   Day   Year

BE SURE EACH MARK IS DARK AND COMPLETELY FILLS THE INTENDED SPACE AS ILLUSTRATED HERE: ● .

#						#						#						#					
1	Ⓐ Ⓑ Ⓒ Ⓓ Ⓔ					41	Ⓐ Ⓑ Ⓒ Ⓓ Ⓔ					81	Ⓐ Ⓑ Ⓒ Ⓓ Ⓔ					121	Ⓐ Ⓑ Ⓒ Ⓓ Ⓔ				
2	Ⓐ Ⓑ Ⓒ Ⓓ Ⓔ					42	Ⓐ Ⓑ Ⓒ Ⓓ Ⓔ					82	Ⓐ Ⓑ Ⓒ Ⓓ Ⓔ					122	Ⓐ Ⓑ Ⓒ Ⓓ Ⓔ				
3	Ⓐ Ⓑ Ⓒ Ⓓ Ⓔ					43	Ⓐ Ⓑ Ⓒ Ⓓ Ⓔ					83	Ⓐ Ⓑ Ⓒ Ⓓ Ⓔ					123	Ⓐ Ⓑ Ⓒ Ⓓ Ⓔ				
4	Ⓐ Ⓑ Ⓒ Ⓓ Ⓔ					44	Ⓐ Ⓑ Ⓒ Ⓓ Ⓔ					84	Ⓐ Ⓑ Ⓒ Ⓓ Ⓔ					124	Ⓐ Ⓑ Ⓒ Ⓓ Ⓔ				
5	Ⓐ Ⓑ Ⓒ Ⓓ Ⓔ					45	Ⓐ Ⓑ Ⓒ Ⓓ Ⓔ					85	Ⓐ Ⓑ Ⓒ Ⓓ Ⓔ					125	Ⓐ Ⓑ Ⓒ Ⓓ Ⓔ				
6	Ⓐ Ⓑ Ⓒ Ⓓ Ⓔ					46	Ⓐ Ⓑ Ⓒ Ⓓ Ⓔ					86	Ⓐ Ⓑ Ⓒ Ⓓ Ⓔ					126	Ⓐ Ⓑ Ⓒ Ⓓ Ⓔ				
7	Ⓐ Ⓑ Ⓒ Ⓓ Ⓔ					47	Ⓐ Ⓑ Ⓒ Ⓓ Ⓔ					87	Ⓐ Ⓑ Ⓒ Ⓓ Ⓔ					127	Ⓐ Ⓑ Ⓒ Ⓓ Ⓔ				
8	Ⓐ Ⓑ Ⓒ Ⓓ Ⓔ					48	Ⓐ Ⓑ Ⓒ Ⓓ Ⓔ					88	Ⓐ Ⓑ Ⓒ Ⓓ Ⓔ					128	Ⓐ Ⓑ Ⓒ Ⓓ Ⓔ				
9	Ⓐ Ⓑ Ⓒ Ⓓ Ⓔ					49	Ⓐ Ⓑ Ⓒ Ⓓ Ⓔ					89	Ⓐ Ⓑ Ⓒ Ⓓ Ⓔ					129	Ⓐ Ⓑ Ⓒ Ⓓ Ⓔ				
10	Ⓐ Ⓑ Ⓒ Ⓓ Ⓔ					50	Ⓐ Ⓑ Ⓒ Ⓓ Ⓔ					90	Ⓐ Ⓑ Ⓒ Ⓓ Ⓔ					130	Ⓐ Ⓑ Ⓒ Ⓓ Ⓔ				
11	Ⓐ Ⓑ Ⓒ Ⓓ Ⓔ					51	Ⓐ Ⓑ Ⓒ Ⓓ Ⓔ					91	Ⓐ Ⓑ Ⓒ Ⓓ Ⓔ					131	Ⓐ Ⓑ Ⓒ Ⓓ Ⓔ				
12	Ⓐ Ⓑ Ⓒ Ⓓ Ⓔ					52	Ⓐ Ⓑ Ⓒ Ⓓ Ⓔ					92	Ⓐ Ⓑ Ⓒ Ⓓ Ⓔ					132	Ⓐ Ⓑ Ⓒ Ⓓ Ⓔ				
13	Ⓐ Ⓑ Ⓒ Ⓓ Ⓔ					53	Ⓐ Ⓑ Ⓒ Ⓓ Ⓔ					93	Ⓐ Ⓑ Ⓒ Ⓓ Ⓔ					133	Ⓐ Ⓑ Ⓒ Ⓓ Ⓔ				
14	Ⓐ Ⓑ Ⓒ Ⓓ Ⓔ					54	Ⓐ Ⓑ Ⓒ Ⓓ Ⓔ					94	Ⓐ Ⓑ Ⓒ Ⓓ Ⓔ					134	Ⓐ Ⓑ Ⓒ Ⓓ Ⓔ				
15	Ⓐ Ⓑ Ⓒ Ⓓ Ⓔ					55	Ⓐ Ⓑ Ⓒ Ⓓ Ⓔ					95	Ⓐ Ⓑ Ⓒ Ⓓ Ⓔ					135	Ⓐ Ⓑ Ⓒ Ⓓ Ⓔ				
16	Ⓐ Ⓑ Ⓒ Ⓓ Ⓔ					56	Ⓐ Ⓑ Ⓒ Ⓓ Ⓔ					96	Ⓐ Ⓑ Ⓒ Ⓓ Ⓔ					136	Ⓐ Ⓑ Ⓒ Ⓓ Ⓔ				
17	Ⓐ Ⓑ Ⓒ Ⓓ Ⓔ					57	Ⓐ Ⓑ Ⓒ Ⓓ Ⓔ					97	Ⓐ Ⓑ Ⓒ Ⓓ Ⓔ					137	Ⓐ Ⓑ Ⓒ Ⓓ Ⓔ				
18	Ⓐ Ⓑ Ⓒ Ⓓ Ⓔ					58	Ⓐ Ⓑ Ⓒ Ⓓ Ⓔ					98	Ⓐ Ⓑ Ⓒ Ⓓ Ⓔ					138	Ⓐ Ⓑ Ⓒ Ⓓ Ⓔ				
19	Ⓐ Ⓑ Ⓒ Ⓓ Ⓔ					59	Ⓐ Ⓑ Ⓒ Ⓓ Ⓔ					99	Ⓐ Ⓑ Ⓒ Ⓓ Ⓔ					139	Ⓐ Ⓑ Ⓒ Ⓓ Ⓔ				
20	Ⓐ Ⓑ Ⓒ Ⓓ Ⓔ					60	Ⓐ Ⓑ Ⓒ Ⓓ Ⓔ					100	Ⓐ Ⓑ Ⓒ Ⓓ Ⓔ					140	Ⓐ Ⓑ Ⓒ Ⓓ Ⓔ				
21	Ⓐ Ⓑ Ⓒ Ⓓ Ⓔ					61	Ⓐ Ⓑ Ⓒ Ⓓ Ⓔ					101	Ⓐ Ⓑ Ⓒ Ⓓ Ⓔ					141	Ⓐ Ⓑ Ⓒ Ⓓ Ⓔ				
22	Ⓐ Ⓑ Ⓒ Ⓓ Ⓔ					62	Ⓐ Ⓑ Ⓒ Ⓓ Ⓔ					102	Ⓐ Ⓑ Ⓒ Ⓓ Ⓔ					142	Ⓐ Ⓑ Ⓒ Ⓓ Ⓔ				
23	Ⓐ Ⓑ Ⓒ Ⓓ Ⓔ					63	Ⓐ Ⓑ Ⓒ Ⓓ Ⓔ					103	Ⓐ Ⓑ Ⓒ Ⓓ Ⓔ					143	Ⓐ Ⓑ Ⓒ Ⓓ Ⓔ				
24	Ⓐ Ⓑ Ⓒ Ⓓ Ⓔ					64	Ⓐ Ⓑ Ⓒ Ⓓ Ⓔ					104	Ⓐ Ⓑ Ⓒ Ⓓ Ⓔ					144	Ⓐ Ⓑ Ⓒ Ⓓ Ⓔ				
25	Ⓐ Ⓑ Ⓒ Ⓓ Ⓔ					65	Ⓐ Ⓑ Ⓒ Ⓓ Ⓔ					105	Ⓐ Ⓑ Ⓒ Ⓓ Ⓔ					145	Ⓐ Ⓑ Ⓒ Ⓓ Ⓔ				
26	Ⓐ Ⓑ Ⓒ Ⓓ Ⓔ					66	Ⓐ Ⓑ Ⓒ Ⓓ Ⓔ					106	Ⓐ Ⓑ Ⓒ Ⓓ Ⓔ					146	Ⓐ Ⓑ Ⓒ Ⓓ Ⓔ				
27	Ⓐ Ⓑ Ⓒ Ⓓ Ⓔ					67	Ⓐ Ⓑ Ⓒ Ⓓ Ⓔ					107	Ⓐ Ⓑ Ⓒ Ⓓ Ⓔ					147	Ⓐ Ⓑ Ⓒ Ⓓ Ⓔ				
28	Ⓐ Ⓑ Ⓒ Ⓓ Ⓔ					68	Ⓐ Ⓑ Ⓒ Ⓓ Ⓔ					108	Ⓐ Ⓑ Ⓒ Ⓓ Ⓔ					148	Ⓐ Ⓑ Ⓒ Ⓓ Ⓔ				
29	Ⓐ Ⓑ Ⓒ Ⓓ Ⓔ					69	Ⓐ Ⓑ Ⓒ Ⓓ Ⓔ					109	Ⓐ Ⓑ Ⓒ Ⓓ Ⓔ					149	Ⓐ Ⓑ Ⓒ Ⓓ Ⓔ				
30	Ⓐ Ⓑ Ⓒ Ⓓ Ⓔ					70	Ⓐ Ⓑ Ⓒ Ⓓ Ⓔ					110	Ⓐ Ⓑ Ⓒ Ⓓ Ⓔ					150	Ⓐ Ⓑ Ⓒ Ⓓ Ⓔ				
31	Ⓐ Ⓑ Ⓒ Ⓓ Ⓔ					71	Ⓐ Ⓑ Ⓒ Ⓓ Ⓔ					111	Ⓐ Ⓑ Ⓒ Ⓓ Ⓔ					151	Ⓐ Ⓑ Ⓒ Ⓓ Ⓔ				
32	Ⓐ Ⓑ Ⓒ Ⓓ Ⓔ					72	Ⓐ Ⓑ Ⓒ Ⓓ Ⓔ					112	Ⓐ Ⓑ Ⓒ Ⓓ Ⓔ					152	Ⓐ Ⓑ Ⓒ Ⓓ Ⓔ				
33	Ⓐ Ⓑ Ⓒ Ⓓ Ⓔ					73	Ⓐ Ⓑ Ⓒ Ⓓ Ⓔ					113	Ⓐ Ⓑ Ⓒ Ⓓ Ⓔ					153	Ⓐ Ⓑ Ⓒ Ⓓ Ⓔ				
34	Ⓐ Ⓑ Ⓒ Ⓓ Ⓔ					74	Ⓐ Ⓑ Ⓒ Ⓓ Ⓔ					114	Ⓐ Ⓑ Ⓒ Ⓓ Ⓔ					154	Ⓐ Ⓑ Ⓒ Ⓓ Ⓔ				
35	Ⓐ Ⓑ Ⓒ Ⓓ Ⓔ					75	Ⓐ Ⓑ Ⓒ Ⓓ Ⓔ					115	Ⓐ Ⓑ Ⓒ Ⓓ Ⓔ					155	Ⓐ Ⓑ Ⓒ Ⓓ Ⓔ				
36	Ⓐ Ⓑ Ⓒ Ⓓ Ⓔ					76	Ⓐ Ⓑ Ⓒ Ⓓ Ⓔ					116	Ⓐ Ⓑ Ⓒ Ⓓ Ⓔ					156	Ⓐ Ⓑ Ⓒ Ⓓ Ⓔ				
37	Ⓐ Ⓑ Ⓒ Ⓓ Ⓔ					77	Ⓐ Ⓑ Ⓒ Ⓓ Ⓔ					117	Ⓐ Ⓑ Ⓒ Ⓓ Ⓔ					157	Ⓐ Ⓑ Ⓒ Ⓓ Ⓔ				
38	Ⓐ Ⓑ Ⓒ Ⓓ Ⓔ					78	Ⓐ Ⓑ Ⓒ Ⓓ Ⓔ					118	Ⓐ Ⓑ Ⓒ Ⓓ Ⓔ					158	Ⓐ Ⓑ Ⓒ Ⓓ Ⓔ				
39	Ⓐ Ⓑ Ⓒ Ⓓ Ⓔ					79	Ⓐ Ⓑ Ⓒ Ⓓ Ⓔ					119	Ⓐ Ⓑ Ⓒ Ⓓ Ⓔ					159	Ⓐ Ⓑ Ⓒ Ⓓ Ⓔ				
40	Ⓐ Ⓑ Ⓒ Ⓓ Ⓔ					80	Ⓐ Ⓑ Ⓒ Ⓓ Ⓔ					120	Ⓐ Ⓑ Ⓒ Ⓓ Ⓔ					160	Ⓐ Ⓑ Ⓒ Ⓓ Ⓔ				

FOR ETS USE ONLY	R1	R2	R3	R4	R5	R6	R7	R8	TR	CS

Directions: Each statement or passage in this test is followed by a question or questions based on its content. After reading a statement or passage, choose the best answer to each question from among the five choices given. Answer all questions following a statement or passage on the basis of what is *stated* or *implied* in that statement or passage; you are not expected to have any previous knowledge of the topics treated in the statements and passages.

Be sure to mark all your answers on your answer sheet and completely fill in the lettered space with a heavy, dark mark so that you cannot see the letter.

Remember, try to answer every question.

1. In 1976 a powerful earthquake devastated the city of Tangshan, China. Scientists had failed to predict the earthquake. But if people had
Line paid attention to the unusual animal behavior
(5) that preceded the earthquake, they would have known it was coming. For animals can often sense an impending earthquake when scientists cannot.

Which of the following, if true, indicates a weakness of the argument above?

(A) A wide variety of phenomena can cause animals to behave strangely.

(B) Scientists use a variety of sophisticated tools to monitor and predict earthquakes.

(C) Many domestic as well as farm animals behaved strangely the day before the Tangshan earthquake.

(D) The city of Tangshan is near a major fault line and will probably be hit by an earthquake again.

(E) Scientists had correctly predicted three major earthquakes in China in the eighteen months prior to the Tangshan earthquake.

Questions 2-3

James Baldwin's eloquent, forceful style has given his work its wide recognition. The intricate sentences, the lyrical prose, the
Line dramatic stance—all these characteristics
(5) contribute to a style that is unique and thus immediately recognizable. But Baldwin's style is more than simply unique; it is a living illustration of what can be achieved in a difficult environment; and
(10) when he uses it to discuss oppression, racial segregation, and inadequate social and cultural opportunities, its sophisticated grace serves as ironic commentary on the problems he considers.

2. Which of the following statements best summarizes the main idea of the passage?

(A) James Baldwin's ironic commentary about racial oppression fills his writings with life and excitement.

(B) James Baldwin has a highly original style that exemplifies what an individual can accomplish even in the face of a difficult environment.

(C) James Baldwin is widely regarded as one of the most important writers of the twentieth century because of his innovations in literary technique.

(D) James Baldwin has often turned to matters with which he is intimately familiar, like racial segregation and inadequate social opportunities, as the subject for his work.

(E) James Baldwin has dedicated his literary work to educating the public at large about the problems that Black Americans face.

3. The passage mentions all of the following as characteristic elements of Baldwin's style EXCEPT

   (A) lyrical prose
   (B) ironic illustrations
   (C) dramatic stance
   (D) intricate sentences
   (E) sophisticated grace

4. A recent article has argued at length that the power of factory supervisors over workers increased after 1900; this point of view, however, completely ignores the fact that, after 1900, personnel departments and seniority systems diminished the power of the supervisors by introducing legal restrictions.

   The statement above is primarily concerned with

   (A) summarizing a point of view
   (B) proposing a compromise
   (C) settling a dispute
   (D) refuting an argument
   (E) exposing a falsification of data

Questions 5- 7

Modern medicine has not yet devised any widely accepted treatment that actively promotes the healing of wounds. Rather, by
Line closing wounds and keeping them moist and
(5) sterile, physicians can only try to make it as easy as possible for nature to take its course. That may soon change: researchers are now exploiting recombinant-DNA technology to produce in large quantities substances that
(10) occur naturally in the body and have a potent stimulatory effect on cell migration and cell division, two processes central to wound healing. These substances, called growth factors, can attach themselves to cells and
(15) stimulate cell growth or movement.

5. Which of the following best summarizes the main idea of the passage?

   (A) Natural cell migration and cell division contribute to wound healing.
   (B) New technological developments may soon alter the way physicians can treat wounds.
   (C) The artificial stimulation of cell growth may have unpredictable consequences.
   (D) Wounds should be kept clean and moist if they are to heal properly.
   (E) In general, physicians have not kept current with the latest developments in the treatment of wounds.

6. The passage implies that growth factors contribute to wound-healing by

   (A) keeping the wound moist and sterile
   (B) making it easier for physicians to encourage the proper treatment of wounds
   (C) encouraging new cell growth and cell movement
   (D) circumventing recombinant-DNA technology
   (E) changing the way physicians treat wounds

7. The primary purpose of the passage is to

   (A) evaluate the efforts of researchers working with recombinant-DNA technology
   (B) summarize the methods physicians use to treat wounds
   (C) examine in detail the biological mechanisms involved in cell division and migration and the way these mechanisms affect wound healing
   (D) stimulate medical researchers to investigate new approaches to the treatment of wounds
   (E) outline the current treatment for wounds and announce new research that seeks to promote wound healing

Questions 8-12

The Native Americans sometimes referred to as "Plains Indians" typically painted the hides they used as robes with designs that
Line either were abstract or depicted scenes from
(5) their lives.

The robes with abstract designs represent the oldest stylistic tradition and were painted by women. These designs seem to follow a distinct tradition: they are simple and
(10) symmetrical, contain geometric elements, and follow conventional patterns. The design generally covers only the back of the robe and seldom appears without a surrounding border pattern. Abstract designs contain
(15) primarily the colors red, yellow, blue, and green, flatly and evenly applied. The most striking aspect of the abstract designs is the contrast in scale and texture they produce— the discrepancy between the delicate tracery
(20) of the designs and the thick, bulky hides on which they are painted.

Life scenes are even better suited to the bulky hides. Most of these scenes are dynamic and, taken together, they form
(25) patterns of great animation that completely cover the robe. Figures are placed on a background lacking sky or earth, are flatly painted in a wide variety of colors, and are sometimes outlined in dark paint. The
(30) main subjects are warriors and horses shown in battles and epic events. These designs usually serve to illustrate the exploits of the men who painted them.

8. The passage provides information for answering most fully which of the following questions?

   (A) What were the sources of the colors that the Plains Indians used to paint the hides?

   (B) When did abstract designs first appear on Plains Indian robes?

   (C) What color did the Plains Indians paint the surface of the hides?

   (D) What colors generally appeared in the abstract designs on Plains Indian robes?

   (E) How did the Plains Indians modify traditional abstract designs to fit specific robes?

9. The phrase "the contrast in scale and texture" (line 18) refers to the contrast between the

   (A) weight of the hide and the quality of the leather

   (B) symmetry of the design and the effect of the colors

   (C) size of the hide and the extent of the design

   (D) complexity of the design and the pattern that the design creates

   (E) delicacy of the design and the bulkiness of the hide

10. It can be inferred from the passage that robes with abstract designs and robes with life scenes differ in all of the following ways EXCEPT the

    (A) amount of the hide covered by the design

    (B) range of colors used in the design

    (C) pattern of the design

    (D) sex of the artist who painted the robe

    (E) type of hide used

11. Which of the following descriptions of life scenes could the author best use to support her claim that such scenes are "dynamic" (line 24) ?

    (A) The scenes are arranged in horizontal rows.

    (B) Horses and riders are often depicted in motion.

    (C) A scene containing more than one figure often shows all the figures in the same pose.

    (D) The horses are painted in colors that are contrary to those seen in nature.

    (E) The figures are represented in varying degrees of realism.

12. Which of the following facts, if true, would most help to explain why abstract designs of robes such as those described in the passage originated before life scenes?

   (A) Pottery, a very early Plains Indian art form, was decorated with abstract designs that later reappeared in other art forms.

   (B) The abstract designs used by the Plains Indians are not derived from the shapes of living creatures.

   (C) The Plains Indians, like their predecessors, probably used highly realistic drawings of animals in ceremonies performed to assure successful hunting.

   (D) The realistic depiction of animals in Plains Indian art occurred before the realistic depiction of people.

   (E) The Plains Indians decorated the surfaces of even the most ordinary household objects with a wide variety of colors.

Questions 13-14 are based on the following excerpt from a commentary on children's literature.

   The publishing of children's books today is not unlike the cookie business: a profitable side avenue of a major industry, turning out, in unprecedented volume and variety, what was once a high-quality product. But most of these new varieties are only sugar and hot air.

13. Which of the following best describes the way in which the claim above is presented?

   (A) A generalization is made and is supported with specific details.

   (B) Irony is used to suggest the opposite of what is stated in the passage.

   (C) An analogy is used to clarify a qualitative judgment.

   (D) Highly emotional language is used to hide the real issue.

   (E) An argument derived from one situation is applied to a variety of other situations.

14. The author's attitude toward the current publishing of children's books can best be described as

   (A) enthusiastic
   (B) tolerant
   (C) uncertain
   (D) uninterested
   (E) disapproving

15. Although not the equal of Ibsen or Chekhov, Elmer Rice was one of the most innovative and imaginative dramatists the United States ever produced. But since socially relevant drama of the 1920's will be remembered primarily for fiery rhetoric rather than for the unemotional intellectualism that characterized Rice's plays, Rice will probably endure as an anonymous and unseen influence rather than as a towering name.

Which of the following can be inferred about Rice from the statement above?

(A) His style was too fiery to be considered great.
(B) He wrote many of his plays anonymously.
(C) He was once as well known as Ibsen or Chekhov.
(D) He did not fully understand the society of the 1920's.
(E) He wrote socially relevant dramas.

16. In the earliest electronic computers, space for the storage of information was a precious resource. Computer programs were therefore written in the most compact form possible. As the cost of computer memory has decreased, the need for succinctness in programs has diminished, and programs have grown increasingly large.

According to the statement above, the decrease in the cost of computer memory has led to

(A) less compact computer programs
(B) an increase in the number of computer programs
(C) the general availability of low-cost personal computers
(D) an increase in the cost of information storage
(E) less computer space being available for information storage

17. In making her crucial contributions to the Civil Rights movement, Ella Baker never sought public attention, nor did many of the other Black women who were important leaders of the movement. Their main concern was not stardom but the well-being of all Black Americans.

The passage above is mainly concerned with which of the following?

(A) Identifying the best-known leaders of the Civil Rights movement

(B) Explaining why many women who were important leaders of the Civil Rights movement are not well known

(C) Describing the most important achievements of the Civil Rights movement

(D) Determining how many of the leaders of the Civil Rights movement were women

(E) Analyzing why public attention to social movements generally focuses more on individuals than on organizations

Questions 18-23

Historians who study middle-class Victorian women have difficulty finding reliable sources of information. The significant lack of
Line extensive autobiographical data has led them
(5) to rely heavily on the serious fiction of the day. But an undiscriminating reliance on such fiction has led some historians, incorrectly, to see the social circumstances of literary characters as typical of those of actual middle-
(10) class Victorian women and has unfortunately reinforced the false image of the idle Victorian woman. Although most popular Victorian novels (those without serious literary ambitions) get closer to the reality of middle-
(15) class women's lives than do the serious novels, the problem of typicality remains. Even household manuals—written for and by middle-class women—must be scrutinized closely to determine the degree to which their
(20) depictions of women's roles are representative of women's actual lives.

A more promising source of information is census and wage data. These throw into doubt the image of the idle woman by undermining
(25) the assumption made by some historians that most middle-class Victorian families employed several domestic servants. The data strongly imply that these households could rarely afford to hire more than a single servant. This
(30) information suggests that, in fact, most middle-class Victorian women had to spend considerable time and energy themselves to maintain their households.

18. According to the author, the uncritical reliance on serious fiction by some historians has resulted in which of the following?

    (A) Outright rejection of information from popular Victorian novels
    (B) Inaccurate generalizations about middle-class Victorian women as a group
    (C) Insufficient consideration of autobiographical data about middle-class Victorian women
    (D) The unsubstantiated assumption that middle-class Victorian households employed no domestic servants
    (E) Overly high estimates of the amount of time that middle-class Victorian women spent on managing their households

19. It can be inferred from the passage that historians might have relied less heavily on serious Victorian fiction as a source of data if which of the following had been available in greater numbers?

    (A) Victorian household manuals
    (B) Popular Victorian novels
    (C) Works of serious fiction from pre-Victorian times
    (D) Autobiographical accounts of Victorian women's lives
    (E) Census and wage data from Victorian times

20. According to the passage, one advantage for historians that popular Victorian novels have over the serious fiction of the day is that the popular novels

    (A) are a more complete source of wage data
    (B) attracted a greater and more diverse readership
    (C) more often portray women drawn from all economic classes
    (D) give a more accurate picture of the lives of middle-class women
    (E) convey a more thorough sense of the circumstances of female domestic servants

21. According to the passage, the kinds of data mentioned in line 27 are significant because they

    (A) emphasize the unique economic circumstances of middle-class households
    (B) call into question the image of the idle Victorian woman
    (C) suggest that the importance of such data in the study of history is debatable
    (D) support the descriptions of middle-class women found in serious Victorian fiction
    (E) undermine the assertion that Victorian household manuals were written by middle-class women

22. The passage strongly suggests that the employment of several domestic servants was uncharacteristic of the

    (A) ideal Victorian family described in household manuals
    (B) typical middle-class household prior to Victorian times
    (C) middle-class families described in Victorian women's autobiographies
    (D) fictional middle-class households described in serious Victorian fiction
    (E) typical middle-class household of Victorian times

23. Which of the following statements best describes the organization of the passage?

    (A) A theory is advanced and then arguments in its favor are introduced.
    (B) A current debate among historians is described and then the author's position is introduced.
    (C) Difficulties regarding the use of certain sources by historians are described and then an alternative source is recommended.
    (D) Individual facts about a historical period are revealed and then a generalization about these facts is made.
    (E) A new approach to historical sources is summarized and then the drawbacks of that approach are suggested.

24. Rembrandt seems to have been his own favorite model. Seventy self-portraits or representations of his face have been preserved, and no moment in the artist's biography is not vividly represented. Such personal statements, expressed with feeling and intensity, are a record of Rembrandt's view of the world and his relationship to it.

The passage implies which of the following about Rembrandt's self-portraits?

    (A) They were used to illustrate Rembrandt's autobiography.
    (B) They accurately depict the world in which Rembrandt lived.
    (C) They reveal Rembrandt's personality and outlook at many times in his life.
    (D) They are more carefully crafted than Rembrandt's portraits of other people.
    (E) They are similar to Rembrandt's paintings of other subjects.

25. Science fiction films often achieve weird effects by simply exaggerating the size of a familiar creature, such as an insect. But that change in size would probably be far more bizarre than any science fiction movie if it actually happened, because the law of gravity dictates that a major change in size means a change in form as well.

If the statements above are true, which of the following must also be true of a bird that became as large as a cow?

(A) It would be recognizable as a familiar form.
(B) Its form would resemble that of a cow.
(C) It would no longer be bizarre.
(D) Its body would be altered in form.
(E) The law of gravity would prevent it from moving.

26. In 1932 many of the highest political leaders in Britain feared that the greatest military threat to Britain was from the air. However, by 1939 a chain of twenty radar stations had been put into operation along the British coast. After the Battle of Britain, in 1941, many of those same leaders believed that radar had succeeded in making Britain an island again.

By the phrase "making Britain an island again," the author most probably means which of the following?

(A) Enabling Britain to remain relatively invulnerable to attacks
(B) Isolating Britain from technological developments taking place in other countries
(C) Enabling Britain to avoid going to war in neighboring countries
(D) Establishing Britain as the most technologically advanced country
(E) Preventing radio communication between Britain and other countries

Questions 27-31

Some very successful advertising campaigns rely on creating what advertisers call "resonance"—the campaigns link a
Line particular product with some widely
(5) recognized positive symbol to induce a favorable view of the product. Consider the recent advertising campaign for personal computers featuring a Charlie Chaplin look-alike as the Little Tramp who, by using his
(10) personal computer, brings order to several comically chaotic business settings. By linking its product with the Little Tramp, beloved for his combination of naive innocence and indomitable spirit, the computer company
(15) acquires a human face and grafts a soul onto its new machine.

The irony of these advertisements and the resonance they create is that Chaplin himself was expressly opposed to mechanization and
(20) the technological goals of speed and efficiency. Those views, evident throughout much of his work, are nowhere more clearly expressed than in the film *Modern Times*, where the Little Tramp as factory worker is driven mad
(25) by the soul-destroying monotony and inhuman pace of the assembly line, comically reducing an entire factory to chaos. The company claims its advertisements "stand fear of technology on its head." In reality, it is the
(30) Chaplin character who is being stood on his head. His original meaning has been expunged, leaving behind only an appealing image to be exploited by the advertiser.

27. Which of the following best expresses the main idea of the first paragraph?

(A) The use of resonance in advertising is well-illustrated by a recent advertising campaign featuring the Little Tramp character.

(B) The Little Tramp character is a good example of a widely recognized cultural symbol with positive associations.

(C) Computers are generally viewed unfavorably by consumers, so advertisements for them often rely on linking them to a positive symbol.

(D) Because computers often help to reduce chaos in the workplace, consumers associate them with the Little Tramp character.

(E) The computer advertisements featuring the Little Tramp character were very successful primarily because the actor appearing in them looked so much like Charlie Chaplin.

28. According to the author, which of the following is true of advertising campaigns that rely on creating resonance?

    (A) They are particularly useful in combating consumer resistance to new products.

    (B) They usually feature historical and cultural figures who would, in fact, have objected to the product advertised.

    (C) They usually rely on irony and humor to achieve their effect.

    (D) They try to induce consumers to associate the product advertised with some appealing and widely known image or person.

    (E) They are more successful than most other kinds of advertising campaigns.

29. Which of the following, if true, would most weaken the author's argument concerning the irony of the computer advertisements?

    (A) *Modern Times* is not considered to be one of Chaplin's best films, because its political and social message overshadows the humorous elements it contains.

    (B) The advertisers who created the campaign doubted that many consumers would recognize their inversion of the plot of *Modern Times*.

    (C) *Modern Times* condemns only the mechanization that dehumanizes the workplace; computerization significantly reduces the drudgery of office work.

    (D) The theme of *Modern Times* is not limited to the effects of mechanization; the film also addresses other social changes.

    (E) *Modern Times* is not the only film by Chaplin in which machines appear as comic props.

30. According to the author, which of the following is true of the actor Charlie Chaplin?

   (A)   He expressly opposed the use of computers.

   (B)   He was beloved for his simplicity and lack of sophistication.

   (C)   He disapproved of increasing speed and efficiency through technology.

   (D)   His films featuring the Little Tramp character are usually serious political or social inquiries.

   (E)   His films are generally quite chaotic and disorganized, but are, nonetheless, very funny.

31. Which of the following best summarizes the passage?

   (A)   It is ironic that most successful advertisements rely on creating appealing images rather than on informing consumers about the product itself.

   (B)   The original meaning of an image or symbol usually changes over time, especially if it is often used in advertising.

   (C)   Although advertisements that use a positive symbol to create resonance can be quite successful, they may also violate the original meaning of that symbol.

   (D)   Linking an advertised product with a widely known positive symbol is called "creating resonance" and is often a successful advertising technique.

   (E)   Advertisements that try to create resonance are most successful when the images they use are familiar to a large number of consumers.

32. In 1843 Emil Du Bois-Reymond became the first person to prove that electricity runs through the nervous system. Working with nerves from animals and with electrodes, he demonstrated the existence of what is now called the action potential, the electro-chemical pulse in our neurons that is nothing less than the language of the brain.

According to the statement above, Emil Du Bois-Reymond was the first person to

(A) demonstrate that electrical pulses exist in the nervous system
(B) insert electrodes into the nerves of animals
(C) coin the term "action potential"
(D) discover the existence of neurons
(E) measure the strength of the electrochemical pulse

33. For the school of painting known as Photo-realism, the painter's only function was to "transfer information" from a photograph to a canvas. Photo-realists sought to remove all evidence of the artist's hand or interpretive vision from their works. However, they did not succeed; even devout Photo-realists "cleaned up" photographs as they painted—sharpening outlines, emphasizing important details, eliminating others.

According to the author, Photo-realist artists tended to produce works that

(A) were indistinguishable from the photographs on which they were based
(B) were based on photographs that had been skillfully retouched before the artists began to work
(C) displayed sharper outlines than did the photographs from which the artists worked
(D) lacked any evidence that they were produced through the interpretive vision of an artist
(E) demonstrated convincingly that the primary function of the artist should be to transfer information from one medium to another

Questions 34-36

Stating that there was "no English precedent for the admission of women to the bar" (i.e., for women to act as lawyers in a
Line courtroom), the United States Supreme
(5) Court in 1878 denied lawyer Belva Lockwood permission to argue cases before the Court, pending the enactment of "special legislation." In response Lockwood herself drafted the necessary legislation and
(10) successfully argued it before the House Judiciary Committee. In February 1879 it was signed into law, and the following month Lockwood became the first woman to argue a case before the Supreme Court. For
(15) Lockwood this would be only one distinction in a lifetime of ground-breaking achievements; in 1884 she became the first woman to appear on a ballot in a presidential election.

34. According to the passage, Lockwood was the first woman in the United States to do which of the following?

(A) Become a lawyer
(B) Draft legislation
(C) Serve on the House Judiciary Committee
(D) Argue a case before the Supreme Court
(E) Vote in a presidential election

35. Which of the following criticisms, if true, would undermine the Supreme Court's argument that "special legislation" was necessary before Lockwood could be allowed to argue before the Supreme Court?

(A) The Supreme Court has the power to override precedent and to establish new judicial procedures.
(B) Being admitted to the bar is not a necessary prerequisite for drafting legislation.
(C) Legislation is more important than precedent in determining who may argue before a United States court.
(D) Most members of the House Judiciary Committee had less experience as lawyers than did Lockwood.
(E) The Supreme Court has no jurisdiction over who may present legislation before the House Judiciary Committee.

36. The author mentions Lockwood's appearance on a presidential ballot as an example of which of the following?

(A) The way Lockwood used legislation to change social conditions
(B) The role of the Supreme Court in the advancement of women's rights
(C) The power of the House Judiciary Committee to review judicial decisions
(D) Lockwood's accomplishments in pursuits previously closed to women
(E) Lockwood's skill in the courtroom

Questions 37-38

During the 1970's a book-banning epidemic broke out in the United States. Statistics collected by associations of teachers
Line and librarians showed an alarming rise in the
(5) incidence of attempts to remove books from the shelves of school and public libraries. In the early seventies, the American Library Association received reports of about 100 such attempts per year. By the late seventies
(10) the number had tripled; by 1981 it had tripled again. In a 1982 survey of school librarians, 34 percent reported having had a book challenged by a parent or a community group that year. What was worse, over half
(15) of those protests met with success—the challenged book was finally removed from the library.

37. According to the passage, in the 1982 survey, school librarians reported which of the following?

(A) Fewer attempts were made to ban books from school libraries than were made in 1981.

(B) Almost all challenged books were removed from school library shelves.

(C) About 100 attempts were made to ban books from school libraries during the year.

(D) Many of the attempts to ban books from school libraries were made by associations of teachers.

(E) More than half of the reported attempts to ban books from school libraries were successful.

38. The author's attitude toward book banning is most clearly revealed in which of the following lists of words?

(A) "epidemic" (line 2); "alarming" (line 4); "worse" (line 14)

(B) "book-banning" (line 1); "attempts" (line 9); "challenged" (line 13)

(C) "Statistics" (line 3); "protests" (line 15); "success" (line 15)

(D) "associations" (line 3); "survey" (line 11); "finally" (line 16)

(E) "incidence" (line 5); "public libraries" (line 6); "removed" (line 16)

39. Slang originates in the effort of ingenious individuals to make language more pungent and picturesque and thus serves to increase the store of striking words, widen the boundaries of metaphor, and provide for new shades of difference in meaning. As some have argued, this is also the aim of poets.

The author attempts to persuade the reader to adopt a positive attitude toward slang by doing which of the following?

(A) Pointing out that most slang is devised by intellectuals

(B) Providing examples of the slang used in normal speech

(C) Refuting a standard criticism of slang

(D) Making a comparison between slang and poetry

(E) Supporting the observation that poets often use slang

40. To this day, the idea that the mass of the materials involved in a chemical reaction remains constant, that matter is conserved, governs the practice of modern chemistry; it would be ridiculous to teach physics and chemistry without this concept, even though, of course, it is not strictly true according to our knowledge of relativity.

With which of the following statements concerning scientific concepts would the author be most likely to agree?

(A)   Outmoded scientific concepts are more likely to be abandoned than modified.

(B)   In science old rules of thumb must be used carefully and with many qualifications.

(C)   There is no more important task in science than the reconciliation of theory and practice.

(D)   The sciences of physics and chemistry are so complicated that explaining them by using simplified concepts introduces unacceptable distortions.

(E)   Certain concepts used in practical applications of chemistry are not strictly and unequivocally true.

Chapter 9
Practice Test, *PPST: Mathematics*

Now that you have studied the content topics and have worked through strategies relating to the *PPST: Mathematics* test, you should take the following practice test. You will probably find it helpful to simulate actual testing conditions, giving yourself 60 minutes to work on the questions. You can cut out and use the answer sheet provided if you wish.

Keep in mind that the test you take at an actual administration will have different questions. You should not expect the percentage of questions you answer correctly in the practice test to be exactly the same as when you take the test at an actual administration, since numerous factors affect a person's performance in any given testing situation.

When you have finished the practice questions, you can score your answers and read the explanations of the best answer choices in chapter 11.

THE **PRAXIS**
S E R I E S
Professional Assessments for Beginning Teachers ®

TEST NAME:
Pre-Professional Skills Test Mathematics

Time—60 minutes

40 Questions

Answer Sheet B

THE PRAXIS SERIES
Professional Assessments for Beginning Teachers ®

DO NOT USE INK

Use only a pencil with soft black lead (No. 2 or HB) to complete this answer sheet.
Be sure to fill in completely the oval that corresponds to your answer choice.
Completely erase any errors or stray marks.

1. NAME

Enter your last name and first initial.
Omit spaces, hyphens, apostrophes, etc.

Last Name (first 6 letters) | F I

(ovals A–Z for name grid)

2.

YOUR NAME: (Print)
Last Name (Family or Surname)   First Name (Given)   M. I.

MAILING ADDRESS: (Print)
P.O. Box or Street Address   Apt. # (if any)

City   State or Province

Country   Zip or Postal Code

TELEPHONE NUMBER: Home ( )   Business ( )

SIGNATURE: **TEST DATE:**

3. DATE OF BIRTH

Month	Day
Jan.	
Feb.	
Mar.	
April	
May	
June	
July	
Aug.	
Sept.	
Oct.	
Nov.	
Dec.	

(Day ovals 0–9)

4. SOCIAL SECURITY NUMBER

(ovals 0–9)

5. CANDIDATE ID NUMBER

(ovals 0–9)

6. TEST CENTER / REPORTING LOCATION

Center Number   Room Number

Center Name

City   State or Province

Country

7. TEST CODE / FORM CODE

0
1

(ovals 0–9)

8. TEST BOOK SERIAL NUMBER

9. TEST FORM

10. TEST NAME

Educational Testing Service, ETS, the ETS logo, and THE PRAXIS SERIES:PROFESSIONAL
ASSESSMENTS FOR BEGINNING TEACHERS and its design logo are registered trademarks of
Educational Testing Service. The modernized ETS logo is a trademark of Educational Testing Service.

ETS Copyright © 1993 by Educational Testing Service, Princeton, NJ 08541. Printed in U.S.A.

MH99232   Q2572-06   51055 • 08916 • CV99M500
I.N. 202973

1   2   3   4

CERTIFICATION STATEMENT: (Please write the following statement below. DO NOT PRINT.)
"I hereby agree to the conditions set forth in the *Registration Bulletin* and certify that I am the person whose name and address appear on this answer sheet."

_____

_____

_____

SIGNATURE: _____   DATE: _____ / _____ / _____
                                                                                                                    Month   Day   Year

---

BE SURE EACH MARK IS DARK AND COMPLETELY FILLS THE INTENDED SPACE AS ILLUSTRATED HERE: ● .

1 Ⓐ Ⓑ Ⓒ Ⓓ Ⓔ	41 Ⓐ Ⓑ Ⓒ Ⓓ Ⓔ	81 Ⓐ Ⓑ Ⓒ Ⓓ Ⓔ	121 Ⓐ Ⓑ Ⓒ Ⓓ Ⓔ
2 Ⓐ Ⓑ Ⓒ Ⓓ Ⓔ	42 Ⓐ Ⓑ Ⓒ Ⓓ Ⓔ	82 Ⓐ Ⓑ Ⓒ Ⓓ Ⓔ	122 Ⓐ Ⓑ Ⓒ Ⓓ Ⓔ
3 Ⓐ Ⓑ Ⓒ Ⓓ Ⓔ	43 Ⓐ Ⓑ Ⓒ Ⓓ Ⓔ	83 Ⓐ Ⓑ Ⓒ Ⓓ Ⓔ	123 Ⓐ Ⓑ Ⓒ Ⓓ Ⓔ
4 Ⓐ Ⓑ Ⓒ Ⓓ Ⓔ	44 Ⓐ Ⓑ Ⓒ Ⓓ Ⓔ	84 Ⓐ Ⓑ Ⓒ Ⓓ Ⓔ	124 Ⓐ Ⓑ Ⓒ Ⓓ Ⓔ
5 Ⓐ Ⓑ Ⓒ Ⓓ Ⓔ	45 Ⓐ Ⓑ Ⓒ Ⓓ Ⓔ	85 Ⓐ Ⓑ Ⓒ Ⓓ Ⓔ	125 Ⓐ Ⓑ Ⓒ Ⓓ Ⓔ
6 Ⓐ Ⓑ Ⓒ Ⓓ Ⓔ	46 Ⓐ Ⓑ Ⓒ Ⓓ Ⓔ	86 Ⓐ Ⓑ Ⓒ Ⓓ Ⓔ	126 Ⓐ Ⓑ Ⓒ Ⓓ Ⓔ
7 Ⓐ Ⓑ Ⓒ Ⓓ Ⓔ	47 Ⓐ Ⓑ Ⓒ Ⓓ Ⓔ	87 Ⓐ Ⓑ Ⓒ Ⓓ Ⓔ	127 Ⓐ Ⓑ Ⓒ Ⓓ Ⓔ
8 Ⓐ Ⓑ Ⓒ Ⓓ Ⓔ	48 Ⓐ Ⓑ Ⓒ Ⓓ Ⓔ	88 Ⓐ Ⓑ Ⓒ Ⓓ Ⓔ	128 Ⓐ Ⓑ Ⓒ Ⓓ Ⓔ
9 Ⓐ Ⓑ Ⓒ Ⓓ Ⓔ	49 Ⓐ Ⓑ Ⓒ Ⓓ Ⓔ	89 Ⓐ Ⓑ Ⓒ Ⓓ Ⓔ	129 Ⓐ Ⓑ Ⓒ Ⓓ Ⓔ
10 Ⓐ Ⓑ Ⓒ Ⓓ Ⓔ	50 Ⓐ Ⓑ Ⓒ Ⓓ Ⓔ	90 Ⓐ Ⓑ Ⓒ Ⓓ Ⓔ	130 Ⓐ Ⓑ Ⓒ Ⓓ Ⓔ
11 Ⓐ Ⓑ Ⓒ Ⓓ Ⓔ	51 Ⓐ Ⓑ Ⓒ Ⓓ Ⓔ	91 Ⓐ Ⓑ Ⓒ Ⓓ Ⓔ	131 Ⓐ Ⓑ Ⓒ Ⓓ Ⓔ
12 Ⓐ Ⓑ Ⓒ Ⓓ Ⓔ	52 Ⓐ Ⓑ Ⓒ Ⓓ Ⓔ	92 Ⓐ Ⓑ Ⓒ Ⓓ Ⓔ	132 Ⓐ Ⓑ Ⓒ Ⓓ Ⓔ
13 Ⓐ Ⓑ Ⓒ Ⓓ Ⓔ	53 Ⓐ Ⓑ Ⓒ Ⓓ Ⓔ	93 Ⓐ Ⓑ Ⓒ Ⓓ Ⓔ	133 Ⓐ Ⓑ Ⓒ Ⓓ Ⓔ
14 Ⓐ Ⓑ Ⓒ Ⓓ Ⓔ	54 Ⓐ Ⓑ Ⓒ Ⓓ Ⓔ	94 Ⓐ Ⓑ Ⓒ Ⓓ Ⓔ	134 Ⓐ Ⓑ Ⓒ Ⓓ Ⓔ
15 Ⓐ Ⓑ Ⓒ Ⓓ Ⓔ	55 Ⓐ Ⓑ Ⓒ Ⓓ Ⓔ	95 Ⓐ Ⓑ Ⓒ Ⓓ Ⓔ	135 Ⓐ Ⓑ Ⓒ Ⓓ Ⓔ
16 Ⓐ Ⓑ Ⓒ Ⓓ Ⓔ	56 Ⓐ Ⓑ Ⓒ Ⓓ Ⓔ	96 Ⓐ Ⓑ Ⓒ Ⓓ Ⓔ	136 Ⓐ Ⓑ Ⓒ Ⓓ Ⓔ
17 Ⓐ Ⓑ Ⓒ Ⓓ Ⓔ	57 Ⓐ Ⓑ Ⓒ Ⓓ Ⓔ	97 Ⓐ Ⓑ Ⓒ Ⓓ Ⓔ	137 Ⓐ Ⓑ Ⓒ Ⓓ Ⓔ
18 Ⓐ Ⓑ Ⓒ Ⓓ Ⓔ	58 Ⓐ Ⓑ Ⓒ Ⓓ Ⓔ	98 Ⓐ Ⓑ Ⓒ Ⓓ Ⓔ	138 Ⓐ Ⓑ Ⓒ Ⓓ Ⓔ
19 Ⓐ Ⓑ Ⓒ Ⓓ Ⓔ	59 Ⓐ Ⓑ Ⓒ Ⓓ Ⓔ	99 Ⓐ Ⓑ Ⓒ Ⓓ Ⓔ	139 Ⓐ Ⓑ Ⓒ Ⓓ Ⓔ
20 Ⓐ Ⓑ Ⓒ Ⓓ Ⓔ	60 Ⓐ Ⓑ Ⓒ Ⓓ Ⓔ	100 Ⓐ Ⓑ Ⓒ Ⓓ Ⓔ	140 Ⓐ Ⓑ Ⓒ Ⓓ Ⓔ
21 Ⓐ Ⓑ Ⓒ Ⓓ Ⓔ	61 Ⓐ Ⓑ Ⓒ Ⓓ Ⓔ	101 Ⓐ Ⓑ Ⓒ Ⓓ Ⓔ	141 Ⓐ Ⓑ Ⓒ Ⓓ Ⓔ
22 Ⓐ Ⓑ Ⓒ Ⓓ Ⓔ	62 Ⓐ Ⓑ Ⓒ Ⓓ Ⓔ	102 Ⓐ Ⓑ Ⓒ Ⓓ Ⓔ	142 Ⓐ Ⓑ Ⓒ Ⓓ Ⓔ
23 Ⓐ Ⓑ Ⓒ Ⓓ Ⓔ	63 Ⓐ Ⓑ Ⓒ Ⓓ Ⓔ	103 Ⓐ Ⓑ Ⓒ Ⓓ Ⓔ	143 Ⓐ Ⓑ Ⓒ Ⓓ Ⓔ
24 Ⓐ Ⓑ Ⓒ Ⓓ Ⓔ	64 Ⓐ Ⓑ Ⓒ Ⓓ Ⓔ	104 Ⓐ Ⓑ Ⓒ Ⓓ Ⓔ	144 Ⓐ Ⓑ Ⓒ Ⓓ Ⓔ
25 Ⓐ Ⓑ Ⓒ Ⓓ Ⓔ	65 Ⓐ Ⓑ Ⓒ Ⓓ Ⓔ	105 Ⓐ Ⓑ Ⓒ Ⓓ Ⓔ	145 Ⓐ Ⓑ Ⓒ Ⓓ Ⓔ
26 Ⓐ Ⓑ Ⓒ Ⓓ Ⓔ	66 Ⓐ Ⓑ Ⓒ Ⓓ Ⓔ	106 Ⓐ Ⓑ Ⓒ Ⓓ Ⓔ	146 Ⓐ Ⓑ Ⓒ Ⓓ Ⓔ
27 Ⓐ Ⓑ Ⓒ Ⓓ Ⓔ	67 Ⓐ Ⓑ Ⓒ Ⓓ Ⓔ	107 Ⓐ Ⓑ Ⓒ Ⓓ Ⓔ	147 Ⓐ Ⓑ Ⓒ Ⓓ Ⓔ
28 Ⓐ Ⓑ Ⓒ Ⓓ Ⓔ	68 Ⓐ Ⓑ Ⓒ Ⓓ Ⓔ	108 Ⓐ Ⓑ Ⓒ Ⓓ Ⓔ	148 Ⓐ Ⓑ Ⓒ Ⓓ Ⓔ
29 Ⓐ Ⓑ Ⓒ Ⓓ Ⓔ	69 Ⓐ Ⓑ Ⓒ Ⓓ Ⓔ	109 Ⓐ Ⓑ Ⓒ Ⓓ Ⓔ	149 Ⓐ Ⓑ Ⓒ Ⓓ Ⓔ
30 Ⓐ Ⓑ Ⓒ Ⓓ Ⓔ	70 Ⓐ Ⓑ Ⓒ Ⓓ Ⓔ	110 Ⓐ Ⓑ Ⓒ Ⓓ Ⓔ	150 Ⓐ Ⓑ Ⓒ Ⓓ Ⓔ
31 Ⓐ Ⓑ Ⓒ Ⓓ Ⓔ	71 Ⓐ Ⓑ Ⓒ Ⓓ Ⓔ	111 Ⓐ Ⓑ Ⓒ Ⓓ Ⓔ	151 Ⓐ Ⓑ Ⓒ Ⓓ Ⓔ
32 Ⓐ Ⓑ Ⓒ Ⓓ Ⓔ	72 Ⓐ Ⓑ Ⓒ Ⓓ Ⓔ	112 Ⓐ Ⓑ Ⓒ Ⓓ Ⓔ	152 Ⓐ Ⓑ Ⓒ Ⓓ Ⓔ
33 Ⓐ Ⓑ Ⓒ Ⓓ Ⓔ	73 Ⓐ Ⓑ Ⓒ Ⓓ Ⓔ	113 Ⓐ Ⓑ Ⓒ Ⓓ Ⓔ	153 Ⓐ Ⓑ Ⓒ Ⓓ Ⓔ
34 Ⓐ Ⓑ Ⓒ Ⓓ Ⓔ	74 Ⓐ Ⓑ Ⓒ Ⓓ Ⓔ	114 Ⓐ Ⓑ Ⓒ Ⓓ Ⓔ	154 Ⓐ Ⓑ Ⓒ Ⓓ Ⓔ
35 Ⓐ Ⓑ Ⓒ Ⓓ Ⓔ	75 Ⓐ Ⓑ Ⓒ Ⓓ Ⓔ	115 Ⓐ Ⓑ Ⓒ Ⓓ Ⓔ	155 Ⓐ Ⓑ Ⓒ Ⓓ Ⓔ
36 Ⓐ Ⓑ Ⓒ Ⓓ Ⓔ	76 Ⓐ Ⓑ Ⓒ Ⓓ Ⓔ	116 Ⓐ Ⓑ Ⓒ Ⓓ Ⓔ	156 Ⓐ Ⓑ Ⓒ Ⓓ Ⓔ
37 Ⓐ Ⓑ Ⓒ Ⓓ Ⓔ	77 Ⓐ Ⓑ Ⓒ Ⓓ Ⓔ	117 Ⓐ Ⓑ Ⓒ Ⓓ Ⓔ	157 Ⓐ Ⓑ Ⓒ Ⓓ Ⓔ
38 Ⓐ Ⓑ Ⓒ Ⓓ Ⓔ	78 Ⓐ Ⓑ Ⓒ Ⓓ Ⓔ	118 Ⓐ Ⓑ Ⓒ Ⓓ Ⓔ	158 Ⓐ Ⓑ Ⓒ Ⓓ Ⓔ
39 Ⓐ Ⓑ Ⓒ Ⓓ Ⓔ	79 Ⓐ Ⓑ Ⓒ Ⓓ Ⓔ	119 Ⓐ Ⓑ Ⓒ Ⓓ Ⓔ	159 Ⓐ Ⓑ Ⓒ Ⓓ Ⓔ
40 Ⓐ Ⓑ Ⓒ Ⓓ Ⓔ	80 Ⓐ Ⓑ Ⓒ Ⓓ Ⓔ	120 Ⓐ Ⓑ Ⓒ Ⓓ Ⓔ	160 Ⓐ Ⓑ Ⓒ Ⓓ Ⓔ

FOR ETS USE ONLY	R1	R2	R3	R4	R5	R6	R7	R8	TR	CS

Directions: Each of the questions or incomplete statements below is followed by five suggested answers or completions. Select the one that is best in each and then fill in the corresponding lettered space on the answer sheet with a heavy, dark mark so that you cannot see the letter.

Remember, try to answer every question.

Special note: Figures that accompany problems in the test are intended to provide information useful in solving the problem. The figures are drawn as accurately as possible except when it is stated in a specific problem that its figure is not drawn to scale. Figures can be assumed to lie in a plane unless otherwise indicated. Position of points can be assumed to be in the order shown, and lines shown as straight can be assumed to be straight. The symbol ⌐ denotes a right angle.

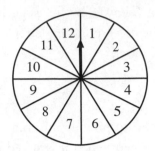

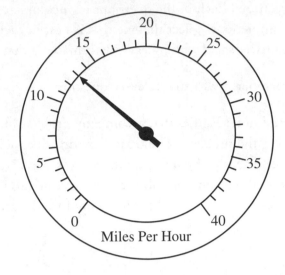

Miles Per Hour

1. On the spinner above, the probability of spinning a number that is a multiple of 3 is

   (A) $\dfrac{1}{12}$

   (B) $\dfrac{3}{12}$

   (C) $\dfrac{4}{12}$

   (D) $\dfrac{5}{12}$

   (E) $\dfrac{8}{12}$

2. A gauge on an exercise bicycle is shown above. The reading on the gauge, in miles per hour, is

   (A) 10.3
   (B) 10.5
   (C) 10.6
   (D) 12
   (E) 13

3. Which of the following numbers is <u>least</u>?

    (A) $\dfrac{1}{7}$

    (B) $\dfrac{11}{70}$

    (C) $\dfrac{101}{700}$

    (D) $\dfrac{1,001}{7,000}$

    (E) $\dfrac{10,001}{70,000}$

4. A 10-gallon tank contains $6\frac{1}{8}$ gallons of gasoline. How many more gallons are needed to fill the tank?

    (A) A little less than 3 gallons
    (B) A little more than 3 gallons
    (C) A little less than 4 gallons
    (D) A little more than 4 gallons
    (E) A little less than 5 gallons

5. A map is drawn to the scale of $\dfrac{3}{4}$ inch = 50 miles. What is the actual distance between two towns that are $1\frac{1}{2}$ inches apart on the map?

    (A) 75 miles
    (B) 100 miles
    (C) 125 miles
    (D) 150 miles
    (E) 200 miles

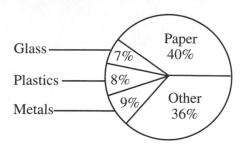

6. The graph above shows the distribution of the content, by weight, of a county's trash. If approximately 60 tons of the trash consists of paper, approximately how many tons of the trash consists of plastics?

    (A) 24
    (B) 20
    (C) 15
    (D) 12
    (E) 5

7. A certain soccer league reported that 12.5 percent of its injured players received ankle injuries last season. There were 128 injured players. Which computation shows the number of players who received ankle injuries?

    (A) 0.0125 × 128
    (B) 0.125 × 128
    (C) 1.25 × 128
    (D) 12.5 × 128
    (E) 125 × 128

x	y
-4	-2
-3	$-\dfrac{3}{2}$
-2	-1
-1	$-\dfrac{1}{2}$
0	0

8. Which of the following is true about the data in the table above?

   (A) As x decreases, y increases.
   (B) As x decreases, y does not change.
   (C) As x increases, y does not change.
   (D) As x increases, y decreases.
   (E) As x increases, y increases.

NUMBER OF COPIES OF FOUR BOOKS
SOLD IN ONE DAY IN A BOOKSTORE

9. If the bookstore sold 60 more copies of book R than book Q, how many books does each [book] in the pictograph represent?

   (A) 3
   (B) 10
   (C) 20
   (D) 30
   (E) 60

7

10. If the perimeter of the rectangle above is 50, what is its length?

   (A) 43
   (B) 36
   (C) 28
   (D) 26
   (E) 18

11. If $3a = 18 - 3b$ what is the value of $a + b$?

   (A) 0
   (B) 6
   (C) 9
   (D) 12
   (E) 15

Questions 12-13 refer to the following graph.

NUMBER OF STUDENTS IN MEDICAL SCHOOLS
IN THE UNITED STATES, 1950-1985
(in thousands)

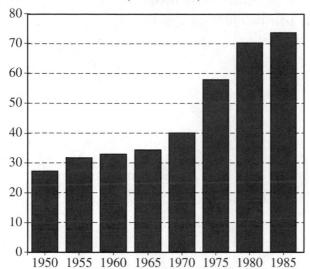

12. In how many of the years shown were there more than twice as many students in medical schools as there were in 1950?

(A) None
(B) One
(C) Two
(D) Three
(E) Five

13. The number of students in medical schools increased by approximately what percent from 1970 to 1980?

(A) 75%
(B) 60%
(C) 50%
(D) 45%
(E) 30%

14. The number 1,000 is how many times 0.1?

(A)   10
(B)   100
(C)   1,000
(D)   10,000
(E)   100,000

15. Which of the following shows a circle with center at (1,1) and a radius of 2?

(A)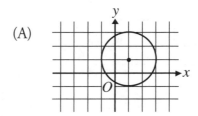

(B)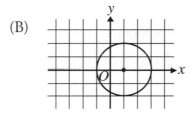

(C)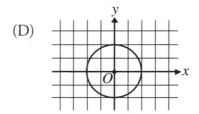

(D)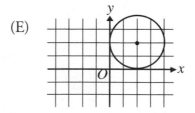

(E)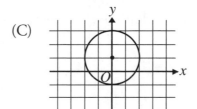

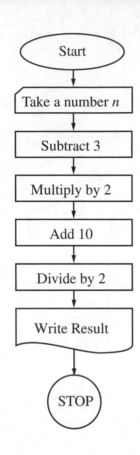

Start

Take a number *n*

Subtract 3

Multiply by 2

Add 10

Divide by 2

Write Result

STOP

16. If *n* = 2, what is the result of the computation outlined in the chart above?

(A) –6
(B) –4
(C) 4
(D) 5
(E) 6

17. A vending machine containing school supplies offers pencils at 2 for a quarter and notebooks at 50 cents each. If the machine accepts only quarters, how many quarters are needed to buy 6 pencils and 2 notebooks?

(A) 16
(B) 10
(C) 8
(D) 7
(E) 5

18. Which of the following numbers, if any, are the same?

I. 1 million
II. 1,000 thousands
III. 10,000 tens

(A) None of them
(B) I and II only
(C) I and III only
(D) II and III only
(E) I, II, and III

19. Which of the following does NOT leave a remainder of 5 when divided into 141?

(A) 136
(B) 68
(C) 34
(D) 16
(E) 8

20. Which of the following is greater than 18.7% ?

    (A) 0.05

    (B) 0.15

    (C) $\dfrac{1}{10}$

    (D) 0.01875

    (E) $\dfrac{1}{5}$

21. There are 8 boys and 13 girls in a choir. What fractional part of the choir is boys?

    (A) $\dfrac{8}{13}$

    (B) $\dfrac{8}{21}$

    (C) $\dfrac{13}{21}$

    (D) $\dfrac{5}{8}$

    (E) $\dfrac{13}{8}$

22. To find 400 times 30, one could multiply 12 by

    (A)   10
    (B)   100
    (C)   1,000
    (D)   10,000
    (E)   100,000

23. If 30% of W = 483, then W =

    (A)   1,610
    (B)   627.9
    (C)   513
    (D)   338.1
    (E)   144.9

24. A set of three points on a line could be a subset of any of the following EXCEPT a

    (A) square
    (B) triangle
    (C) cube
    (D) cylinder
    (E) circle

ROBIN'S TEST SCORES

88, 86, 98, 92, 90, 86

25. In an ordered set of numbers, the median is the middle number if there is a middle number; otherwise, the median is the average of the two middle numbers. If Robin had the test scores given in the table above, what was her median score?

    (A) 86
    (B) 89
    (C) 90
    (D) 92
    (E) 95

Questions 26-27 refer to the following table.

DAYTIME RATES
FOR DIRECT-DIALED CALLS

Miles Between Parties	First Minute	Each Additional Minute
1-10	$0.23	$0.15
11-22	$0.28	$0.19
23-55	$0.31	$0.21
56-124	$0.33	$0.24
125-292	$0.33	$0.26
293-430	$0.34	$0.28
431-925	$0.36	$0.30
926-1,910	$0.37	$0.31
1,911-3,000	$0.40	$0.32

26. The cost of a 50-minute direct-dialed daytime call between two parties 500 miles apart is

   (A) $14.00
   (B) $14.70
   (C) $15.06
   (D) $15.36
   (E) $17.00

27. If the cost of a 20-minute direct-dialed daytime call was $6.26, which of the following could be the distance between the parties?

   (A)   50 miles
   (B)   360 miles
   (C)   480 miles
   (D)   900 miles
   (E) 1,250 miles

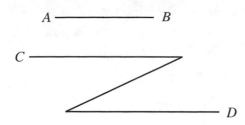

28. If the length of *AB* in the figure above represents 0.3 mile, which of the following is most likely the length, in miles, of the road shown from *C* to *D*?

(A) 0.012
(B) 0.12
(C) 1.2
(D) 0.9
(E) 3

29. If $B = 2(G - 5)$, then $G =$

(A) $2(B - 5)$

(B) $\dfrac{B + 10}{2}$

(C) $\dfrac{B}{2}$

(D) $2B + 5$

(E) $\dfrac{B - 5}{2}$

30. Which of the following expressions is NOT equivalent to the others?

(A) $2^2 \times 10 \times 12$
(B) $2^3 \times 6 \times 10$
(C) $2^4 \times 5 \times 6$
(D) $2^5 \times 3 \times 10$
(E) $4^2 \times 5 \times 6$

31. In one year, a funding agency spent the following amounts on five projects.
Project 1: $19,256,413
Project 2: $7,986,472
Project 3: $11,010,218
Project 4: $754,194
Project 5: $4,918,975
The total amount spent on these five projects, in millions of dollars, was most nearly

(A) 40
(B) 41
(C) 42
(D) 43
(E) 44

32. A square-topped cake is uniformly iced on its top and sides. Which of the following figures shows a way to slice the cake so that each piece has the same amount of icing?

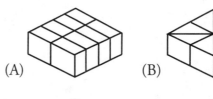

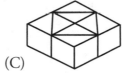 (A)   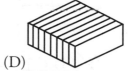 (B)

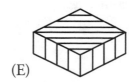 (C)   (D)

(E)

33.

If $= \dfrac{T - S}{R}$, then =

(A) 2
(B) 1
(C) –1
(D) –2
(E) –5

34. The four shapes below are made up of identical squares and identical right triangles. If two sides of each triangle have equal length, which of the four shapes, if any, has the least perimeter?

(A)

(B)

(C)

(D)

(E) All have the same perimeter.

35. On a certain day, high tide occurred at 8:54 a.m. and again at 9:26 p.m. What was the length of time between the two high tides?

(A) 11 hr 12 min
(B) 12 hr 32 min
(C) 13 hr 12 min
(D) 13 hr 20 min
(E) 14 hr 20 min

36. Which of the figures below could be used to <u>disprove</u> the statement "If all sides of a polygon are equal in length, then all angles of the polygon are equal in measure"?

(A)

(B)

(C)

(D)
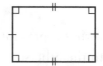

(E)

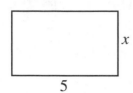

5

37. If the width of the rectangle above is doubled and its length is halved, then the area of the new rectangle is given by the formula

(A) $A = 2\frac{1}{2}x$

(B) $A = 5x$

(C) $A = 7\frac{1}{2}x$

(D) $A = 10x$

(E) $A = 20x$

In a design all isosceles triangles are shaded.

In the design some isosceles triangles are right triangles.

---

38. Which of the following conclusions about the design is valid if the statements above are true?

(A) All right triangles are shaded.
(B) All right triangles are isosceles.
(C) Some right triangles are shaded.
(D) No right triangles are shaded.
(E) No right triangles are isosceles.

39. What number is halfway between $\frac{2}{3}$ and $\frac{3}{4}$?

(A) $\frac{5}{14}$

(B) $\frac{7}{12}$

(C) $\frac{13}{18}$

(D) $\frac{17}{24}$

(E) $\frac{8}{9}$

40. Which of the following numbers is written in scientific notation?

(A) $4,136.28 \times 10^2$
(B) 413.628×10^3
(C) 41.3628×10^4
(D) 4.13628×10^5
(E) 0.413628×10^6

Chapter 10
Practice Test, *PPST: Writing*

▶ ▶ ▶ ▶ ▶ ▶ ▶ ▶ ▶ ▶ ▶ ▶

Now that you have studied the content topics and have worked through strategies relating to the *PPST Writing* test, you should take the following practice test. You will probably find it helpful to simulate actual testing conditions, giving yourself 60 minutes to work on the questions. You can cut out and use the answer sheet provided if you wish.

Keep in mind that the test you take at an actual administration will have different questions. You should not expect the percentage of questions you answer correctly in the practice test to be exactly the same as when you take the test at an actual administration, since numerous factors affect a person's performance in any given testing situation.

When you have finished the practice questions, you can score your answers and read the explanations of the best answer choices in chapter 11.

THE **PRAXIS**
S E R I E S ®
Professional Assessments for Beginning Teachers ®

TEST NAME:
Pre-Professional Skills Test Writing

Time—60 minutes

38 Multiple-choice Questions

1 Essay

THE PRAXIS SERIES
Professional Assessments for Beginning Teachers®

Answer Sheet A

DO NOT USE INK

Use only a pencil with soft black lead (No. 2 or HB) to complete this answer sheet.
Be sure to fill in completely the oval that corresponds to the proper letter or number.
Completely erase any errors or stray marks.

1. NAME
Enter your last name and first initial.
Omit spaces, hyphens, apostrophes, etc.

Last Name (first 6 letters)   F I

A B C D E F G H I J K L M N O P Q R S T U V W X Y Z

2.

YOUR NAME: _____ _____ M.I.
(Print)   Last Name (Family or Surname)   First Name (Given)

MAILING ADDRESS: _____ _____ Apt. # (if any)
(Print)   P.O. Box or Street Address

_____ _____
City   State or Province

_____ _____
Country   Zip or Postal Code

TELEPHONE NUMBER: (___) _____ (___) _____
                    Home   Business

SIGNATURE: _____   TEST DATE: _____

3. DATE OF BIRTH

Month	Day
Jan.	0 0
Feb.	1 1
Mar.	2 2
April	3 3
May	4
June	5
July	6
Aug.	7
Sept.	8
Oct.	9
Nov.	
Dec.	

4. SOCIAL SECURITY NUMBER

0 1 2 3 4 5 6 7 8 9 (repeated columns)

5. CANDIDATE ID NUMBER

0 1 2 3 4 5 6 7 8 9 (repeated columns)

6. TEST CENTER / REPORTING LOCATION

Center Number _____ Room Number _____

Center Name _____

City _____ State or Province _____

Country _____

7. TEST CODE / FORM CODE

0 1 2 3 4 5 6 7 8 9 (repeated columns)

8. TEST BOOK SERIAL NUMBER
_____

9. TEST FORM
_____

10. TEST NAME
_____

51055 • 09244 • TF72R200 • Printed in U.S.A.

MH98334   Q2570-06   I.N. 203230

1 2 3 4

ETS®

PAGE 2

CERTIFICATION STATEMENT: (Please write the following statement below. DO NOT PRINT.)
"I hereby agree to the conditions set forth in the Registration Bulletin and certify that I am the person whose name and address appear on this answer sheet."

_____

_____

_____

SIGNATURE: _____ DATE: _____ / _____ / _____
                                                          Month   Day   Year

BE SURE EACH MARK IS DARK AND COMPLETELY FILLS THE INTENDED SPACE AS ILLUSTRATED HERE: ●

1 Ⓐ Ⓑ Ⓒ Ⓓ Ⓔ   13 Ⓐ Ⓑ Ⓒ Ⓓ Ⓔ   25 Ⓐ Ⓑ Ⓒ Ⓓ Ⓔ   37 Ⓐ Ⓑ Ⓒ Ⓓ Ⓔ
2 Ⓐ Ⓑ Ⓒ Ⓓ Ⓔ   14 Ⓐ Ⓑ Ⓒ Ⓓ Ⓔ   26 Ⓐ Ⓑ Ⓒ Ⓓ Ⓔ   38 Ⓐ Ⓑ Ⓒ Ⓓ Ⓔ
3 Ⓐ Ⓑ Ⓒ Ⓓ Ⓔ   15 Ⓐ Ⓑ Ⓒ Ⓓ Ⓔ   27 Ⓐ Ⓑ Ⓒ Ⓓ Ⓔ   39 Ⓐ Ⓑ Ⓒ Ⓓ Ⓔ
4 Ⓐ Ⓑ Ⓒ Ⓓ Ⓔ   16 Ⓐ Ⓑ Ⓒ Ⓓ Ⓔ   28 Ⓐ Ⓑ Ⓒ Ⓓ Ⓔ   40 Ⓐ Ⓑ Ⓒ Ⓓ Ⓔ
5 Ⓐ Ⓑ Ⓒ Ⓓ Ⓔ   17 Ⓐ Ⓑ Ⓒ Ⓓ Ⓔ   29 Ⓐ Ⓑ Ⓒ Ⓓ Ⓔ   41 Ⓐ Ⓑ Ⓒ Ⓓ Ⓔ
6 Ⓐ Ⓑ Ⓒ Ⓓ Ⓔ   18 Ⓐ Ⓑ Ⓒ Ⓓ Ⓔ   30 Ⓐ Ⓑ Ⓒ Ⓓ Ⓔ   42 Ⓐ Ⓑ Ⓒ Ⓓ Ⓔ
7 Ⓐ Ⓑ Ⓒ Ⓓ Ⓔ   19 Ⓐ Ⓑ Ⓒ Ⓓ Ⓔ   31 Ⓐ Ⓑ Ⓒ Ⓓ Ⓔ   43 Ⓐ Ⓑ Ⓒ Ⓓ Ⓔ
8 Ⓐ Ⓑ Ⓒ Ⓓ Ⓔ   20 Ⓐ Ⓑ Ⓒ Ⓓ Ⓔ   32 Ⓐ Ⓑ Ⓒ Ⓓ Ⓔ   44 Ⓐ Ⓑ Ⓒ Ⓓ Ⓔ
9 Ⓐ Ⓑ Ⓒ Ⓓ Ⓔ   21 Ⓐ Ⓑ Ⓒ Ⓓ Ⓔ   33 Ⓐ Ⓑ Ⓒ Ⓓ Ⓔ   45 Ⓐ Ⓑ Ⓒ Ⓓ Ⓔ
10 Ⓐ Ⓑ Ⓒ Ⓓ Ⓔ   22 Ⓐ Ⓑ Ⓒ Ⓓ Ⓔ   34 Ⓐ Ⓑ Ⓒ Ⓓ Ⓔ
11 Ⓐ Ⓑ Ⓒ Ⓓ Ⓔ   23 Ⓐ Ⓑ Ⓒ Ⓓ Ⓔ   35 Ⓐ Ⓑ Ⓒ Ⓓ Ⓔ
12 Ⓐ Ⓑ Ⓒ Ⓓ Ⓔ   24 Ⓐ Ⓑ Ⓒ Ⓓ Ⓔ   36 Ⓐ Ⓑ Ⓒ Ⓓ Ⓔ

FOR ETS USE ONLY	R	ESSAY	R / ESSAY	CS

LAST NAME (first two letters) [ ][ ]   FIRST INITIAL [ ]   DATE OF BIRTH (month and day only)   MONTH [ ][ ]   DAY [ ][ ]

TEST CODE / FORM CODE

TEST DATE: _____ / _____ / _____
Mo.   Day   Year

CANDIDATE ID NUMBER: _____

TEST BOOK SERIAL NUMBER: _____

I agree to give Educational Testing Service permission to use my responses anonymously in its educational research and for instructional purposes. I understand that I am free to mark "No," with no effect on my score or its reporting.

◯ Yes   ◯ No

(ESSAY) Begin your essay on this page. If you need more space, continue on page 4.

36-3 MH98308

Continuation of essay from page 3. Write below only if you need more space.

SECTION 1

MULTIPLE-CHOICE QUESTIONS

Time—30 minutes

Directions: In each of the sentences below four portions are underlined and lettered. Read each sentence and decide whether any of the underlined parts contains a grammatical construction, a word use, or an instance of incorrect or omitted punctuation or capitalization that would be inappropriate in carefully written English. If so, note the letter printed beneath the underlined portion and completely fill in the corresponding lettered space on the answer sheet with a heavy, dark mark so that you cannot see the letter.

If there are no errors in any of the underlined portions, fill in space E. <u>No sentence has more than one error.</u>

Remember, try to answer every question.

EXAMPLES: **Sample Answers:**

1. He spoke <u>bluntly</u> and <u>angrily</u> to <u>we</u> <u>spectators</u>.   1. Ⓐ Ⓑ ● Ⓓ Ⓔ
               A   B   C   D

    <u>No error</u>
       E

2. Margaret <u>insists</u> <u>that</u> this hat <u>, coat, and scarf</u> <u>,</u>   2. Ⓐ Ⓑ Ⓒ ● Ⓔ
                A   B   C   D

    are hers. <u>No error</u>
                   E

Part A

21 Questions

(Suggested time—10 minutes)

1. In some of the new computer industries ,
   A   B
   more problems result from poor business
                     C
   decisions as from lack of technical expertise.
            D
   No error
   E

2. Although the amount of registered nurses in
                  A
   the United States has increased every year
                  B
   since 1983, there are still not enough nurses to
   C   D
   meet the demand for their services. No error
                                        E

3. Chairs as we know them today were virtually
                                      A
   unheard of until the sixteenth century, when
             B
   they began to replace stools and benches as a
             C   D
   more comfortable mode of seating. No error
                                      E

4. Contrary to its reputation for aggressive
               A
   brutality, the sperm whales that were observed
                                        B
   around the Galápagos Islands proved to be
                       C
   timid and sociable . No error
             D   E

5. Some experts believe that unless the number
                 A
   of vehicles on the road is regulated, neither
   the improved combustion engines or the new
                                  B
   fuels now being tested by automobile
              C
   manufacturers will significantly reduce air
   pollution in the next decade. No error
                          D   E

6. Born in 1887, Marcus Garvey came to the
   A
   United States in 1916, two year's after
                        B
   founding the Universal Negro Improvement
   C
   Association in his native Jamaica. No error
              D   E

7. That women generally live longer than men
   A   B
   has been reflected not only in lower annuity
   payments to women and also in higher life
   C   D
   insurance premiums for men. No error
                              E

8. <u>The plan to preserve</u> the prison
   A
   <u>as a national monument</u> led to objections
   B
   <u>from those who believe</u> that its cell blocks
   C
   represent a sordid part of the nation's history,

   one that <u>is best forgotten.</u> <u>No error</u>
   D E

9. Between 1947 <u>to</u> 1973, the average worker's
   A
   earnings, when adjusted for inflation, <u>rose</u>
   B
   61 percent, <u>reflecting a</u> <u>rise in</u> productivity.
   C D
   <u>No error</u>
   E

10. <u>Because</u> federal Superfund dollars are used to
    A
    clean up hazardous waste sites, states that have

    large numbers <u>of such sites</u> <u>will suffer from</u>
    B C
    cuts in appropriations more than

    <u>those that are not.</u> <u>No error</u>
    D E

11. The first documented human flight in a

    balloon took place <u>in</u> 1783, <u>in which</u> two men
    A B
    <u>sailed over</u> Paris, covering five and one-half
    C
    miles <u>in</u> about 23 minutes. <u>No error</u>
    D E

12. In their study *Women in Europe from*

    Prehistory to the Present, Bonnie Anderson and

    Judith Zinsser insist that, <u>although</u> differences
    A
    of historical era, class, and nationality

    <u>are crucial</u> to the study of women <u>,</u> these
    B C
    differences are all outweighed

    <u>by what they call</u> "similarities of gender."
    D
    <u>No error</u>
    E

13. The bank's reputation for making <u>both</u> safe
    A
    and profitable investments has been shaken by

    scandals <u>,</u> <u>that have forced</u> <u>the resignations of</u>
    B C D
    several prominent bank officials. <u>No error</u>
    E

14. A preliminary study suggests that alcoholism

    and drug abuse are <u>most</u> prevalent <u>in</u> <u>rural</u>
    A B C
    than in <u>urban areas.</u> <u>No error</u>
    D E

15. Anita Brookner, an art historian <u>known for</u>
    A
    her work on eighteenth-century <u>french</u>
    B
    painting, has also <u>recently</u> earned a reputation
    C
    <u>as a major</u> novelist. <u>No error</u>
    D E

16. In an effort <u>to compensate</u> for diminished
          A
    vacation traffic <u>,</u> many airlines <u>now direct</u>
                    B   C
    <u>their advertising</u> at the business traveler.
            D
    <u>No error</u>
        E

17. <u>Early in</u> the century, many travelers <u>went from</u>
        A   B
    Pittsburgh to Cincinnati on a 1,200-ton

    riverboat, the Virginia <u>;</u> a steamer that
                            C
    <u>regularly provided</u> transportation along the
            D
    Ohio River. <u>No error</u>
                    E

18. <u>First</u> published in 1949, Simone de Beauvoir's
        A
    The Second Sex <u>remains</u> a penetrating and
                        B
    relevant <u>interpretation of</u> the relationship
                    C
    <u>among</u> women and men. <u>No error</u>
        D   E

19. Mayan astronomers developed a precise

    calendar <u>that permitted</u> rulers and priests
                    A
    <u>to predict with great accuracy</u> such phenomena
                    B
    <u>like</u> eclipses <u>of the Sun and Moon.</u> <u>No error</u>
        C   C   E

20. Horace Pippin, an African American artist <u> </u>
                                                  A
    worked on several drafts of a war narrative

    <u>before</u> he turned <u>from writing to</u> drawing and
        B   C
    <u>finally</u> to painting. <u>No error</u>
        D   E

21. The giant trees <u>of the rain forest</u> absorb carbon
                            A
    dioxide <u>as they</u> grow but <u>release it</u> into the
                B   B
    atmosphere when they burn <u>or</u> rot. <u>No error</u>
                                    D   E

Part B

17 Questions

(Suggested time — 20 minutes)

Directions: In each of the following sentences some part of the sentence or the entire sentence is underlined. Beneath each sentence you will find five ways of writing the underlined part. The first of these repeats the original, but the other four are all different. If you think the original sentence is better than any of the suggested changes, you should choose answer A; otherwise you should mark one of the other choices. Select the best answer and completely fill in the corresponding lettered space on the answer sheet with a heavy, dark mark so that you cannot see the letter.

This is a test of correctness and effectiveness of expression. In choosing answers, follow the requirements of standard written English; that is, pay attention to acceptable usage in grammar, diction (choice of words), sentence construction, and punctuation. Choose the answer that expresses most effectively what is presented in the original sentence; this answer should be clear and exact, without awkwardness, ambiguity, or redundancy.

Remember, try to answer every question.

EXAMPLES: **Sample Answers:**

1. <u>While waving</u> goodbye to our friends, the   1. Ⓐ Ⓑ ● Ⓓ Ⓔ
    airplane took off, and we watched it disappear
    in the sky.

    (A) While waving
    (B) Waving
    (C) As we were waving
    (D) While we are waving
    (E) During waving

2. Modern travelers seem to prefer speed <u>to comfort</u>.   2. ● Ⓑ Ⓒ Ⓓ Ⓔ

    (A) to comfort
    (B) than comfort
    (C) rather than being comfortable
    (D) instead of being comfortable
    (E) more than comfort

22. The successful effort to clean the Thames has allowed the authorities to rescind the law that made it mandatory <u>for you to spend a night in the hospital for observation if one happened to fall into the river</u>.

    (A) for you to spend a night in the hospital for observation if one happened to fall into the river
    (B) for one to spend a night for observation in the hospital if you happened to fall into the river
    (C) that you should spend a night in the hospital for observation should you have happened to fall into the river
    (D) for people happening to fall into the river that they should spend a night in the hospital for observation
    (E) for people who happened to fall into the river to spend a night in the hospital for observation

23. In many areas water was long considered a free commodity, available to the farmer <u>at not any more than the price to transport it</u>.

    (A) at not any more than the price to transport it
    (B) at no more than costs of transportation
    (C) for not any more than are the costs of its transportation
    (D) for no more than the price of transporting it
    (E) only for the price that it costs to transport it

24. Completing seven triple-jumps, <u>Kristi Yamaguchi's performance was the most technically difficult free-style program</u> of any of the female competitors at the 1989 United States National Figure Skating Championships.

    (A) Kristi Yamaguchi's performance was the most technically difficult free-style program
    (B) Kristi Yamaguchi's free-style program was of the most technical difficulty
    (C) Kristi Yamaguchi performed the most technically difficult free-style program
    (D) the free-style program of Kristi Yamaguchi was the most technically difficult
    (E) the performance of Kristi Yamaguchi's free-style program was of the most technical difficulty

25. During the seventh and eighth centuries A.D., Damascus <u>flourished as</u> the capital of the Umayyad Empire, which stretched from Spain to India.

    (A) flourished as
    (B) flourishes, being
    (C) has flourished, being
    (D) flourishes, since it was
    (E) flourished in that it was

26. Lithography was invented in Germany by a Bavarian playwright, Aloys Senefelder, who found that <u>his scripts can be duplicated cheap</u> by printing them from greasy crayons and inks applied to slabs of local limestone.

   (A) his scripts can be duplicated cheap
   (B) he can duplicate his scripts cheap
   (C) he can cheaply duplicate his scripts
   (D) he could duplicate his scripts cheap
   (E) he could duplicate his scripts cheaply

27. The curator of the new art exhibit believes that Max Ernst is to Dada and Surrealism <u>the way that Picasso is to</u> twentieth-century art as a whole.

   (A) the way that Picasso is to
   (B) what Picasso is to
   (C) what Picasso means for
   (D) the way that Picasso has meaning for
   (E) how Picasso has been for

28. The lynx is endowed with a heavy <u>coat and is enabled by it</u> to function well in extreme cold.

   (A) coat and is enabled by it
   (B) coat by which it is enabled
   (C) coat that enables it
   (D) coat, thus enabled by it
   (E) coat, and thus it is enabled

29. There is some evidence that garlic <u>may be capable to</u> play a role in providing protection against vascular disease.

   (A) may be capable to
   (B) may be can
   (C) can maybe
   (D) can perhaps
   (E) perhaps can be capable to

30. <u>As against what government analysts had expected</u>, the drop in home mortgage interest rates did not stimulate the housing market.

   (A) As against what government analysts had expected
   (B) Contrary with what government analysts were expecting
   (C) In contrast to the expectations government analysts had
   (D) Opposite of government analysts' expectations
   (E) Contrary to the expectations of government analysts

31. Advocates of women's rights have accused the regulatory agencies <u>with being lax as to enforcing</u> antidiscrimination laws.

   (A) with being lax as to enforcing
   (B) of being lax in enforcing
   (C) with being lax on the enforcement of
   (D) as to being lax for the enforcement of
   (E) with laxness on enforcing

32. Because freight rates for grain are subsidized in Canada, it costs no more to ship 100 pounds of grain 700 miles from Saskatchewan to ports on the Great Lakes <u>as sending</u> a letter.

   (A) as sending
   (B) as it does to send
   (C) as to send
   (D) than sending
   (E) than it does to send

33. In the 1950's and 1960's, the acceptance by employers of substantial health and pension plans <u>which were part of a contract settlement made union officials to be</u> the executive officers of large funds requiring investment expertise.

    (A) which were part of a contract settlement made union officials to be
    (B) which were part of contract settlements converted union officials into
    (C) included in the contract settlement made union officials to be
    (D) as part of contract settlements made union officials
    (E) as part of a contract settlement converted union officials into

34. Unlike the United States, <u>in Japan there is no</u> tax incentive for art patronage in the form of a charitable deduction.

    (A) in Japan there is no
    (B) Japan does not offer a
    (C) Japanese law provides no
    (D) the Japanese do not have a
    (E) Japan's laws do not provide for

35. Before it was known to be a carcinogen, asbestos was widely used <u>to be insulation and fireproofing</u>.

    (A) to be insulation and fireproofing
    (B) for insulation and fireproof
    (C) as insulation and for fireproofing
    (D) to be insulation and for fireproofing
    (E) as insulation and as fireproof

36. Defendants in Florida do not have the right to close their trials to television cameras, <u>as defendants in some other states do</u>.

    (A) as defendants in some other states do
    (B) as defendants have it in some other states
    (C) which they do in some other states
    (D) which in some other states they have
    (E) like defendants have in some other states

37. <u>To play wind instruments, it requires not only manual dexterity but also breath control as well</u>.

    (A) To play wind instruments, it requires not only manual dexterity but also breath control as well.
    (B) To play wind instruments requires both manual dexterity and breath control as well.
    (C) Playing wind instruments requires not manual dexterity only but breath control too.
    (D) Playing wind instruments, it requires manual dexterity and breath control.
    (E) Playing wind instruments requires both manual dexterity and breath control.

38. <u>As recent as 30 years ago there were</u> no Saudi universities for women.

    (A) As recent as 30 years ago there were
    (B) Just as recent as 30 years ago there was
    (C) As recently as 30 years ago was there
    (D) As recently as 30 years ago there were
    (E) Just as recent as 30 years ago there were

SECTION 2

ESSAY

Time—30 minutes

Directions: You will have 30 minutes to plan and write an essay on the topic presented on page 218. Read the topic carefully. You will probably find it best to spend a little time considering the topic and organizing your thoughts before you begin writing. DO NOT WRITE ON A TOPIC OTHER THAN THE ONE SPECIFIED. An essay on a topic of your own choice will not be acceptable. In order for your test to be scored, your response must be in English.

The essay question is included in this test to give you an opportunity to demonstrate how well you can write. You should, therefore, take care to write clearly and effectively, using specific examples where appropriate. Remember that how well you write is much more important than how much you write, but to cover the topic adequately, you will probably need to write more than a paragraph.

Your essay will be scored on the basis of its total quality—i.e., holistically. Each essay score is the sum of points (0-6) given by two readers. When your total writing score is computed, your essay score will be combined with your score for the multiple-choice section of the test.

You are to write your essay on the answer sheet; you will receive no other paper on which to write. Please write neatly and legibly. To be certain you have enough space on the answer sheet for your entire essay, please do NOT skip lines, do NOT write in excessively large letters, and do NOT leave wide margins. You may use the bottom of page 218 for any notes you may wish to make before you begin writing.

GO ON TO THE NEXT PAGE

SECTION 2

ESSAY

Time—30 minutes

Read the opinion stated below.

"Letter grading systems should be replaced by pass/fail grading systems."

Discuss the extent to which you agree or disagree with this point of view. Support your position with specific reasons and examples from your own experience, observations, or reading.

The space below is for your **NOTES**. Write your essay in the space provided on the answer sheet.

DO NOT TURN BACK TO SECTION 1 OF THIS TEST.

Chapter 11

Right Answers and Explanations for the Practice Tests

▶   ▶   ▶   ▶   ▶   ▶   ▶   ▶   ▶   ▶   ▶   ▶

Scoring Your Sample Tests

Separate instructions are given for scoring each of the three *Pre-Professional Skills* Tests.

When you actually take the *PPST*, you will have questions that are very similar to the questions in the sample tests in this book, but they will not be identical. Because of the difference in questions, the tests you actually take may be slightly more or less difficult than the tests printed in this book. Therefore, you may not get the same number of questions right on an actual test as on the sample tests.

NOTE: The **data** in tables 1–6 apply only to the *PPST* sample tests in this book. The actual tests you take will have different answer tables and different conversion tables.

The *PPST: Reading* Test

To score your *PPST: Reading* sample test:

- Count the number of questions you answered correctly. The correct answers are in Table 1.

- Use Table 2 to find the scaled score corresponding to the number of questions answered correctly. You can compare your scaled score to the passing score required by your state or institution. (Passing state scores are available on the Praxis Web site at www.ets.org/praxis.)

- Score report category R-1 contains 25 questions measuring literal comprehension. The 15 questions in category R-2 assess reading skills in critical and inferential comprehension. Count the number of questions you answered correctly in each of these categories. This may give you some idea of your strengths and weaknesses.

Table 1: *PPST: Reading* Sample Test

Answers to Practice Test Questions and Percentages of Examinees Answering Each Question Correctly

Question	Score Report Category	Correct Answer	Percentage of Examinees Choosing Correct Answer
1	R-2	A	73%
2	R-1	B	75
3	R-1	B	85
4	R-1	D	55
5	R-1	B	91
6	R-2	C	86
7	R-1	E	84
8	R-1	D	63
9	R-1	E	81
10	R-2	E	52
11	R-2	B	60
12	R-2	A	41
13	R-1	C	67
14	R-2	E	91
15	R-2	E	53
16	R-1	A	50
17	R-1	B	88
18	R-1	B	88
19	R-2	D	67
20	R-1	D	84
21	R-1	B	66
22	R-2	E	75
23	R-1	C	71
24	R-2	C	72
25	R-2	D	90
26	R-1	A	80
27	R-1	A	69
28	R-1	D	83
29	R-2	C	53
30	R-1	C	72
31	R-1	C	57
32	R-1	A	91
33	R-1	C	68
34	R-1	D	90
35	R-2	A	42
36	R-1	D	85
37	R-1	E	75
38	R-2	A	83
39	R-1	D	51
40	R-2	E	55

NOTE: Percentages are based on the test records of 2,250 examinees who took the 50-minute version of the *PPST: Reading* test in November 1992.

* In general, questions may be considered as easy, average, or difficult based on the following percentages:

Easy questions	=	75% or more answered correctly
Average questions	=	55% - 74% answered correctly
Difficult questions	=	less than 55% answered correctly

Table 2: *PPST: Reading* **Sample Test**
Conversion Table

Number Right	Scaled Score
40	187
39	186
38	186
37	185
36	184
35	183
34	182
33	181
32	180
31	179
30	178
29	177
28	177
27	176
26	175
25	174
24	173
23	172
22	171
21	170
20	169
19	168
18	168
17	167
16	166
15	165
14	164
13	163
12	162
11	161
10	160
9	159
8	159
7	158
6	157
5	156
4	155
3	154
2	153
1	152
0	151

The *PPST: Mathematics* Test

To score your Mathematics sample test:

- Count the number of questions you answered correctly. The correct answers are in Table 3.

- Use Table 4 to find the scaled score corresponding to the number of questions answered correctly. You can compare your scaled score to the passing score required by your state or institution. (Passing state scores are available on the Praxis Web site at www.ets.org/praxis.)

- Score report category M-1 contains 20 questions measuring conceptual knowledge and procedural knowledge; category M-2 contains 10 questions measuring understanding of and use of representations of quantitative information; and category M-3 contains 10 questions measuring understanding and use of informal geometry and measurement and reasoning in a quantitative context.

- Count the number of questions you answered correctly in each of the categories. This may give you some idea of your strengths and weaknesses.

Table 3: *PPST: Mathematics* Sample Test
Answers to Practice Test Questions and Percentages of Examinees Answering Each Question Correctly

Question	Score Report Category	Correct Answer	Percentage of Examinees Choosing Correct Answer
1	M-1	C	81%
2	M-3	E	89
3	M-1	A	54
4	M-1	C	71
5	M-3	B	82
6	M-2	D	63
7	M-1	B	73
8	M-2	E	74
9	M-2	C	89
10	M-3	E	71
11	M-1	B	72
12	M-2	D	79
13	M-2	A	28
14	M-1	D	69
15	M-2	A	88
16	M-1	C	84
17	M-1	D	92
18	M-1	B	58
19	M-1	D	81
20	M-1	E	69
21	M-1	B	81
22	M-1	C	90
23	M-1	A	63
24	M-3	E	67
25	M-2	B	48
26	M-2	C	88
27	M-2	E	50
28	M-3	C	66
29	M-1	B	61
30	M-1	D	79
31	M-1	E	75
32	M-3	B	80
33	M-1	A	68
34	M-3	A	33
35	M-3	B	80
36	M-3	B	45
37	M-1	B	51
38	M-3	C	61
39	M-2	D	51
40	M-1	D	37

Table 4: *PPST: Mathematics* Sample Test
Conversion Table

Number Right	Scaled Score
40	190
39	189
38	188
37	187
36	186
35	185
34	184
33	183
32	182
31	181
30	180
29	179
28	178
27	177
26	176
25	175
24	174
23	173
22	172
21	171
20	170
19	169
18	168
17	167
16	166
15	165
14	164
13	163
12	162
11	161
10	160
9	159
8	158
7	157
6	155
5	154
4	153
3	152
2	151
1	150
0	150

NOTE: Percentages are based on the test records of 2,250 examinees who took the 50-minute version of the *PPST: Mathematics* test in November 1992.

* In general, questions may be considered as easy, average, or difficult based on the following percentages:

Easy questions = 75% or more answered correctly
Average questions = 55% - 74% answered correctly
Difficult questions = less than 55% answered correctly

The *PPST: Writing* Test

To score your *PPST: Writing* sample test:

- Count the number of questions you answered correctly in the multiple-choice section of the test. The correct answers are in Table 5.

- Score report category W-1 contains 9 questions measuring knowledge of grammatical relationships; category W-2 contains 12 questions assessing understanding of structural relationships; and category W-3 contains 17 questions assessing understanding of idiom and word choice, mechanics, and correct usage. Count the number of questions you answered correctly in each of these categories. This may give you some idea of your strengths and weaknesses.

- Essays from actual administrations of the *PPST: Writing* test are read and rated by at least two writing experts. The readers use a rating scale of 1 to 6, where 6 is best. (Zero is used for "off-topic" essays.) The essay score is the sum of the two ratings and can therefore range from 2 to 12. Because it is impossible for you to score your own essay, you might want to try using three different values of essay scores in combination with your score on the multiple-choice section to see how your overall score would vary depending on how well you did on the essay. A score of 8 would be about average. You might also want to try a low score of 3 or 4, for example, and a high score, say, of 11 or 12.

- Use Table 6 to find your possible scaled scores. In the column on the left, find the number of questions you answered correctly on the multiple-choice section. Look across the top of Table 6 to the column with the essay score you are using. Go across the row and down the column to find the scaled scores for different combinations of multiple-choice section and essay scores. You can compare your scaled score to the passing score required by your state or institution. (Passing state scores are available on the Praxis website at www.ets.org/praxis.)

Table 5: *PPST: Writing* Sample Test

Answers to Practice Test Questions and Percentages of Examinees Answering Each Question Correctly

Question	Score Report Category	Correct Answer	Percentage of Examinees Choosing Correct Answer
1	W-2	D	83%
2	W-3	A	33
3	W-3	E	68
4	W-1	A	57
5	W-2	B	70
6	W-3	B	73
7	W-2	D	69
8	W-3	E	63
9	W-2	A	83
10	W-1	D	54
11	W-1	B	52
12	W-3	E	46
13	W-3	B	73
14	W-2	A	68
15	W-3	B	78
16	W-3	E	67
17	W-3	C	65
18	W-2	D	60
19	W-1	C	70
20	W-3	A	92
21	W-3	E	68
22	W-1	E	67
23	W-3	D	66
24	W-2	C	56
25	W-3	A	87
26	W-1	E	68
27	W-2	B	63
28	W-1	C	89
29	W-3	D	84
30	W-3	E	70
31	W-3	B	75
32	W-2	E	54
33	W-2	D	45
34	W-2	B	70
35	W-1	C	69
36	W-3	A	48
37	W-2	E	80
38	W-1	D	64

NOTE: Percentages are based on the test records of 2,250 examinees who took the 60-minute version of the *PPST: Writing* test in November 1992.

* In general, questions may be considered as easy, average, or difficult based on the following percentages:

Easy questions = 75% or more answered correctly
Average questions = 55% - 74% answered correctly
Difficult questions = less than 55% answered correctly

Table 6: *PPST: Writing* Sample Test

Conversion Table

Multiple-Choice Section (# Right)	Essay Score (Sum of Two Readings)												
	0	1	2	3	4	5	6	7	8	9	10	11	12
0	150	150	152	154	155	157	158	160	162	163	165	166	168
1	150	151	152	154	156	157	159	160	162	164	165	167	168
2	150	151	153	155	156	158	159	161	163	164	166	167	169
3	150	152	153	155	157	158	160	161	163	165	166	168	169
4	151	152	154	156	157	159	160	162	164	165	167	168	170
5	151	153	154	156	158	159	161	162	164	166	167	169	170
6	152	153	155	157	158	160	161	163	165	166	168	169	171
7	152	154	155	157	159	160	162	163	165	167	168	170	172
8	153	154	156	158	159	161	162	164	166	167	169	170	172
9	153	155	157	158	160	161	163	165	166	168	169	171	173
10	154	155	157	159	160	162	163	165	167	168	170	171	173
11	154	156	158	159	161	162	164	166	167	169	170	172	174
12	155	156	158	160	161	163	164	166	168	169	171	172	174
13	155	157	159	160	162	163	165	167	168	170	171	173	175
14	156	157	159	161	162	164	165	167	169	170	172	173	175
15	156	158	160	161	163	164	166	168	169	171	172	174	176
16	157	158	160	162	163	165	166	168	170	171	173	174	176
17	157	159	161	162	164	165	167	169	170	172	173	175	177
18	158	159	161	163	164	166	167	169	171	172	174	175	177
19	158	160	162	163	165	166	168	170	171	173	174	176	178
20	159	160	162	164	165	167	168	170	172	173	175	176	178
21	159	161	163	164	166	167	169	171	172	174	175	177	179
22	160	161	163	165	166	168	169	171	173	174	176	177	179
23	160	162	164	165	167	168	170	172	173	175	176	178	180
24	161	162	164	166	167	169	170	172	174	175	177	178	180
25	161	163	165	166	168	169	171	173	174	176	177	179	181
26	162	163	165	167	168	170	172	173	175	176	178	180	181
27	162	164	166	167	169	170	172	174	175	177	178	180	182
28	163	165	166	168	169	171	173	174	176	177	179	181	182
29	163	165	167	168	170	171	173	175	176	178	179	181	183
30	164	166	167	169	170	172	174	175	177	178	180	182	183
31	164	166	168	169	171	172	174	176	177	179	180	182	184
32	165	167	168	170	171	173	175	176	178	179	181	183	184
33	165	167	169	170	172	173	175	177	178	180	181	183	185
34	166	168	169	171	172	174	176	177	179	180	182	184	185
35	166	168	170	171	173	174	176	178	179	181	182	184	186
36	167	169	170	172	173	175	177	178	180	181	183	185	186
37	167	169	171	172	174	175	177	179	180	182	183	185	187
38	168	170	171	173	174	176	178	179	181	182	184	186	187

Explanations of Answers to the Sample Tests

Reading

1. Choice A is the best answer. The author of the passage argues that people would have known that an earthquake was about to occur if they had paid attention to the unusual animal behavior that preceded the earthquake. This argument is weakened, however, if unusual animal behavior can occur for a wide variety of reasons. If there is no necessary link between unusual animal behavior and earthquakes, there would be no sure way for people to know that an earthquake was about to occur on the basis of animal behavior.

2. Choice B is the best answer because it summarizes the points the passage makes about Baldwin's style. The passage as a whole discusses the characteristics of Baldwin's writing style. It describes Baldwin's style as unique or original, and also states that Baldwin's style illustrates or exemplifies what someone can achieve in a difficult environment.

3. Choice B is the best answer. The passage mentions "intricate sentences," "lyrical prose," and "dramatic stance" as characteristic elements of Baldwin's style in lines 3–4. In line 12–13, "sophisticated grace" is also mentioned as a characteristic element of Baldwin's style. Choice B, "ironic illustrations," is the best response because such illustrations are not mentioned in the passage as a characteristic element of Baldwin's style.

4. Choice D is the best answer. The passage begins by stating the conclusion of an argument made in a recent article: factory supervisors had increased power over workers after 1900. The passage then goes on to dispute that conclusion by mentioning that the power of supervisors was actually diminished after 1900 by the introduction of legal restrictions. Thus, the passage is primarily concerned with refuting an argument.

5. Choice B is the best answer because it summarizes the main idea of the passage. The passage begins by discussing the current treatment of wounds. The passage then states that these treatment procedures may soon change and goes on to discuss the new technology that may lead to a change in the way physicians treat wounds. Choices A and D can be eliminated because they focus on only part of the passage; C and E can be eliminated because they make claims that are not supported by the passage.

6. Choice C is the best answer. The passage states that growth factors stimulate cell growth and movement. The passage also states that cell migration or movement and cell division or growth are central to wound-healing. From these two statements it can be inferred that growth factors contribute to wound-healing by encouraging new growth and cell movement.

7. Choice E is the best answer because it summarizes the primary purpose of the passage. The passage begins by briefly describing the current treatment of wounds followed by physicians. It then goes on to announce new research into the promotion of wound-healing.

8. Choice D is the best answer. Lines 15–16 state that abstract designs were painted in "red, yellow, blue, and green." Thus, only the question posed in choice D can be answered fully on the basis of the information in the passage. The passage does not provide enough information to answer the questions in the other options.

9. Choice E is the best answer. The phrase "contrast in scale and texture" is found in line 18 of the passage. Lines 19–21 indicate the nature of the contrast mentioned in line 18. These lines state that there is a discrepancy between the delicacy of the design and the thickness of the hides.

10. Choice E is the best answer. Choice A can be eliminated because lines 11–14 state that abstract designs cover the back of the robe only, whereas lines 24–26 state that life scenes cover the whole robe. Choice B can be eliminated because lines 15–16 state that abstract designs "contain primarily the colors red, yellow, blue, and green," whereas lines 27–28 state that life scenes are painted in a "wide variety of colors." Choice C can be eliminated because lines 9–14 state that the robes with abstract designs follow conventional patterns and usually appear with a surrounding border pattern, whereas lines 24–26 state that the robes with life scenes "form patterns of great animation that completely cover the robe." Choice D can be eliminated because lines 6–8 state that abstract designs were painted by women, whereas lines 31–33 state that life scenes were painted by men. Choice E is the best answer because the passage does NOT state that the type of hide used in abstract designs differs from the type used in life scenes. In fact, the passage suggests that abstract designs and life scenes were painted on the same type of hide.

11. Choice B is the best answer. The word "dynamic" means active, showing energy and force. The motion of horses and riders, which the passage tells us are depicted in battle, is active and shows energy and force. Thus, B best supports the claim in lines 23–24 that the scenes are dynamic.

12. Choice A is the best answer. The question asks for the answer choice reporting a fact that, if true, would best help to explain why the use of abstract designs predated the use of life scenes on painted robes. One plausible explanation is that the Native Americans sometimes referred to as "Plains Indians" were already using abstract designs in some other art form and transferred the use of these designs when they first began to paint robes. This explanation is made even more plausible by lines 6–8 of the passage, which state that abstract designs represent the oldest stylistic tradition of the Plains Indians. Thus, Choice A is best because it offers a plausible explanation for why the use of abstract designs on painted robes predated the use of life scenes.

13. Choice C is the best answer. The author compares the publishing of children's books to the cookie business and then states that, although the publishing industry once turned out a high-quality product, it now turns out a product that is devoid of any real content—"sugar and hot air." Thus, the author uses the comparison between publishing children's books and the cookie business to make a judgment about the quality of the children's books being published today.

14. Choice E is the best answer. The author compares the books published by current publishers of children's books to cookies made only of "sugar and hot air." This comparison suggests that the author finds current children's books to be devoid of any important or useful content. Choice E correctly describes the author's attitude—"disapproving."

15. Choice E is the best answer. In offering a reason why Rice's name will not endure, the passage states that a certain class of plays— socially relevant dramas of the 1920's—will be remembered for fiery rhetoric rather than for unemotional intellectualism. The reason offered would be irrelevant if Rice had not written plays that belonged to this particular class of plays. Therefore, the passage suggests that Rice's plays were socially relevant dramas.

16. Choice A is the best answer. The author states that the earliest electronic computers had very little space for the storage of information and, as a result, computer programs were written in very compact forms. However, the author goes on to say that because computer memory does not cost as much as it did originally, computer programs have grown increasingly large.

17. Choice B is the best answer. The passage states that neither Ella Baker nor many other Black women who played an important role in the civil rights movement sought public attention because they were more concerned with making contributions to the civil rights movement than with becoming famous. The information contained in the passage thus explains why many women who were important civil rights leaders are not well known. The other answer choices can be eliminated because the passage does not identify the best-known leaders of the civil rights movement, specify how many of the movement's leaders were women, or analyze public response to social movements.

18. Choice B is the best answer. Lines 3–6 state that historians of middle-class Victorian women have had to rely heavily on the serious fiction of the day because of the lack of extensive autobiographical data. Because Victorian women in serious fiction were typically idle, some historians have incorrectly concluded that actual middle-class Victorian women were idle. This reliance has therefore led some historians to make inaccurate generalizations about middle-class Victorian women.

19. Choice D is the best answer. In lines 3–6 the passage states that historians relied on serious Victorian fiction because there was a lack of extensive autobiographical data about women. Therefore, the passage suggests that they would have been less likely to rely on serious Victorian fiction if there had been a significant amount of autobiographical data.

20. Choice D is the best answer. Lines 12–16 state that middle-class women are portrayed more realistically in popular Victorian novels than in serious fiction. This more realistic portrayal of middle-class women is an advantage to historians studying the actual conditions of women's lives.

21. Choice B is the best answer. Lines 22–23 introduce a source of data about middle-class Victorian women's lives that is more promising than is the fiction of the day. Lines 23–27 indicate that the data mentioned in line 23 (census and wage data) are significant because they undermine the assumption that middle-class Victorian families employed several servants, and thus throw into doubt the image of the idle Victorian woman.

22. Choice E is the best answer. Lines 23–27 indicate that census and wage data strongly imply that middle-class Victorian families "could rarely afford to hire more than a single servant." Thus, the passage suggests that it was uncharacteristic for middle-class Victorian families to employ several domestic servants.

23. Choice C is the best answer. In the first paragraph, the author points out the weakness in using either serious or popular fiction as a source of information about middle-class Victorian women. Serious fiction has presented a portrait of middle-class women that has led historians to conclude inaccurately that middle-class Victorian women were idle; and popular fiction, even though it provides a more realistic portrait of middle-class women's lives than does serious fiction, is still not completely reliable. However, census and wage data, which the author introduces in the second paragraph, are alternate sources of information about middle-class Victorian women that can provide an accurate picture of the actual circumstances of middle-class Victorian women's lives. Thus, C best describes the organization of the passage.

24. Choice C is the best answer. The passage indicates that Rembrandt painted self-portraits at many points in his life. It also indicates that Rembrandt's self-portraits expressed personal feelings about the world and his place in it. Thus, the passage suggests that Rembrandt's self-portraits show his personality and his attitudes at many different periods in his life.

25. Choice D is the best answer because it is supported by the statements in the passage. The passage says that a major change in the size of a creature would also always mean a change in its form. Thus, if a bird were to change its size and become as large as a cow, it follows that the bird's form would change as well.

26. Choice A is the best answer. The first sentence states that British rulers in 1932 worried about wartime aerial threats to their country. The next sentence states that in 1939 the British built radar stations along their coast. It can be inferred that the purpose of the radar stations was to detect enemy airplanes. The last sentence of the passage suggests that the radar was successful in helping to protect Britain from aerial attacks. Thus, with the phrase "making Britain an island again" the author suggests that the radar chain around its coast defended Britain from attacks by air in the same way that the ocean around Britain defended it from attack before the invention of the airplane.

27. Choice A is the best answer because it most accurately describes the main topic of the first paragraph, which introduces the concept of resonance in advertising and illustrates it with the specific example of the Little Tramp ads. The other answer choices are incorrect because they incorrectly identify the main topic of the paragraph as being computers or the computer advertising campaign or the Little Tramp, rather than the general advertising strategy under discussion.

28. Choice D is the best answer. Lines 1–6 of the passage discuss advertising campaigns that rely on creating resonance. The passage states that in these campaigns, advertisers link a product with some positive image or symbol to create a favorable view of that product in the public's mind.

29. Choice C is the best answer. The author argues that the computer advertisements discussed in the passage are ironic because they use Charlie Chaplin to create favorable feelings about a machine used in the workplace, when in reality Chaplin was opposed to "mechanization and the technological goals of speed and efficiency" (lines 19–20). In the film *Modern Times*, according to the author, Chaplin sees the "soul-destroying monotony and inhuman pace of the assembly line" (lines 25–26) as forces that drive workers mad. However if computers make work less monotonous and reduce drudgery, they make the workplace better. Because Chaplin presumably would have been in favor of an improved workplace, the author's argument would thus be weakened.

30. Choice C is the best answer. In lines 19–20, the author states that Chaplin was "opposed to mechanization and the technological goals of speed and efficiency."

31. Choice C is the best answer because it best summarizes the whole passage, whose first paragraph explains the concept of resonance by using the Little Tramp campaign as an example, and whose second paragraph argues that the use of Charlie Chaplin in the ad campaign is ironic because the original meaning of the symbol has been completely changed in the ads. The other answer choices are incorrect either because they accurately describe only a part of the passage (choice D) or because they introduce information or ideas not included in the passage (choices A, B, and E).

32. Choice A is the best answer. The first sentence in the passage indicates that Emil Du Bois-Reymond was the first person "to prove that electricity runs through the nervous system," and the second sentence states that he "demonstrated the existence of… the electrochemical pulse in our neurons."

33. Choice C is the best answer. The first two sentences of the passage indicate that Photo-realist artists sought to produce works that resembled as closely as possible the photographs on which they were based. However, the last sentence of the passage indicates that the Photo-realists did not succeed in doing so. They did change aspects of the photographs they were working from; the passage states that they included sharper outlines in their paintings than the outlines in the original photographs.

34. Choice D is the best answer. Lines 13–14 of the passage state that Lockwood became the first woman to argue a case before the Supreme Court.

35. Choice A is the best answer. The Supreme Court's argument was that legislation was needed before Lockwood could argue a case before the Court because there was no English precedent for women to act as lawyers in a courtroom. However, if the Supreme Court has the power to override precedent and to establish new judicial procedures, it does not matter that there was no precedent. The Court can on its own establish that women can argue cases before the court.

36. Choice D is the best answer. In lines 13–14, the author states that Lockwood was the first woman to argue a case before the Supreme Court. In lines 14–17, the author adds that for Lockwood this was "only one distinction in a lifetime of groundbreaking achievements." By "groundbreaking achievements" the author means that Lockwood was the first woman to accomplish certain things. Immediately after this statement, the author mentions that Lockwood was the first woman to appear on a presidential ballot. Thus, the author mentions Lockwood's appearance on a presidential ballot to provide another example of Lockwood's accomplishments in pursuits previously closed to women.

37. Choice E is the best answer. Lines 11–14 of the passage give the percentage of librarians in a 1982 survey who reported having a book challenged. Lines 14–17 state that in over half such cases, the challenged book was removed from the library. Thus, the passage indicates that more than half of the reported attempts to ban books from libraries were successful.

38. Choice A is the best answer. The three words listed in choice A reveal the author's attitude toward book-banning. The word "epidemic" suggests diseases, "alarming" suggests something dangerous, and "worse" suggests something bad—all carry a negative tone. The author of the passage has a disapproving attitude toward book-banning that is revealed by the choice of these negative words.

39. Choice D is the best answer. In the first sentence of the passage, the author makes several positive statements about slang, including statements about its effects on vocabulary, metaphor, and meaning. In the second sentence, the author suggests that poets aim for the same results. The passage therefore suggests that the writing of poets—poetry—and slang have some elements in common. By comparing slang to something valuable like poetry, the author is attempting to convince the reader that slang is positive.

40. Choice E is the best answer. According to the passage, the principle that matter is conserved is important in the practice of modern chemistry. However, the passage ends by stating that this principle is not strictly true. Therefore, it can be inferred that the author would be likely to agree that some concepts used in practical applications of chemistry are not necessarily true.

Mathematics

1. The multiples of 3 shown on the spinner are 3, 6, 9, and 12, so there are 4 chances in 12 of the spinner stopping on a multiple of 3. The answer is C.

2. The reading on the gauge shown is between 10 and 15. Since the interval between 10 and 15 is marked off in fifths, each subdivision represents 1, and the reading is thus 13. The answer is E.

3. Fractions are easy to compare if they have the same denominator. Convert each fraction to one with a denominator of 7 by dividing the numerator and the denominator by the same number.

$$\frac{1}{7} = \frac{1}{7}$$

$$\frac{11 \div 10}{70 \div 10} = \frac{1.1}{7}$$

$$\frac{101 \div 100}{700 \div 100} = \frac{1.01}{7}$$

$$\frac{1,001 \div 1,000}{7,000 \div 1,000} = \frac{1.001}{7}$$

$$\frac{10,001 \div 10,000}{70,000 \div 10,000} = \frac{1.0001}{7}$$

Since $\frac{1}{7}$ has the smallest numerator, $\frac{1}{7}$ is less than the other four fractions, and the answer is A.

4. If there were 6 gallons in the tank, 4 more gallons would be needed to fill the 10-gallon tank. Since $6\frac{1}{8}$ is a little more than 6, a little less than 4 gallons is needed. The answer is C.

5. The scale is the relation between a distance on a map and the distance it represents on the ground. If $\frac{3}{4}$ inch represents 50 miles, then $1\frac{1}{2}$ inches, which is $2 \times \frac{3}{4}$ inch, represents $2 \times 50 = 100$ miles. The answer is B.

6. The circle graph shows the distribution of the trash content *in percentages,* but the question asks for the *weight* of the plastic content in tons. From the graph we see that plastics account for 8% of the total weight of the trash. The problem states that 60 tons of the trash consist of paper; the graph shows that this amount equals 40% of the total, so

    $$60 = 0.4 \times \left(\text{total weight}\right)$$

    and the total weight is $\dfrac{60}{0.4} = 150$ tons.

    The weight of plastics equals 8% of 150 tons or $\left(0.08\right)\left(150\right) = 12$ tons.

    There is another, slightly faster, way to solve this problem. We use the fact that the *ratio* of plastics to paper in the trash is the same, whether the two amounts are given as percents or in tons. This gives us the proportion.

    $$\frac{\text{tons of plastic}}{\text{tons of paper}} = \frac{8\%}{40\%} = \frac{1}{5}$$

    or

    $$\frac{\text{tons of plastic}}{60} = \frac{1}{5}$$

    $$\text{tons of plastic} = \frac{60}{5} = 12$$

    The answer is D.

7. The problem tells us that 128 players were injured and that the number of players with ankle injuries was 12.5% of this total. Since $12.5\% = \dfrac{12.5}{100} = 0.125$, the number of players with ankle injuries was 0.125×128. The answer is B.

8. The numbers in the table follow a pattern, and you are asked to select a description of that pattern. The values of x in the table correspond to points on the number line. As x moves from -4 to 0, that is, from left to right on the number line, its value increases.

    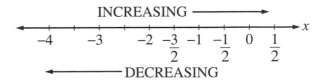

    Similarly, the value of y increases from -2 to 0. Thus, it can be seen that as x increases, y increases. The answer is E.

9. In a pictograph, each symbol represents the same quantity, and there are 3 more book symbols in the row for book R than in the row for book Q. Since the bookstore sold 60 more copies of book R than book Q, the 3 book symbols represent 60 books. Therefore, 1 book symbol represents 20 books. The answer is C.

10. The opposite sides of a rectangle are equal in length, and the perimeter of a rectangle is the sum of those lengths. If you label the given figure and write an equation for the perimeter, you can find the length ℓ of the rectangle.

    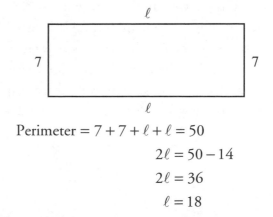

    $$\text{Perimeter} = 7 + 7 + \ell + \ell = 50$$
    $$2\ell = 50 - 14$$
    $$2\ell = 36$$
    $$\ell = 18$$

The length of the given rectangle is therefore 18, and the answer is E.

11. To find $a+b$, add $3b$ to both sides of the equation.

$$3a + 3b = 18 - 3b + 3b$$
$$3a + 3b = 18$$
$$3(a+b) = 18$$

Divide both sides of the equation by 3.

$$\frac{3(a+b)}{3} = \frac{18}{3}$$
$$a + b = 6$$

The answer is B.

12. There is information for eight different years in the bar graph. The vertical scale goes from 0 to 80,000. The zeros are left off the scale because the title tells you to read the numbers in thousands. To find the number of students in any one year, read the height of the corresponding bar off the left-hand scale and multiply that height by 1,000.

The bar for 1950 has a height of about 27, so the number of students in 1950 was about 27,000. You have to find the number of years in which there were more than twice as many—that is, more than 54,000 students. To do this, count the number of bars that are higher than 54. These are the bars for 1975, 1980, and 1985. Thus, there were three years in which there were more than twice as many students as in 1950. The answer is D.

13. To compute a percent increase, you need the increase in the number of students and the number of students before the increase.

The graph shows that the number of students in 1970 was 40,000 and the number of students in 1980 was 70,000, an increase of 30,000 students. To find the percent increase, divide this number by the base number, that is, the number of students before the increase, or 40,000.

$$\frac{30,000}{40,000} = \frac{3}{4} = 0.75 = 75\%$$

The answer is A.

14. Since $0.1 = \frac{1}{10}$, you can multiply each of the answer choices by $\frac{1}{10}$.

10 times $\frac{1}{10}$ is 1.

100 times $\frac{1}{10}$ is 10.

1,000 times $\frac{1}{10}$ is 100.

10,000 times $\frac{1}{10}$ is 1,000.

100,000 times $\frac{1}{10}$ is 10,000.

Since 1,000 is 10,000 times $\frac{1}{10}$, or 0.1, the answer is D.

15. The question asks you to look at each of the circles and find the one that has a center at (1,1) and radius 2, but the scale is not given. First, find a point that could be (1,1). In the rectangular coordinate system, the point (1,1) is 1 unit to the right of the origin, O, along the x-axis, and 1 unit up along the y-axis. The circles in choices A an E could have their center at (1,1), because in each the distances along the x-axis and the y-axis are equal; but then the radius of the circle in choice E would be 1, with each grid line representing $\frac{1}{2}$. In choice A, with each grid line representing 1 unit, the radius of the circle is 2. The answer is A.

16. The problem gives a set of instructions to follow, one step at a time, in the order given, and you are told the number $n = 2$. Thus, starting with the second step, the computation is as follows.

$$2 - 3 = -1$$
$$-1 \times 2 = -2$$
$$-2 + 10 = 8$$
$$8 \div 2 = 4$$

The result is 4, so the answer is C.

17. This is what you are given in this problem.

- 2 pencils cost 1 quarter (25¢)
- 1 notebook costs 2 quarters (50¢)
- The machine takes only quarters

To find the number of quarters needed to buy 6 pencils and 2 notebooks, you can draw a picture and then count the number of quarters needed.

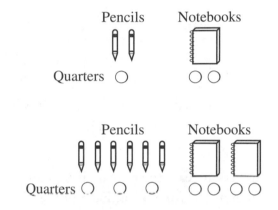

You need 7 quarters, so the answer is D.

18. 1 million (I) is the same as 1,000,000.

1,000 thousands (II) is the same as $1,000 \times 1,000 = 1,000,000$.

Thus, 1 million and 1,000 thousands are the same, and the answer is B.

19. One way of doing this problem is to divide 141 by each of the given numbers and find the remainder that is different from 5.

$$\frac{141}{136} = 1\,R\,5$$

$$\frac{141}{68} = 2\,R\,5$$

$$\frac{141}{34} = 4\,R\,5$$

$$\frac{141}{16} = 8\,R\,13$$

$$\frac{141}{8} = 17\,R\,5$$

If 141 is divided by 16, the remainder is NOT equal to 5, so the answer is D.

20. Numbers are easy to compare if they are written in the same form. Each of the numbers in the problem can be converted to a decimal, and then the decimal can be compared to $0.187 = 18.7\%$. Remember that adding zeros at the end of a decimal does not change the value of the decimal.

$0.05 = 0.050$ and is less than 0.187.

$0.15 = 0.150$ and is less than 0.187

$\dfrac{1}{10} = 0.100$ and is less than 0.187.

0.01875 is less than 0.18700.

$\dfrac{1}{5} = 0.200$ and is greater than 0.187.

Since 0.187 is less than $0.200 = \dfrac{1}{5}$, the answer is E.

21. You are given that there are 8 boys and 13 girls in a choir, so the total number of boys and girls in the choir is 21, as represented in the picture.

ⒷⒷ G ⒷⒷ
ⒷⒷ G G G ⒷⒷ
G G G G G G G G G

The fraction of the choir that is boys is, therefore, $\dfrac{\text{number of boys}}{\text{total}} = \dfrac{8}{21}$. The answer is B.

22. This question asks you to think of 400×30 as 12 times some number. Because $400 = 4 \times 100$ and $30 = 3 \times 10$, you can write 400×30 as $4 \times 100 \times 3 \times 10$. Since the order in which you multiply does not matter, you can write 400×30 as $4 \times 3 \times 100 \times 10$, which is $12 \times 1,000$. The answer is C.

23. You are told that 483 is 30% of a number W. This means that 483 is $\dfrac{30}{100}$ or $\dfrac{3}{10}$ of W, so

$$W = \frac{10}{3}(483) = \frac{10(483)}{3} = 10(161) = 1,610.$$

The answer is A.

24. The question asks you to think of three points on a line and, if possible, to visualize the three points on each of the given figures.

You can visualize the three points on a square.

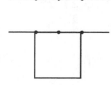

You can visualize the three points on a triangle.

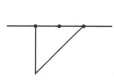

You can visualize the three points on a cube.

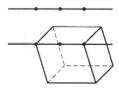

You can visualize the three points on a cylinder.

If you think about a circle, you CANNOT visualize the three points on a circle.

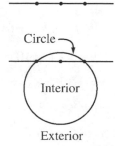

Since two of the points on the line can be on the circle but the third one cannot be, the answer is E.

25. The problem gives a set of test scores and the definition of median. The first part of the definition tells you to order the scores, that is, to arrange them in order from smallest to largest. Here are the numbers ordered from smallest to largest:

$$86, 86, 88, 90, 92, 98$$

Because there is an even number of scores (6), there are two middle numbers in the set, 88 and 90, and the average of the two middle numbers is

$$\frac{88+90}{2} = \frac{178}{2} = 89$$

Thus the median of Robin's scores is 89 and the answer is B. (Notice that the median of a set of numbers need not be one of the numbers in the set.)

26. The question asks you to compute the cost of a 50-minute call when the parties are 500 miles apart. The range $431 - 925$ miles in the table gives the rates for parties 500 miles apart. The cost of the first minute is $0.36, and the cost of each additional minute is $0.30. This information can be represented in an equation. Cost = $0.36 + 49($0.30) where 49 is the number of additional minutes.

Cost = $0.36 + 14.70 = $15.06, so the answer is C.

27. In this question, you are given that the cost of a 20-minute call was $6.26, and you have to find the distance between the parties who were on the phone for 20 minutes. If the additional-minute rate for the whole 20 minutes is used, the approximate cost of each minute is the cost of the call divided by the

number of minutes, or $6.26 ÷ 20$ which is about $0.31 per minute. The row in which each additional minute costs $0.31 is the row with $926 - 1,910$ miles between the parties. Only the distance given in E could be the miles between the parties.

This result can be checked by using the cost of the first minute and the cost of each additional minute listed in the eighth row to compute the total cost of the call.

$$0.37 + 19(\$0.31) = \$6.26$$

The answer is E.

28. You are given a line segment, *AB*, that represents 0.3 mile—that is, about $\frac{1}{3}$ of a mile—and are asked to estimate the distance from *C* to *D*. By inspection you can see that each of the 3 segments of the road is a little longer than *AB*; so the distance from *C* to *D* is greater than $3 \times \frac{1}{3}$ or 1 mile. Only two choices are greater than 1 mile: 1.2 and 3. For the distance to be 3, each of the segments would have to be about 3 times as long as *AB*. Thus the answer is C.

29. One way to solve the equation $B = 2(G - 5)$ for *G* is to multiply $(G - 5)$ by 2.

$B = 2G - 10$

Add 10 to both sides of the equation.

$B + 10 = 2G - 10 + 10 = 2G$

Divide both sides of the equation by 2.

$$\frac{B + 10}{2} = \frac{2G}{2} = G$$

The answer is B.

30. All five choices can be easily compared if they are expressed in the same form. One way to do this is to factor all choices completely.

(A) $2^2 \times 10 \times 12 =$
    $2^2 \times 2 \times 5 \times 2 \times 2 \times 3 =$
    $2^5 \times 3 \times 5$

(B) $2^3 \times 6 \times 10 =$
    $2^3 \times 2 \times 3 \times 2 \times 5 =$
    $2^5 \times 3 \times 5$

(C) $2^4 \times 5 \times 6 =$
    $2^4 \times 5 \times 2 \times 3 =$
    $2^5 \times 3 \times 5$

(D) $2^5 \times 3 \times 10 =$
    $2^5 \times 3 \times 2 \times 5 =$
    $2^6 \times 3 \times 5$

(E) $4^2 \times 5 \times 6 =$
    $(2 \times 2)^2 \times 5 \times 2 \times 3 =$
    $2^2 \times 2^2 \times 5 \times 2 \times 3 =$
    $2^5 \times 3 \times 5$

Choice D is NOT equivalent to the others and therefore is the answer.

Another way to express all choices in the same form is to perform all the indicated operations.

(A) $2^2 \times 10 \times 12 = 4 \times 10 \times 12 = 480$

(B) $2^3 \times 6 \times 10 = 8 \times 6 \times 10 = 480$

(C) $2^4 \times 5 \times 6 = 16 \times 5 \times 6 = 480$

(D) $2^5 \times 3 \times 10 = 32 \times 3 \times 10 = 960$

(E) $4^2 \times 5 \times 6 = 16 \times 5 \times 6 = 480$

Choice D is NOT equivalent to the others and therefore is the answer.

31. This problem gives five amounts and asks for an estimate of the sum of the amounts to the nearest million dollars. You can round each amount in the list and then add these rounded numbers. Because the answer choices are consecutive numbers, however, it is advisable to round to the nearest tenth of a million dollars before adding.

   Project 1: $19.3

   Project 2:   8.0

   Project 3:   11.0

   Project 4:   0.8

   Project 5:   4.9

   Total: $44.0 million

The answer is E.

32. You are given five different ways to slice a cake and are asked to pick the one way that gives pieces each with the same amount of icing. By examining each of the ways, you can see that only choice B shows that each slice of the cake has the same size and is iced on top and on one side only.

Each slice of the cake cut this way has the same amount of icing.

In choices A and C, it can be seen that a corner piece of the cake has more icing than a piece that is not a corner.

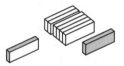

In choice D, the two end slices have more icing than any of the other slices.

In choice E, a slice from the middle of the cake has more icing than a slice closer to the corner pieces of the cake. The answer is B.

33. Although this problem has an unusual look, it requires only the substitution of the given values $T = 12$, $S = -4$, and $R = 8$, in the expression $\dfrac{T - S}{R}$. Substituting gives

$$\frac{T - S}{R} = \frac{12 - (-4)}{8} = \frac{12 + 4}{8} = \frac{16}{8} = 2,$$

so the answer is A.

34. The problem asks you to examine four shapes and decide if the distance around any one of them—the perimeter—is less than the distance around any of the other three. When we think about perimeter, we think about the lengths of the line segments that are joined at end points to make up the shape. We do not think about any of the line segments drawn inside.

Each shape can be thought of as being made from 6 lengths, and each length is either short or long. The shapes in choices B, C, and D are made from 4 short lengths and 2 long lengths, and the shape in choice A is made from 6 short lengths. Thus, the perimeter of the shape in choice A is least, so the answer is A.

35. Two times within a 24-hour period are given, and you are asked to find the number of hours and minutes between the two times. From high tide in the morning at 8:54 a.m. to noon is 3 hours 6 minutes, and from noon to high tide at 9:26 p.m. in the evening is 9 hours 26 minutes. Adding the two times gives 12 hours 32 minutes, so the answer is B.

The problem can also be solved by subtraction, but you must be careful when subtracting times because you cannot regroup in the usual way. Since there are 24 hours in a day, 9:26 p.m. can be expressed as 21 hours 26 minutes and the subtraction problem can be solved as follows.

Hours	Minutes
20	
~~21~~	$26 + 60$
$-\ 8$	$-\ 54$
12	32

The amount of time between the two high tides was 12 hours 32 minutes, and the answer is B.

36. You are given five figures, called polygons, to look at. One of them shows that the statement in the question is not always true. Examine the first part of the statement, "if all sides of a polygon are equal in length." This means that you have to look only at the figures in which the sides are equal in length. (The little marks on the sides of the figures tell which sides are equal in length.) Choices D and E do not have sides that are equal in length and can therefore be eliminated. You now look at the three figures that remain to find the one that does not have angles all equal in measure. That figure is the one example needed to disprove the statement. The figure in choice A is an equilateral triangle, so all angles have equal measure. The figure in choice C is a square with all right angles. By carefully looking at the figure in choice B, you see that the angles in the figure do not all have equal measure. The answer is B.

37. The formula for the area A of a rectangle is $A = \text{length} \times \text{width}$. The length of the rectangle shown is 5 and the width is x. The area of a rectangle with length $\frac{1}{2}(5)$ and width $2(x)$ is

$$A = \frac{1}{2}(5) \times 2(x) = 5x.$$ The answer is B.

38. In this question you are asked to use logical reasoning to draw a conclusion.

An isosceles triangle has two equal sides, and a right triangle has one 90° angle. A triangle can be both an isosceles triangle and a right triangle.

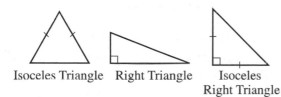

Isoceles Triangle   Right Triangle   Isoceles Right Triangle

One way to represent the two statements in the box is by a Venn diagram.

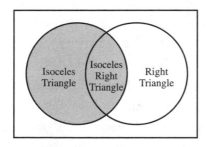

From the Venn diagram you see that only the statement in choice C is true, so the answer is C.

39. The question asks you to find the number halfway between $\frac{2}{3}$ and $\frac{3}{4}$. The number you are looking for is greater than $\frac{2}{3}$ and less than $\frac{3}{4}$. Write $\frac{2}{3}$ and $\frac{3}{4}$ as fractions with a common denominator in order to find the fraction that is halfway between them. Common denominators of 3 and 4 include 12 and 24, so you can write

$$\frac{2}{3} = \frac{8}{12} = \frac{16}{24} \qquad \frac{3}{4} = \frac{9}{12} = \frac{18}{24}$$

The fraction $\frac{17}{24}$ is halfway between $\frac{16}{24}$ and $\frac{18}{24}$, so the answer is D.

Alternatively, the problem can be solved by finding the average of $\frac{2}{3}$ and $\frac{3}{4}$, since the average of two numbers is halfway between the numbers.

$$\frac{\frac{2}{3} + \frac{3}{4}}{2} = \frac{\frac{8}{12} + \frac{9}{12}}{2} = \frac{17}{12} \times \frac{1}{2} = \frac{17}{24}$$

The answer is D.

40. In scientific notation, a positive number is written as a number between 1 and 10 multiplied by a power of 10. For example, 125,000 can be written as 1.25×10^5.

$$\underset{\text{A number between 1 and 10}}{\overset{\text{A power of 10}}{125,000 = 1.25 \times 10^5}}$$

Although 125,000 is also equal to 12.5×10^4 or 125×10^3, neither is written in scientific notation because neither 12.5 nor 125 is a number between 1 and 10. All of the answer choices are numbers multiplied by a power of 10, but only 4.13628 is a number between 1 and 10. The answer is therefore D.

Writing—Part A

1. A grammatical error occurs at D, where the word "as" is incorrectly used. A comparative construction beginning with "more" should be completed by a phrase beginning with "than" rather than with "as": "more X than Y." The word at D should be "than."

2. The error occurs at A. The word "amount" is used to refer to quantities that can be measured but not counted, and is normally followed by a singular noun (e.g., "large amount of snow"). The word required at A is "number," which is used for quantities that can be counted, and is usually followed by a plural noun ("number of registered nurses").

3. Because there are no grammatical, idiomatic, logical, or structural errors in this sentence, the best answer is E.

4. A noun-pronoun agreement error occurs at A. The possessive pronoun that is used to refer to the plural noun "whales" must also be plural.

Thus, the singular pronoun "its" should be replaced by "their."

5. The error occurs at B. The correct form for an expression of negation that includes "neither" is "neither X nor Y." The error can be corrected by substituting "nor" for "or" at B.

6. The error occurs at B. An apostrophe should not be used to form the plural of "year." The correct plural of "year" is "years."

7. An error of idiom occurs at D. The construction begun by "not only" is correctly completed by "but also." The "and" at D therefore produces an unidiomatic expression. The word at D should be "but."

8. Because there are no grammatical, idiomatic, logical, or structural errors in this sentence, E is the best answer.

9. An error of idiom occurs at A. Because the idiomatic form of this expression is "between X and Y," the correct word at A would be "and."

10. The error occurs at D. In this sentence, the construction "more than" is used to compare those districts that "have large numbers" of certain kinds of students with those districts that do not have large numbers of them. "Are" cannot grammatically substitute for "have" because it would produce the implied construction "those that are not have large numbers," which is ungrammatical and nonsensical here. Thus, the phrase "those that do not" is called for at D.

11. The error occurs at B. The conjunction "when" is needed to refer to 1783 and introduce a clause that describes that date as the time when something occurred; "in which" is not an idiomatic way to refer to dates.

12. There are no grammatical, idiomatic, logical, or structural errors in this sentence, so E is the best answer.

13. The error occurs at B. The clause "that have forced..." is a restrictive clause, one that is essential to the meaning of the sentence. A restrictive clause is not preceded by a comma, because it is part of the main idea and should not be separated from it; thus, the comma at B is incorrect. On the other hand, a nonrestrictive clause, one that is not essential and could be removed from the sentence without altering its meaning, must be preceded by a comma to indicate that it is not essential to the main idea and can be separated from it. A nonrestrictive clause would also normally use the relative pronoun "which," rather than "that."

14. The error occurs at A. The construction "most...than" is incorrect because "most" is a superlative, whereas "than" functions as part of a comparison. A construction in which "than" is used to make a comparison is usually begun by "more"; thus, the word at A should be "more," not "most."

15. An error in capitalization occurs at B. Because words that name nationalities should be capitalized, the letter at B should be a capital "F."

16. There are no errors of grammar, idiom, logic, or structure in this sentence; therefore, E is the best answer.

17. An error of punctuation occurs at C. The semicolon is typically used to separate independent clauses; a comma is needed at A to set off the noun phrase "a steamer...," which modifies "the *Virginia.*"

18. The error occurs at D. When a "relationship" involves only two elements, the appropriate connecting word is "between"; "among" is used with three or more elements. Therefore, the error at D can be corrected by changing "among" to "between."

19. The error occurs at C. In phrases presenting examples, the word that should normally be used in combination with "such" is "as," not "like." The use of "like" is unidiomatic here.

20. The error occurs at A. The phrase "a Black American artist" is not the subject of the verb "worked"; "Horace Pippin" is the subject. The phrase "a Black American artist" is an appositive phrase that provides additional information about "Horace Pippin," and as such it should be set off by commas from the rest of the sentence. Therefore, a comma should be placed at A.

21. There are no errors in grammar, idiom, logic, or structure in this sentence, so E is the best answer.

Writing—Part B

22. The best answer is E. Choices A and B lack consistency in the use of pronouns: "you" and "one" should not be used together in a sentence to refer to the same person. Also, the wording of A is awkward and confusing because "one happened to fall into the river" is closer to "hospital" and to "observation" than to any word it could logically modify. Choices C and D are incorrect because they use the unidiomatic "that you should spend" and "that they should spend," respectively. The appropriate way of completing the phrase "made it mandatory" is with the infinitive "to spend." Choice E both uses the idiomatic "to spend" and avoids the "you-one" confusion by using "people."

23. The best answer, D, is idiomatic, logical, and unambiguous. Choices A and C are wordy and awkward, and both use a phrase that is unidiomatic in this context, "not any more," rather than "no more." Choice B is awkwardly and unclearly phrased: "available at...costs of" should be "available for...the price of," and the word "transportation" does not clearly refer to "water." In choice E, "the price that it costs" is redundant, and "only" confusingly suggests that water will be available "only" if the farmer pays a price equal to the costs of transportation.

24. The best answer is C. The opening phrase, "Completing seven triple-jumps," should be completed by a noun that identifies the person who performed the jumps. Only choice C supplies that noun. In the other four choices, either the "program" (B and D) or the "performance" (A and E) is illogically credited with completing the jumps, and is thus illogically compared with "female competitors."

25. Because this sentence discusses only past time ("During the seventh and eighth centuries"), the appropriate tense for the verb is the past tense "flourished." Choices B and D use the present tense "flourishes," and choice C uses the present perfect tense "has flourished." Also, in D, "since it was" changes the meaning of the sentence by introducing the idea of a cause-effect relationship—that is, that Damascus flourished *because* it was the capital. Similarly, in E, the phrase "in that" is roughly equivalent to "since" or "because." A, which uses the past tense and is logically clear and grammatically correct, is the best choice.

26. There should be consistency of verb tenses in the sentence. Because the first two verbs, "was invented" and "found," are in the past tense,

the next verb should be the past tense "could" rather than the present tense "can." Also, the word that modifies the verb "duplicated" should be an adverb such as "cheaply," not an adjective such as "cheap." The only choice that contains both the past tense "could" and the adverb "cheaply" is E, which is the best answer.

27. This sentence requires that the comparison between Ernst and Picasso be completed by a parallel construction beginning with "what": "*W* is to *X* what *Y* is to *Z*." Choices A and D are wrong because they use "the way that." Choice E is wrong because it uses "how" instead of "what." Choice C begins with "what" but uses "means for" rather than "is to." Similarly, choices D and E substitute "means for" and "has meaning for," respectively, for "is to." Choice B, the best answer, is the only option in which this parallel construction is used correctly.

28. Choices A, B, D, and E are wordy and use a weak passive voice, "(is) enabled." Furthermore, D is incomplete: the words following the comma bear no clear grammatical relationship to the rest of the sentence. Choice C, the best answer, is clear and to the point and uses the active voice, "enables."

29. Choice D, the best answer, is both grammatically and idiomatically correct. Choices A and E use the incorrect phrase "capable to"; the correct form is "capable of (playing)." Choice C is redundant. Choice B is incorrect on two counts: grammatically, the adverb "maybe," rather than the verb form "may be," is required to modify the verb "can"; but even if this error were corrected, "maybe can" would still be unidiomatic.

30. The opening phrase of A, "As against what," and the opening phrase of D, "Opposite of," are awkward and unidiomatic in this context. Choice B uses "Contrary with," which is unidiomatic in this context; "contrary to" is required. Choice C is awkward and wordy. Choice E, the best answer, is clear, idiomatic, and grammatically correct.

31. Choice B, the only choice to use the correct phrasing, is the best answer. The correct phrase is "to accuse (a party) of" an offense. Also, it is appropriate to say that one is lax "in performing" an action. Thus, the prepositions "with" in A, C, and E, and "as to" in D are incorrect. Similarly, A uses "as to enforcing," C uses "on the enforcement of," D uses "for the enforcement of," and E uses "on enforcing"— all wordy or unidiomatic in context.

32. A comparative construction beginning with "more" is properly completed by a phrase beginning with "than": "more *X* than *Y*." Thus, A, B, and C are incorrect because they use "as" instead of "than." Also, the "no more…than" comparison requires a parallel construction: "it costs no more *to ship*…than (it does) *to send*." In A and D, "sending" is not parallel to "to ship." Choice E is the best answer: it preserves the parallelism and uses "than" rather than "as."

33. Choice D is the best answer. The phrase "as part of contract settlements" is clearer than the more awkward and wordy phrasing of A, B, C, and E. Also, the "made…to be" construction is ungrammatical as used in A and C, and "converted…into" in B and E misleadingly implies a total change in the functions of the officials, rather than the addition of a new function to their existing duties.

34. In a comparison using "like" or "unlike," the things being compared must be of the same type. Because the first noun in this comparison is the name of a country, "the United States," the second term must also be the name of a country, "Japan." Only B, the best answer, follows this logical structure. Choice A lacks the parallel construction of a proper comparison because it introduces the preposition "in." Choices C and E substitute the laws of the country, and D its people, for the name of the country itself.

35. When "used" is followed by a noun such as "insulation" or "fireproofing," the correct idioms are "used as" and "used for." Thus, in choices A and D, the infinitive "to be" is incorrect. In choices B and E, the adjective or verb form "fireproof" is incorrectly used as a noun, instead of the proper form of the noun, "fireproofing." Choice C, which uses both this noun and the correct idioms, is the best answer.

36. The sense of this sentence is that defendants in Florida *do not* have a right that defendants in some other states *do*. The verb "do" must be repeated in the second part of the sentence to parallel the verb "do" in the first part. It is not necessary to repeat "have." Choices B, D, and E fail to repeat "do," and the referent of "it" is unclear in B. In C and D, the pronoun "they" lacks a logical antecedent; grammatically, it refers to "Defendants in Florida," not to defendants in other states. Choice E is also wrong because the correct usage before comparisons containing a subject and verb ("defendants have") is "as," not "like." Choice A, the best answer, maintains the "do" parallel and contains no unclear reference.

37. To be grammatically correct, this sentence must provide one clear subject and a concise indication of the two requirements, "manual dexterity" and "breath control." Choices A and D are ungrammatical because "it" wrongly introduces a second grammatical subject for the verb "requires." In choice A, the use of both "also" and "as well" is redundant, since both have the same meaning. In B, "as well" used with "both" is unidiomatic; only "both" is required. In C, "only" should be placed immediately after "not." In choice E, the best answer, "Playing" makes a better subject for "requires" than does "To play...," and the rest of the sentence is clear and concise.

38. The subject of the sentence is "universities," a plural noun. Because the verb must agree with the subject, the singular verb "was," as used in choices B and C, should be "were." The adjective "recent" in A, B, and E is incorrect; because the word has to modify the verb "were," the adverb form, "recently," is correct. Also in C, the correct word order, "there was," is reversed. Choice D, the best answer, correctly uses the adverb and the plural verb.

Essay:

Response that Received a Score of 6

Essay	Explanation of Score
The debate as to whether a precise grading system, or the development of a pass/fail system in the schools would be better is a discussion which is a topic of great consideration in today's educational system. There are many questions which need to be asked when considering this debate. In what ways are children learning differently in the late 1990s as compared to any other time? Are teachers teaching differently, and in what ways are teachers organizing their classrooms? Most importantly, where is the motivation coming from for children to learn? All of these issues need to be addressed before a decision can be made about the grading systems used, and whether or not there needs to be one unanimous choice made on the issue. However, while there is support for both precise grading systems and pass/fail grading systems, precise grading systems seem to provide more motivation for academic achievement among students in America. Today, children learn much differently than they did even ten years ago. Mostly, this is because of the increase in resources and their accessibility. The improvement in the public library systems and the introduction of computers as the norm in schools, as well as the continually increasing popularity of the internet, makes learning much more of an every day activity, if not something that is enjoyable. Because of the availability of these resources every student is on equal ground when it comes to projects, papers, and other tasks. In this case, a precise grading system seems to be in order, because if everyone has the same opportunities, then everyone should be taking advantage of those opportunities. In communities where these resources might not be as readily available to students, it is important that parents and teachers encourage the discovery and use of these tools for education. The way in which a teacher organizes his or her classroom is also a factor to consider in this debate. While no one should praise only the excellent students for the achievement and ignore the struggling students, it is important that success is recognized. If success is not recognized, then where is the motivation for learning? Most children at a young age, and maybe not until college, do not appreciate learning for learning's sake. It takes something more than the information a book has to offer to make a student want to read it. It is how the teacher presents it and what the student will be expected to learn from the book which makes reading the book a task which will be completed. The biggest factor, though, is probably what the other students will know that drives one student to learn.	This essay begins by considering both sides of the debate, then ends the first paragraph in favor of "precise grading systems." Three clear reasons are given in support of that choice (new educational techniques, teacher organization, motivation), each well explained in its own paragraph. The essay is very clear, very well organized, and its reasons in support of a precise grading system are fully developed. It builds logically from beginning to end, with ideas and sentences nicely linked together. There are sentences of varied lengths and rhythm (including both simple and complex sentences), providing a fluent and enjoyable read; precise word choices ("consideration, unanimous, academic achievement, conjure, flying colors") help to keep the reader interested.

Motivation to do well in school comes mainly from competition. No one student wants to be left behind the others when he or she knows he can do well. The word competition may conjure negative images in people's minds, but in reality it is probably the biggest driving force leading to academic achievement among America's students. There are scholarships and awards given to those who achieve in various areas of their school experience. Things like this make learning something worthwhile. When a student can get an A,B,C,D or F in a class, the motivation for getting an A is high. An A is definitely better than a C (average) or a D (barely passing) and obviously better than an F. In a pass/fail system however, a student can only pass or fail. There is no distinction between passing with flying colors or barely passing. In many cases, a student might do just enough work to pass, whereas in a precise grading system, a student might work diligently to earn an A. The motivation is obvious: everyone can see how hard a student worked to earn that A. In a pass/fail system, however, every student that passes is on equal ground—just where they were when they began the class.

Pass/fail systems can definitely work in some classrooms, depending on the subject and age level. In beginning classrooms where the focus is learning basic concepts, a pass/fail system would be appropriate and applicable. In a more advanced classroom, however, where the emphasis is on applying basic concepts to different tasks and forming new ideas, the use of a precise grading system would definitely produce more effort from the students, and better results in the end. Precise grading systems encourage learning based on the outcome, and those who are successful in grade school and high school understand the expectations that university will hold, and work more diligently to meet those expectations.

Response that Received a Score of 5

Essay	Explanation of Score
Competition encourages students to strive toward individual and group-oriented goals. Rewards, such as higer letter grades, are incentives for students as individuals and as teammates in organized group environments. Letter grades are important in stimulating the student intellectually. Thomas Jefferson, Alexander Hamilton, and Benjamin Franklin are examples of well-educated, intellectual, self-interested, and motivated heroes of the past. These men were well-educated and they were given the opportunity to lead a new country as a result of the American Revolution. These men were competitive and they wanted to be remembered. They stood out in a crowd. Our society is still a very competitive society. Many still believe that only the strong survive. Would these men still be as competitive and goal oriented enough to establish a new Government, if competition and desire were taken away from them? Would they still be aspiring towards new goals if they did not strive together as a team in defeating the British? Where did they learn how to survive as individuals and as American colonists? Letter grades are fundamental in motivating students who wish to excel at their own personal achievements. If one student is weak in one subject area, such as Mathematics, it is important to record the students progress, or lack of progress, in order to help the student improve. If the student is left alone and just passes the course, will this help him/her in the outside world? Will the lack of goals help students make the transition into a world that is highly competitive? No, it will not. Even Employment Angencies give standardized tests to potential employees. The test scores are vital in determining what types of jobs the employee will interview for. Another example is the Praxis tests. No one can teach in public schools without passing these tests. Scores are set and there are no if, and's, or but's about it. If you do not pass, even if it is only by one point, the person must retake the test. Is this important? Yes. This is extremely important because society needs self-motivated, intelligent individuals at the head of the classroom. Test scores are not the only factor involved in the development of a good teacher, however, scores are a fundamental of the entire process. Society is also very team oriented. Sports, politics, education are just a few of the situations students will find themselves in throughout their lifetimes. How does one team defeat the other? How does the Environmental Protection Agency get it's laws passed? How did the states amend the Articles of Confederation? How does a country win a war?	This insightful essay establishes the writer's position in favor of letter grades, although some lapses do occur. The writer's position is made clear ("letter grades are incentives for students"), along with the connection between letter grades and competition; the writer tells us letter grades made great men such as Jefferson, Hamilton, and Franklin work very hard. While much of the essay does logically explain the idea of competition (in the form of letter grades) helping to motivate a student, occasionally the writing loses focus: What does the paragraph about testing tell us about letter grades? How does the list of rhetorical questions ("How did the states amend the Articles of Confederation? How does a country win a war?") help the writer's argument? While this essay does take a clear position and largely defends it, its focus is occasionally lost. Sharpening up this explanation would certainly help this otherwise well-written and thoughtful essay.

Motivation has become less important to many individuals today. Most people just try to get by and they lack the desire needed for improving themselves in all areas of life. If this were untrue, there would not be as many homeless people, abandoned children, or drug abusers in our world today. Children need to learn skills that will help them make the transition into a highly competitive and sometimes scary society.	

Response that Received a Score of 4

Essay	Explanation of Score
Grades play an important role in school. I think that a precise grading scale would work better for students than a pass/fail system. Any type of grading system will cause competition, but I think a little competition is good for students. Competition, if controlled, teaches students how to get along with others and also pushes them to try harder. A precise grading system would cause a little more competition than any other type of grading system.	This essay is for the "precise grading system" and says why (to motivate students). The explanation for choosing letter grades discusses motivating students, but also includes a specific example from the writer's life when he or she saw the effect of letter grading versus pass/fail; this example helps bring the writer's argument to life. The essay is organized—building from its clear introduction through its explanation of ideas—and easy to follow. More specifics and more explanation would help the piece, as would variety in language; there are few interesting words, and the constant repetition of certain phrases ("precise grading system…grades…teachers…students…pass/fail") makes the reading somewhat monotonous. Better word choices and sentences of different lengths would help to give this essay a little more sparkle.
Precise grades motivate students to work their hardest. A precise grading system not only gives students motivation, it also gives them a reasonable goal to work towards. Say for instance, an average student could aim for a B, while an above average student could set their goal for an A. Instead of both just trying to pass.	
I personally think that a pass/fail grading system would put more strain and pressure on a student than a precise grading system. If I were on a pass/fail system then I would feel that if I made one mistake then I would be that much closer to failing. This would make me nervous and I would second guess myself more often then usual and I wouldn't perform as well. If I was on a precise grading system, I would feel that I had a little room for mistakes.	
Another reason I think precise grading is important, is because it is a good way of telling where a student stands. In a pass/fail grading system the teacher would only know if you passed of failed, but in a precise grading system teachers would be able to see how well a student did on an assignment or test and they could see how they stand with the rest of the class.	
I have seen students that were graded both by pass/fail and by a precise scale. One teacher assigned the students a paper, they were graded on a pass/fail. These students were happy with passing. This seemed reasonable, because they did pass. But in another classroom where the teacher assigned the same paper and graded these student's using a precise scale. These students were not happy unless they got a grade higher than a C. These papers were way above passing, yet they were unhappy. This made me realize that students are and will be more motivated with letter grades rather than pass/fail.	
Students decide for themselves how hard they are going to try, but by using a precise grading system, students will compete a little with each other and try to better themselves. A precise grading system would not only be useful for the students, but for teachers as well. Teachers would be able to tell how each student was doing in each subject and then could offer whatever help was needed for that student.	

Response that Received a Score of 3

Essay	Explanation of Score
What is happening in schools is it is getting to easy for kids to get out of working hard. Going to a pass/fail grading system would play right into their hands. They want the easy way out, and what is easier then passing or failing? Here are someways that we can get the kids back into the grading system. First lets challlenge the kids to do better. Then we make the children want to get a higher grade. Finally we can relax on the grading scale. I will explain in detail what I mean in my steps below. Let's go back to the days when kids wanted to learn, ok that was never true. If we can not make them want to go to school, we can at least make them want to learn. We can start to change the classroom to make it more challenging and to bring back the energy to do well in school. This gets the kids to stop thinking some much on the grades, but rather on the learning. That would be the first step to reintroducing the grading scale. Making the classroom fun will hopefully get the kids minds of the grades and learning will take place and the grades will go up and they will not worry about pass/fail. Rather they will be thinking A or B. Taking the hassle out of learning will promote the kids to learn rather then to force them to learn. The final step for the kids and the teachers to keep the grade scale is to relax on the grading. I feel that you have to grade appriately for the student. If he is a little slower, do not be as harsh as with your honor student. Also give more credit for group work. Group work will promote energy in learning because you are a part of something and you feel more at liberty to speak and interact. So I am in totally favor of keeping the grading scale because I feel that it promotes self worth and motivation to work harder. I do not think it would be in anyone's best interest to go to the pass/fail method. That just promotes laziness. Because if you can get away with medicore work, then why try hard. If you really think about the current grading system, it is almost the same idea. You have four letter grades which are passing and only one that is failing. I think you have a better chance with the grading system rather then without. To make the children to stop thinking about failing you should make the class fun, interest them in things that will strike an interest, and finally take the grading system for what it is worth, a degree of passing.	This writer has an obvious position ("I am totally in favor of keeping the grading scale"), but the reasons explaining why the writer feels this way are not very clear. Instead of approaching the argument with a clear starting point, the essay instead seems to be jumping around. Many ideas are like the following sentence, which changes in mid-thought: "Let's go back to the days when kids wanted to learn, ok that was never true." The writer has obviously not thought his or her position through, which is evident from the lack of organization and unclear explanation. While there is focus and explanation in this essay, better organization could certainly have helped it.

Response that Received a Score of 2

Essay	Explanation of Score
Some people argue that giving grades to students puts too much emphasis on competition and not enough emphasis on learning. While, others argue that without a precise grading system, students would not work as hard to excel. Students receiving grades in school encourages them to suceed and prepares them for thier future. Receiving grades will continue throughout the students lives. For example when entering the work force you will be graded on your job preformance. In school if a students strived to achieve then this wil contiune in their job preformance. Some students might not of been motivated in school to achieve high grades but they are outstanding in the job field that they have choosen. The aspect of grading will still be a part of them because they were graded for preformance in school. Grades are important in our lives they give us encouragement to achieve. This process will continue through out our lives.	This essay may be a discussion of the benefits of grades, but it never discusses whether or not letter grades should be replaced by a pass/fail system. That is the topic addressed in the prompt, so this essay lacks a clear position or thesis. The arguments make sense, but they are not being given to support a thesis; the writer is rambling. Odd word choices and mistakes in grammar also confuse the reader, and it is often not easy to understand the writer's point. This essay needs a more clear focus, better explanation, and language that is easier to follow.

Response that Received a Score of 1

Essay	Explanation of Score
I think we should use the same grading system we already have, not Pass/Fail. That way kids will keep working at their homework. I believe the only thing that would happen the other way would be terribul. People would just skip school all the time because, students wouldnt have to worry about there grades. Instead the schools should remain having the grades they way they always have.	This brief essay does have a clear position ("we should use the same grading system...not Pass/Fail"), but gives only one vague reason to support it ("the other way would be terrible"). The writer does tell us the terrible result would be that kids would skip school, but never tells us why they would skip. We are told students "wouldn't have to worry about their grades" any longer, but again we are not told why. Language problems do not interfere with the reader's understanding in this essay, but a lack of explanation does make it hard for the reader to know what the writer is getting at.

Chapter 12

Are You Ready? Last-Minute Suggestions

► ► ► ► ► ► ► ► ► ► ►

Checklist

Complete this checklist to determine if you're ready to take your test.

❏ Do you have your appointment for the computer-based test or your admission ticket for the paper-and-pencil test?

❏ Do you know the topics that will be covered in each section of the test?

❏ Have you reviewed any textbooks, study notes, and course readings that relate to the topics covered?

❏ Do you know how long the test will take and the number of questions it contains? Have you considered how you will pace your work?

❏ Are you familiar with the test directions and the types of questions for your test?

❏ If you are taking the *PPST: Writing* test in paper-and-pencil format, are you aware that you must use a pencil, not a pen, to write your essay?

❏ If you are taking the test on computer, have you familiarized yourself with the appearance of the screens and the use of the buttons?

❏ Are you familiar with the recommended test-taking strategies and tips?

❏ Have you practiced by working through the practice test questions at a pace similar to that of an actual test?

❏ If you are repeating a *PPST* test, have you analyzed your previous score report to determine areas where additional study and test preparation could be useful?

Appendix A
Study Plan Sheet

▶   ▶   ▶   ▶   ▶   ▶   ▶   ▶   ▶   ▶   ▶   ▶

Study Plan Sheet

See Chapter 1 for suggestions on using this Study Plan Sheet.

STUDY PLAN						
Content covered on test	How well do I know the content?	What material do I have for studying this content?	What material do I need for studying this content?	Where could I find the materials I need?	Dates planned for study of content	Dates completed

Appendix B
For More Information

▶   ▶   ▶   ▶   ▶   ▶   ▶   ▶   ▶   ▶   ▶   ▶

For More Information

Educational Testing Service offers additional information to assist you in preparing for the Praxis Series™ Assessments. *Tests at a Glance* booklets and the *Registration Bulletin* are both available without charge (see below to order). You can also obtain more information from our website: **www.teachingandlearning.org**.

General Inquires

Phone: 800-772-9476 or 609-771-7395 (Monday-Friday, 8:00 A.M. to 7:45 P.M., Eastern time)
Fax: 609-771-7906

Extended Time

If you have a learning disability or if English is not your primary language, you can apply to be given more time to take your test. The *Registration Bulletin* tells you how you can qualify for extended time.

Disability Services

Phone: 866-387-8602 or 609-771-7780
Fax: 609-771-7906
TTY (for deaf or hard-of-hearing callers): 609-771-7714

Mailing Address

ETS—The Praxis Series
P.O. Box 6051
Princeton, NJ 08541-6051

Overnight Delivery Address

ETS—The Praxis Series
Distribution Center
225 Phillips Blvd.
Ewing, NJ 08628

Appendix C
Complete List of Topics Covered

► ► ► ► ► ► ► ► ► ► ► ►

As you study for the *PPST*, you may find it helpful to have the topics covered in each section of the test listed in one place. This appendix contains representative descriptions of the topics covered in all three categories (Reading, Math, and Writing) of the *PPST*. It does not introduce any new information; all of the topics listed below are also discussed in chapters 4, 5, 6, and 7.

Topics Covered in the *PPST: Reading* Test

I. Literal Comprehension

Literal comprehension content measures the ability to understand accurately and completely the explicit content of a written message. There are four types of questions:

- Main idea questions involve identifying summaries or paraphrases of the main idea or primary purpose of a reading selection.

- Supporting idea questions involve identifying summaries or paraphrases of supporting ideas.

- Organization questions involve recognizing how a reading selection is organized, how it uses language, how the ideas in a selection are related to one another, or how key phrases and transition words are used in a reading selection.

- Vocabulary questions involve identifying the meanings of words as they are used in the context of a reading selection.

II. Critical and Inferential Comprehension

Critical and inferential comprehension content measures the ability to evaluate a reading selection and its messages. There are three types of questions:

- Argument evaluation questions involve determining the strengths and weaknesses of arguments in a reading selection, determining the relevance of evidence presented in the reading selection to the assertions made in the selection, or judging whether material presented is fact or opinion.

- Inferential reasoning questions involve drawing inferences and implications from the directly stated content of a reading selection, determining the logical assumptions underlying a selection, or determining the author's attitude toward the material discussed.

- Generalization questions involve recognizing situations that are similar to the material in a reading selection, drawing conclusions about the material in a selection, or applying ideas from the selection to new situations.

Topics Covered in the *PPST: Mathematics* Test

I. Conceptual Knowledge

Demonstrate number sense and operation sense—that is, an understanding of the foundational ideas of numbers, number properties, and operations defined on numbers (whole numbers, fractions, and decimals).

- Order: demonstrate an understanding of order among whole numbers, fractions, and decimals.

- Equivalence: demonstrate an understanding that a number can be represented in more than one way.

- Numeration and place value: demonstrate an understanding of how numbers are named, place value, and order of magnitude of numbers.

- Number properties: demonstrate an understanding of the properties of whole numbers without necessarily knowing the names of the properties.

- Operation properties: demonstrate an understanding of the properties (commutative, associative, and distributive) of the basic operations (addition, subtraction, multiplication, and division) without necessarily knowing the names of the properties; recognize equivalent computational procedures.

II. Procedural Knowledge

Demonstrate an understanding of the procedures required to represent quantitative relationships and the ability to plan, execute, interpret, or complete operations to solve problems.

- Computation: perform computations; adjust the result of a computation to fit the context of a problem; identify numbers or information or operations needed to solve a problem.

- Estimation: estimate the result of a calculation; determine the reasonableness of an estimate.

- Ratio, proportion, and percent: solve problems involving ratio, proportion, and percent.

- Probability: interpret numbers used to express simple probability; assign a probability to a possible outcome.

- Equations: solve simple equations and inequalities; predict the outcome of changing some number or condition in a problem.

- Algorithmic thinking: demonstrate an understanding of the algorithmic point of view—that is, follow a given procedure; recognize various ways to solve a problem; identify, complete, or analyze a procedure; discover patterns in a procedure.

III. Representations of Quantitative Information

Demonstrate an ability to interpret visual displays of quantitative information, to retrieve information from data, to determine whether statements based on data are true or false, to recognize relationships in and make inferences from data, and to represent a given set of data graphically.

- Interpretation: read and interpret visual displays of quantitative information, such as bar graphs, line graphs, pie charts, pictographs, tables, stemplots, scatterplots, schedules, simple flowcharts, and diagrams; recognize relationships in data; determine an average, a range, a mode, or a median.

- Trends: given a data display, observe groupings, make comparisons, and make predictions or extrapolations.

- Inferences: given a data display, draw conclusions or make inferences from the data.

- Patterns: identify and recognize patterns in data, such as variation.

- Connections: demonstrate an understanding of the relationship between numerical values in a table, the symbolic rule relating table values, and the corresponding graphical representation of the table and the rule; choose a graph appropriate to represent a given set of data; recognize quantitative relationships in symbols or in words.

IV. Measurement and Informal Geometry

Demonstrate a basic understanding of measurement, of the U.S. Customary and metric systems of measurement, and of geometric properties and relationships. At least half of the questions will focus on informal geometry.

- Systems of measurement: demonstrate basic literacy in the U.S. Customary and metric systems of measurement; convert from one unit to another within the same system; recognize and use appropriate units for making measurements; read a calibrated scale.

- Measurement: determine the measurements needed to solve a problem; recognize and use geometric concepts in making linear, area, and volume measurements; solve measurement problems by using a formula, estimating, employing indirect measurement, using rates as measures, making visual comparisons, using scaling/proportional reasoning, or using a nonstandard unit.

- Geometric properties: recognize and use geometric properties and relationships in both pure and real-world situations, such as recognizing a symmetrical design or determining a distance using the Pythagorean relationship.

V. Formal Mathematical Reasoning

Demonstrate the ability to use the basics of logic in a quantitative context.

- Logical connectives and quantifiers: interpret statements that use logical connectives (and, or, if...then) as well as quantifiers (some, all, none).

- Validity of arguments: use deductive reasoning to determine whether an argument (a series of statements leading to a conclusion) is valid or invalid.

- Generalization: identify an appropriate generalization, an example that disproves an inappropriate generalization, or a hidden assumption.

Topics Covered in the *PPST: Writing* Test

I. Grammatical Relationships

- Identify errors in
  - Adjectives
  - Adverbs
  - Nouns
  - Pronouns
  - Verbs

II. Structural Relationships

- Identify errors in
  - Comparison
  - Coordination
  - Correlation
  - Negation
  - Parallelism
  - Subordination

III. Idiom/Word Choice, Mechanics, and No Error

- Identify errors in

  — Idiomatic expressions

  — Word choice

  — Capitalization

  — Punctuation

- Identify sentences free from error.

IV. Essay

- Write an essay that is appropriate for the assigned task and for the intended audience.

- Organize and develop ideas logically, making clear connections between them.

- Provide and sustain a clear focus or thesis.

- Use supporting reasons, examples, and details to develop clearly and logically the ideas presented in the essay.

- Demonstrate facility in the use of language and the ability to use a variety of sentence structures.

- Construct effective sentences that are generally free of errors in standard written English.

NOTES